Russia in the Changing International System

Emel Parlar Dal • Emre Erşen
Editors

Russia in the Changing International System

palgrave
macmillan

Editors
Emel Parlar Dal
Department of International Relations
Marmara University
Istanbul, Turkey

Emre Erşen
Department of Political Science
and International Relations
Marmara University
Istanbul, Turkey

ISBN 978-3-030-21831-7   ISBN 978-3-030-21832-4 (eBook)
https://doi.org/10.1007/978-3-030-21832-4

This Palgrave Macmillan imprint is published by the registered company Springer Nature
Switzerland AG
The registered company address is: Gewerbestrasse 11, 6330 Cham, Switzerland

ACKNOWLEDGMENTS

We would like to thank the editorial staff of the *Rising Powers Quarterly* journal for their valuable support and assistance.

CONTENTS

NOTES ON CONTRIBUTORS

Philipp Casula holds a PhD in sociology from University of Basel, Switzerland. In his thesis he analysed the domestic politics of contemporary Russia in terms of hegemony and populism. His research interests include the cultural history of post-colonial Russia, especially the relations of the USSR with the Middle East and their cultural representation in the Soviet media and academia. He is also interested in contemporary populism and nationalism in Europe.

Nikolay Dobronravin is a professor at the School of International Relations, St. Petersburg State University, Russia. His research interests include world politics and African and Islamic studies. He has published extensively on West Africa, boundary studies and energy policy. His chapters entitled "Oil, Gas, and Modernization of Global South: African Lessons for Post-Soviet States" and "Oil, Gas, Transit and Boundaries: Problems of the Transport Curse" were included in Vladimir Gel'man and Otar Marganiya (eds.), *Resource Curse and Post-Soviet Eurasia: Oil, Gas, and Modernization* (2010). He also wrote a chapter for *From Bi-polar to Multipolar World: The Latin American Vector of International Relations* (2018).

Emre Erşen is an associate professor at Marmara University's Department of Political Science and International Relations in Istanbul, Turkey. He received his PhD from the same department. He conducted research at the Higher School of Economics (Moscow, Russia), Institute for Human Sciences (Vienna, Austria), University of Kent (Canterbury, UK) and Jagiellonian University (Krakow, Poland) as a visiting scholar. He has written for a number of academic publications including *Geopolitics, Turkish Studies, Energy Policy, Insight Turkey, Journal of Eurasian Studies* and *Perceptions: Journal of International Affairs*. He has also contributed many conference papers and book chapters on Turkish-Russian relations, Eurasianism and Turkish geopolitics. He is the co-editor of *Turkey's Pivot to Eurasia: Geopolitics and Foreign Policy in a Changing World Order* (2019, with Seçkin Köstem).

Sergii V. Glebov is an associate professor at the Department of International Relations, leading research fellow at the Centre for International Studies and Dean of the School of International Relations at the Institute of Social Sciences, Odessa Mechnikov National University (ONU). He received his PhD in 2002. In 2000/2001, he was a visiting scholar at the Centre for European Studies, University of Exeter, UK, and at Columbia University, Harriman Institute, New York City, USA, in 2003. He received several individual and institutional fellowships, including from HESP/AFP Open Society Institute (Budapest, Hungary), Carnegie Foundation and Jean Monnet Program. His research interests include foreign and security policy of Ukraine, international relations in the Black Sea-Caspian region, European and Euro-Atlantic security, Russian foreign policy and Ukraine's relations with NATO and EU.

Regina Heller is a senior researcher at the Institute for Peace Research and Security Policy at the University of Hamburg (IFSH). She studied Political Science and East Slavic Studies at the University of Mainz, Middlebury College, VT/USA, and University of Hamburg. After her exam in Hamburg, she worked as a project manager at the Conflict Prevention Network (CPN) at the Stiftung Wissenschaft und Politik in Ebenhausen and Berlin; as a coordinator of the research project "International Risk Policy" at the Center for Transatlantic Foreign and Security Policy at the Free University Berlin; and as the project manager of the "German-American-Russian Dialogue" at the Aspen Institute Berlin. In 2006, she received her PhD from Hamburg University on the topic of human rights and norm socialization in Russia. Since 2008, she is a member of the scientific advisory council of the Cologne Forum for International Relations and Security Policy. Throughout the academic year 2014/2015, she held a substitute professorship for International Relations at the Helmut Schmidt University Hamburg and University of the German Armed Forces.

Emre İşeri is a professor and chair of the Department of International Relations at Yaşar University, İzmir, where he teaches Introduction to International Political Economy, Energy Politics, American Foreign Policy, Middle Eastern Politics and Turkish Foreign Policy. He received his PhD in international relations from Keele University, UK. His research interests include energy politics, political communication, Eurasian/ Middle Eastern politics and Turkish foreign policy. His publications have appeared in various books as well as academic journals including *Geopolitics, Journal of Balkan and Near Eastern Studies (JBNES), Turkish Studies, Energy Policy, Security Journal, South European Society and Politics (SESP), European Journal of Communication, Environment and Planning C: Politics and Space* and *Alternatives: Global, Local, Political.*

Victor Jeifets is a professor at the School of International Relations, St. Petersburg State University, Russia, and director of the Center for Iberoamerican Studies at the same university. His research interests include international relations and communist studies. He has published extensively on Russian foreign policy as well as Latin American history and politics. His recent publications include *América Latina en la Internacional Comunista, 1919–1943* (Santiago: Ariadna Editores, 2015, 2018); *El Partido Comunista de Argentina y la III Internacional* (Mexico: Nostromo, 2013); "Reflexiones sobre el centenario de la participación rusa en la Primera Guerra Mundial: entre el olvido histórico y los mitos modernos," *Anuario Colombiano de Historia Social y de Cultura* 42, no. 2 (2015): 177–201; "Rusia, Ukrania y los países del Oeste: en vísperas de la Paz Fría," *Patria: Análisis Político de la Defensa* 2 (2014): 70–86, and "Russia and Latin America: Renewal Versus Continuity," *Portuguese Journal of Social Science* 17, no. 2 (2018): 213–228. He also edited a book entitled *From Bi-polar to Multipolar World: The Latin American Vector of International Relations* (2018).

Marcin Kaczmarski (PhD) is a lecturer at the School of Social & Political Sciences in University of Glasgow. Prior to joining the University of Glasgow, he was a visiting scholar at the Chengchi University in Taiwan, Slavic-Eurasian Research Center in Japan, Aleksanteri Institute in Finland and Kennan Institute in Washington, DC. He combined research and teaching with policy-oriented analysis for the Finnish Institute of International Affairs in Helsinki and Centre for Eastern Studies in Warsaw. His research focuses on Russia-China relations, comparative regionalism, Russia's foreign and security policy and the role of rising powers in international politics. He is the author of *Russia-China Relations in the Post-crisis International Order* (2015). He also published articles in leading academic journals including *International Affairs, International Politics* and *Europe-Asia Studies.*

Alexey Khlebnikov is an expert on Russian foreign policy towards the Middle East and North Africa region at the Russian International Affairs Council (RIAC). He holds an MA in global public policy from the University of Minnesota, Hubert Humphrey School of Public Affairs and a BA and MA in Middle Eastern studies from Lobachevsky State University of Nizhny Novgorod. He was Edmund Muskie Fellow (2012–2014) in the US and a research fellow at the Johns Hopkins University School of Advanced International Studies (SAIS) in 2013.

Alexander Libman is Professor of Social Sciences and Eastern European Studies at the Ludwig Maximilians University of Munich. Prior to that, he worked as an associate at the German Institute for International and Security Affairs SWP (Berlin) and as an assistant professor of the Frankfurt School of Finance & Management. He holds a PhD degree from the University of Mannheim. His research interests include Russian subnational politics, impact of historical legacies on the evolution of post-communist countries and Eurasian regionalism. His most recent publications include *Authoritarian Regionalism in the World of International Organizations* (2019, with Anastassia Obydenkova) and *Re-evaluating Regional Organizations: Beyond the Smokescreen of Official Mandates* (Palgrave Macmillan 2017, with Evgeny Vinokurov). In addition, his articles appeared in journals including *World Politics, Comparative Political Studies, Comparative Politics, Review of International Political Economy* and *Journal of Democracy.*

Andrey Makarychev is a guest professor at the Johan Skytte Institute of Political Science. His area of expertise and teaching includes Russian and European studies and EU-Russia relations. He published extensively on a variety of topics related to Russian foreign policy including co-edited volumes *Russia's Changing Economic and Political Profiles* (2014) and *Mega-events in Post-Soviet Eurasia: Shifting Borderlines of Inclusion and Exclusion* (Palgrave Macmillan 2016); a monograph *Russia and the EU in a Multipolar World* (Ibidem 2014), and a co-authored monograph *Celebration Borderlands in a Wider Europe: Nations and Identities in*

Ukraine, Georgia and Estonia (2016). His research articles on the EU, Russia and the common neighbourhood countries were published in peer-reviewed journals such as *Problems of Post-communism, Journal of International Relations and Development, Europe-Asia Studies, Journal of Eurasian Studies, Demokratizatsiya* and *European Urban and Regional Studies.*

Volkan Özdemir is an associate professor affiliated with EPPEN-Institute for Energy Markets and Policies in Ankara, Turkey. He is an expert on Russian, Caspian and Turkish energy markets, gas trade, pricing and geopolitics. He received his BA degree from the Department of International Relations at the Middle East Technical University, Ankara, and his MA degree from Uppsala University, Sweden, with his thesis on energy cooperation and security in the Caspian region. In 2013, he received his PhD degree in economics from the Moscow International Institute of Energy Policies of the MGIMO University, Russia, with his research on world gas markets and the economic aspects of Turkish-Russian gas relations. He later worked at the Undersecretariat for Foreign Trade of the Turkish Prime Ministry, Turkish Ministry of Energy and Natural Resources and Petroleum Pipeline Company-BOTAŞ. In addition to his professional experience, he has been teaching courses on energy economics, security and diplomacy in different universities and publishing extensively on energy issues.

Emel Parlar Dal is an associate professor at Marmara University's Department of International Relations. After graduating from Galatasaray University, she received her MA and PhD degrees at Paris 1 Panthéon-Sorbonne and Paris 3 Nouvelle Sorbonne Universities in France. She received the Swiss government's scholarship and conducted research as a visiting fellow at the Graduate Institute of International and Development Studies in Geneva during 2010–2011. In 2013, she conducted research as an academic visitor at St. Anthony's College Middle East Centre of the Oxford University. Her articles on Turkish foreign policy, rising powers and Turkey in global governance were published in academic journals including *Third World Quarterly, International Politics, International Journal* and *Turkish Studies.* She is the editor of *Middle Powers in Global Governance: The Rise of Turkey* (Palgrave Macmillan 2018) and co-editor of *Violent Non-state Actors and the Syrian Civil War* (2017).

Richard Sakwa joined the University of Kent in 1987 and was promoted to professorship in 1996. While completing his doctorate on Moscow politics during the Civil War (1918–1921) he spent a year on a British Council scholarship at Moscow State University (1979–1980), and then worked for two years in Moscow in the 'Mir' Science and Technology Publishing House. Before moving to Kent, he lectured at the University of Essex and the University of California, Santa Cruz. He is Associate Fellow of the Russia and Eurasia Programme at the Royal Institute of International Affairs, Chatham House, Honorary Senior Research Fellow at the Centre for Russian, European and Eurasian Studies (CREES) at the University of Birmingham and since September 2002 a member of Academy of Learned Societies for the Social Sciences.

Alexander Sergunin is Professor of International Relations at Moscow State Institute of International Relations, St. Petersburg State University and Nizhny Novgorod State University, Russia. He received his PhD in history from Moscow State University and habilitation in political science from St. Petersburg State University. His fields of research and teaching include Russian foreign policy and international relations theory. His most recent publications include *Explaining Russian Foreign Policy Behavior: Theory and Practice* (2016), *U.S. Ballistic Missile Defense System: Past, Present, Future* (2015) (with Valery Konyshev and Valeria Shatzkaya), *Contemporary Military Strategy* (2014) (with Valery Konyshev) and *Contemporary International Relations Theories* (2013) (with Valery Konyshev et al.).

Jeanne L. Wilson is Shelby Cullom Davis Professor of Russian Studies and Professor of Political Science at Wheaton College, Norton, MA. She is also a research associate at the Davis Center for Russian and Eurasian Studies, Harvard University, Cambridge, MA. Her research interests include the comparative examination of Russian and Chinese foreign policy behaviour with respect to national identity and integration into the global international system.

CHAPTER 1

Russia and the Changing International System: An Introduction

Emel Parlar Dal and Emre Erşen

INTRODUCTION

What kind of an actor is Russia in the current international system, which has recently been marked by substantive structural and normative changes as a result of the ongoing power shift from the Global North to the Global South? Should Russia be conceived as a great power or a rising power in world politics? Or should it rather be categorized as a "near" great power? How can Russia's perceptions about the changing international order be critically assessed? What are Russia's motives, roles and strategies with regard to key regional and global issues? Does the Russian leadership have an alternative interpretation of the international order that significantly differs from the "liberal" understanding of the Western states? This volume seeks to address these questions and attempts at scrutinizing Russia as a unique actor, which plays the dual role of a traditional great power and a rising power in the international system. The implications of this duality in

E. Parlar Dal (✉)
Department of International Relations, Marmara University, Istanbul, Turkey

E. Erşen (✉)
Department of Political Science and International Relations,
Marmara University, Istanbul, Turkey

© The Author(s) 2020
E. Parlar Dal, E. Erşen (eds.), *Russia in the Changing International System*, https://doi.org/10.1007/978-3-030-21832-4_1

1

Russia's actorness are important in terms of not only understanding the Russian elites' response to the emerging post-hegemonic international order but also evaluating the development of Moscow's policies in the sphere of global governance.

There is a growing literature on Russia's vision of the changing international system (e.g. Sakwa 2017; Radin and Reach 2017; Miskimmon and O'Loughlin 2017; Tsereteli 2018). However, the existing literature still lacks a comprehensive study that evaluates Russia's interactions with the international system in the light of its policies with regard to multiple regions and various state and non-state actors. On the other hand, the Russian foreign policy literature is dominated with country-specific, geography-oriented and issue-based studies. This volume, in contrast, aims to provide a broader and more integrative approach to understand the evolution of Russian responses to key regional and global issues and Russia's engagements with a number of international institutions including the Eurasian Economic Union (EAEU), Shanghai Cooperation Organization (SCO), Collective Security Treaty Organization (CSTO) and BRICS.

This volume also seeks to diversify the conceptual and empirical accounts regarding Russia's evolving role in the international system. In doing so, it tries to provide answers to the following research questions:

- How do the Russian leaders view the international order and perceive their country's role as an international actor?
- How does Russia perceive the concept of "rising powers"? What are the contradictions between Russia's roles as a great power and a rising power?
- What are the main determinants of Russia's claim to be a great power? Which global and regional aspirations determine the perceptions of the Russian leadership regarding their country's great power status?
- How are the discourses of "anti-Westernism" and "post-Westernism" employed in the redefinition of Russia's relations with other actors of the international system?
- What is the significance of the "East" or "Asia" in Russia's views about the international system? What is the relevance of organizations such as the EAEU, BRICS, CSTO and SCO in the evolution of this perception?
- How do the issues of Ukraine, Crimea and Syria influence or legitimize Russia's claims about the international order? How does Russia perceive the concept of "regional hegemony" particularly in the former Soviet Union and the Middle East?

The duality in Russia's actorness in the international system creates certain confusion in the IR literature and thus must be exposed with a specific focus on Moscow's recent foreign policy actions. It is important to approach this subject from different angles using various case studies and focus on the "realist-idealist", "regional-global" and "political-economic" implications of Russia's activism in the international system. What separates this volume from the previous studies on Russian foreign policy is that it elaborates on Russia's global governance policies—particularly in the regional institutions—and adopts an encompassing perspective to the strategies pursued by Moscow in key issue areas like energy, security, regional conflicts, international political economy and international organizations. The chapters of the volume also shed a light on Russia's perceptions about the transformation in the world order and the responses developed by Russian policymakers to the ongoing security challenges and economic issues at both the material and normative levels. Structured around various topics like post-Westernism, multipolarity and regional hegemony, the chapters offer a comprehensive understanding of Russian foreign policy in the face of regional and global challenges.

In this introductory chapter, we argue that Russia's role in the changing international system as well as its main motives and instruments in its regional and global engagements should be evaluated in accordance with its multiple actorness in the international system, its distinct interpretation of the international order and its mixed approach to multilateralism. It is clear that Russia's reading of the present world order differs significantly from the interpretation of its Western counterparts. In fact, the Russian vision of world politics is far from being "Western" at the normative level, since it does not act as a "norm taker" in the current international structure and rather tends to impose its own norms by challenging the norm diffusion strategies initiated by the Western powers. Against this background, it is important to grasp how Russia's "illiberal" approach to the international order shapes its foreign policy outcomes as well as its problematic relations with the West.

RUSSIA'S MULTIPLE ACTORNESS IN THE CHANGING INTERNATIONAL SYSTEM

Russia is traditionally regarded as a great power in the IR literature due to its large geographical size, rich energy resources, advanced nuclear capabilities and permanent seat at the United Nations Security Council

(UNSC). These capabilities enable Russia to project significant geopolitical influence in various regions including Eastern Europe, Asia-Pacific, Middle East, Caucasus and Central Asia. Yet, it should be recalled that Russia has been struggling with major economic and social problems. Its population has been in decline since the collapse of the Soviet Union, while its economic indicators have been deteriorating due to the fluctuating energy prices as well as the ongoing Western economic sanctions. This has urged Russia to associate itself in a more visible way with groupings such as BRICS and SCO, through which it has successfully developed stronger political and economic links with rising powers such as China and India.

At the same time, however, Russia itself can be viewed as a rising power, since it has some significant similarities with other rising powers in terms of its positional, behavioural and functional power. More importantly, it shares a strong ideological affinity with other rising powers in terms of challenging the Western supremacy in international relations and strives to create an alternative to the Western-dominated world order (Oğuzlu and Parlar Dal 2013). Moscow also tries to use its strategic realignment with the rising powers to advance its influence in global and regional politics.

In short, Russia can be defined as a "multifaceted actor" that is capable of playing different roles depending on the context as well as the changing global and regional circumstances. Yet, it should be noted that Russia's adaptation to post-bipolar world order has not been without tensions, as it has pursued different status policies at two different fronts. On the one hand, it has sought to maintain its great power status despite the domestic political, economic and social difficulties it has encountered since the early 1990s. Its military involvement in the disputes in Georgia and Ukraine, in particular, proves that Russia pursues policies that aim to challenge the existing rules and norms of the international order. On the other hand, Moscow has striven to upgrade its status in the hierarchy of states and chosen to act as a rising power in the multipolar international system—in a very similar way with other rising powers like China, India and Brazil.

It can be claimed that this duality of roles in the international system gives significant leverage to Russia in global governance as it is able to pursue different policies depending on the type of its actorness. For instance, in the field of security governance, Russia prefers to act more like a great power, while in economic governance or in other global governance issue areas, it acts as a rising power that holds limited power capacity in both material and ideational terms compared with other great powers—particularly the US.

Russia's evolving relationship with China is especially important in terms of understanding the contradictions between its roles as a great power and a rising power (Charap et al. 2017). Compared with China, Russia has limited capacity to expand its influence outside its borders mainly due to its relatively weak trading state posture as well as the lack of adequate resources in financing and infrastructure investments in extra regional geographies. For instance, China's influence in Latin America, sub-Saharan Africa and the Persian Gulf is much more prominent than the Russian influence. Partly due to this factor, Russia seems to have been following a two-layered policy towards China that is simultaneously based on cooperation and rivalry (Kaczmarski 2015). Moscow and Beijing pursue similar status-seeking strategies in international institutions like BRICS, G20 and SCO, while Central Asia, for instance, is perceived as a theatre of great power competition by the Russian leaders where China is treated more like a rival than a partner. Still, it should be noted that the Russian strategy towards China is not in the form of direct confrontation, and Moscow seeks more advantageous terms of cooperation with China in regional and global politics. In short, it can be argued that Moscow follows a highly pragmatic and multi-approach policy towards China.

Encountering the Liberal International Order: The Russian Way

A second question that needs to be addressed is what kind of an international order Russia hopes to preserve in the post–Cold War period. Answers to this question, however, vary depending on the four key features of Russia's interpretation of the existing international order.

(a) Normativeness: The normative dimension of Russia's understanding of the international order can be regarded as a reaction to the Western rules and norms about international law. Yet, it should be mentioned that Russia does not propose a concrete alternative to the West in this sphere. It rather prefers to advocate a flux model of normative order which it claims to be more comprehensive and fairer than the Western model (Romanova 2018). For instance, Moscow rejects the implementation of the Responsibility to Protect (R2P) and views this doctrine against the principles of state sovereignty and non-intervention (Averre and Davies 2015). In a similar way, it does not view the norms that are related with human rights and liberal democracy as supreme. Thus, Russia's normativeness is actually quite thin, communitarian and limited.

(b) Emphasis on sovereignty: State sovereignty is a key principle in Russia's understanding of the international order which means that no state is permitted to intervene in the internal affairs of another state with the claim that basic human rights are violated by national governments. In this sense, Russia views the R2P doctrine as a pretext of the Western powers to achieve regime change in other countries by the use of military force. It should also be noted that Russia's dedication to the principle of sovereignty and non-intervention in this regard is quite similar with the approach of other rising powers.

(c) Revisionism: Russia constantly demands the revision of the international order in accordance with the principles of justice, fairness and equality. In Georgia and Ukraine, this has even resulted in direct military intervention which has been defended by President Putin on the grounds of challenging the US-led international order. Revisionism in this regard is a key element of the Russian leadership's populist discourse regarding international relations (Allison 2017). However, it should be emphasized that Russia's revisionism is not full-fledged, but partial (Clunan 2018). This means that Moscow does not seek to re-establish a brand new international order on the ruins of the existing order and rather aims to preserve some of the traditional principles (e.g. balance of power and sphere of influences) of the existing order that serve the Russian interests.

(d) Multilateralism: Russian discourse about the international order strongly advocates multi-purposed and multi-regional cooperation within the framework of international institutions in specific issue areas such as climate change, international trade, conflict management and economic governance. On the other hand, its permanent membership in the UNSC gives Russia significant leverage in the field of international security and conflict management. It should also be remembered that Moscow has underlined in various occasions that it rejects the unilateral actions of the Western powers.

An important dimension of Russia's understanding of the international order is related with how the Russian leadership perceives its relations with the US. Especially in the Caucasus and Middle East, Russia has gradually expanded its influence vis-à-vis the West in the past decade and become much more engaged in the reshaping of the international order in line with its own national interests. It can even be argued in this regard that Russia seeks to benefit from the lack of a clear US strategy in the Trump era and exploit the tensions among NATO members over issues like defence spending and nuclear disarmament. Russia sees the liberal values promoted by the Western countries as functional instruments of interventionism that have been frequently employed in the name of democracy against other countries (Clunan 2018; Holm and Tjalve 2018).

In this sense, the Russian leaders argue that the international order does not necessarily need to be liberal. Yet, this is not very surprising when one considers the evolution of the Russian regime in the 2000s as well as the identity, ideology and foreign policy preferences that have defined Putin's Russia (Pieper 2019; Götz and Merlen 2019; Clunan 2018). The rise of "competitive authoritarianism" which is used by scholars to define the populist and nationalist governments around the world also makes it easy for Russia to challenge the liberal values of the West and advocate illiberal strategies in both the domestic and international spheres (Levitsky and Way 2010). The illiberal turn in some of the countries of Eastern Europe in particular seems to have strengthened Moscow's claim that the international order does not need to be exclusively liberal.

It is also not surprising to view that the Russian leadership has been long advocating the continuity of a "multipolar world order" in which Russia holds a "special" role as a great power—a perception that is inherited from the Cold War period. It can be argued that the existence of multiple power poles in the international system provides additional leverage to the Kremlin which places Russia higher than the other rising powers in the hierarchy of states in the international system. This leverage has been positively welcomed and actively used by the Russian leaders in their diplomatic dealings with other countries and institutions around the world.

There is still no consensus among the Western analysts whether Russia maintains its status as a great power and a counterbalance to the US in the international order. Despite its serious economic weaknesses, its impressive military potential and diplomatic influence nevertheless enable Moscow to play the role of a hegemon in specific regions. Russia actively uses its deepening political and economic partnership with China to protect this image. Yet, it should be underlined that the Russian perceptions about a rising China are somewhat unpredictable (Parlar Dal 2019). The gradual decline in the US hegemony and growth of China's material and soft power at the global level may currently seem to be working to Russia's favour in terms of challenging the West in global politics. However, the Russian leaders must seriously take into consideration the rise of China while reshaping their policies, as Russia can easily be perceived as China's "junior partner" in the longer term considering the significant asymmetry of economic power between the two states.

RUSSIA'S IN-BETWEEN ROLE IN MULTILATERALISM

In the current age of multilateralism, Russia seems to have been pursuing a balanced and pragmatic strategy vis-a-vis the other rising powers as well as the West (Macfarlane 2006). Its prudent approach towards China's expansion of power on the global scale and its emphasis on cooperation rather than competition in its relations with China also justify its strong attachment to multilateralism at both the policy level and institutional level (Charap et al. 2017). Russia's institutionalism is also diverse and multidimensional. Its membership in both major global governance institutions and regional and/or informal institutions is a clear evidence of its twofold global governance strategy between the Global North and the Global South. This also illustrates that Russia tries to establish a delicate balance between its rising power status and great power status. Here, it should be underlined that this duality of roles strengthens Russia's hand in many issue areas including security and climate change. In short, remaining in this grey area enables Russia to preserve its distinct and in-between approach regarding multilateralism.

Russia is also a champion of socialization in the international institutions where it has a membership. The Russian leaders frequently express their interest in active cooperation with other actors in the international institutions (Ministry of Foreign Affairs 2018). In Russia's view, the current international order is not based on multilateralism, but a nuanced unilateralism. In this regard, Moscow believes the US dominance in major international organizations and the unilateral US actions in the international system must be balanced by the increasing contribution of other states in the global governance structures.

However, it should be emphasized that Russia seems to prefer a loose multilateral system rather than a stronger one. It also tends to strike a delicate balance between multilateralism and bilateralism in its foreign policy. In addition, the Russian view of multilateralism is pluralist rather than solidarist. Its reticence in supporting the demands of rising powers like Brazil and India for reform in the UNSC is a clear illustration of its nuanced approach to multilateralism, which seems to be favouring status quo rather than genuine change in the international system. On the other hand, Russia is not among the countries with the highest financial contribution to UN and its agencies, while its military and ideational contribution to the UN is also remarkably weak—particularly when one considers Moscow's strong rhetorical support to multilateral institutions. Against this background, it can actually be argued that Russia is still a fragile actor in multilateralism due to the large gap between its motivations and its de facto contribution to global governance.

OUTLINE OF THE CHAPTERS

The chapters of this volume seek to examine Russia's role, position and policies in the changing international order and global governance architecture. In his chapter (Chap. 2), Richard Sakwa argues that after a quarter century of stasis, the pattern of world order is changing and the inter-cold war period of the cold peace is giving way not to a thaw, but to the re-entrenchment of bipolar confrontation between the expansive liberal international order and the resistance of a group of states including Russia. In his view, like the First Cold War, the second is also about the conflicting views of world order as the US-led liberal international order is challenged by the emergence of a putative anti-hegemonic alignment between Russia, China and their allies in the emerging alternative architecture of world affairs. Therefore, the clash between Russia and the West is only an early version of the challenges against the long-term stasis in international affairs. Sakwa concludes that although the sinews of a post-Western world are emerging, it remains to be seen whether bodies like the SCO or BRICS will be able to sustain the multilateralism of the last seven decades in the absence of the hegemon that had provided the security and support for such multilateralism to thrive.

Andrey Makarychev elaborates on Russia's European policies and argues that despite the current conflicts between Russia and the EU, the latter remains a key reference point in a plethora of Russian discourses that are Europe-centric in the sense of playing with different arguments aimed at vindicating Russia's belonging to Europe through loosely defined history, geography and culture, but also through accentuating Russia's military presence and ability to interfere in European domestic processes. The chapter traces the trajectory of Russia's EU policies since the beginning of the 1990s until the present, compares Russian and European approaches to international relations and discusses Russia's rhetorical manoeuvring under the conditions of drastic deterioration of relations with the West after 2014. Makarychev additionally focuses on Russia's policies towards the EU from the viewpoint of broader debates on post-liberal international order and shares some critical insights on the state of communication between Russia and Europe.

In Chap. 4, Jeanne L. Wilson discusses the goals and motivations of Russia as a regional actor and argues that under the presidency of Boris Yeltsin in the 1990s, Russia neither possessed the will nor the capability to assume a dominant role in its relations with its neighbours, while Vladimir Putin came to office with the goal of reversing the decline in Russia's presence in the post-Soviet space. Putin's new foreign policy has included various efforts to project Russian influence in the post-Soviet space through the establishment or strengthening of regional structures: CSTO, SCO and EAEU. The chapter argues that Putin's efforts simultaneously serve as a means of redesigning the role of Russia as the hegemonic leader of a regional bloc which is a role that validates Moscow's claim to be a great power. These efforts, however, have been challenged by a number of factors which include the regional and global implications of Russia's annexation of Crimea as well as the Russian leadership's increasing tendency to conceive of Eurasian integration as a civilizational project.

In his chapter that focuses on the EAEU, Alexander Libman argues that this organization has become a major topic for discussions about Russia's attempts to resurge as a regional and even a global power as well as the subject of major controversy. However, in the political and scholarly discourse about the EAEU, there exist multiple and partly overlapping images of this organization. The chapter reviews the perceptions of the EAEU in Eurasia and beyond, arguing that both the Russian and international observers share an important common feature in their view of the EAEU: the focus on the geopolitical role of the organization and in particular its alleged ability to enhance Russia's influence in the global arena. Libman indicates, however, that the research on the EAEU faces an important problem: the institutional design of this regional organization does not seem to be particularly suitable to promote the Russian hegemony.

Marcin Kaczmarski elaborates on Russia's relations with China and argues that there is some kind of an informal division of labour between these two countries in the current global governance architecture. Russia remains active in the realm of international security governance, whereas China has increased the level of its participation in areas of economic, financial and environmental governance. These differences are ascribed to the different potential of both states as well as their related varied scope of interests in a well-functioning global governance system. However, Kaczmarski argues that this division of labour has evolved in the last couple of years. Beijing has increased its engagement with international security governance, while Moscow has lost some of its (already limited) interest in such areas as environmental or economic governance. The chapter aims at exploring this shift and its implications. Rather than analysing Sino-Russian relations in distinct areas of global governance, it proposes a different approach and identifies three patterns of interactions between the two countries: direct cooperation, parallel activities and contradictory/divergent activities.

Taking a geopolitical economic perspective, Emre İşeri and Volkan Özdemir argue that at a time of critical geopolitical economic changes (i.e. power shifts and volatile energy prices), Russia has been pursuing different foreign policy lines on the two sides of the Eurasian landmass. On the one hand, it has been intensifying its economic ties with Asia-Pacific, particularly with China. On the other hand, it has been pursuing an assertive policy against the interests of the Western powers (e.g. in Georgia, Ukraine and Syria). How do these geopolitical changes interact with Russia's different foreign policy orientations as an aspiring great power and an energy giant? To answer this question, the chapter adopts a neo-classical realist approach to argue that at a time of profound global changes, the geopolitical economic perceptions of the Russian elites regarding their resource-rent based country's role in the Eurasian landmass have created such a duality in its foreign policy. The authors conclude that the Russian elites' sense of geopolitical exposure and economic policy preferences have not only prompted this discrepancy in Russian foreign policy but also undermined Russia's great power prospects in the twenty-first century.

In his chapter that focuses on Russia's policies towards BRICS, Alexander Sergunin argues that Russia's approach about this grouping represents a combination of ideational and material motives. On the one hand, BRICS is important for Moscow in terms of enhancing its status in international relations. On the other hand, the Kremlin prioritizes its economic and strategic partnership with the BRICS countries, since they are important for Russia's wellbeing and sustainable development as well as its efforts for counter-balancing the West in the global geoeconomic and geopolitical arena. For Sergunin, Russia's active participation in BRICS indicates that Moscow prefers to redesign its foreign policy in a way to support and further develop international norms, rules and institutions as well as non-coercive and soft power methods. The BRICS framework in this regard provides Moscow with not only additional authority in the world community but also legitimacy to its international activities. All these factors explain why the Kremlin attaches great importance to the BRICS and why strengthening BRICS and its role in global politics is viewed in Moscow as a basis for solidifying Russia's political and economic position in the international arena.

The chapter by Sergii V. Glebov (Chap. 9) aims to evaluate the regional and global impacts of the conflict in Ukraine in relation with the challenges posed by Russia to the security of the Euro-Atlantic community. Relations between Russia and the Western countries are currently going through a period of a clash of principles and interests at all the systemic levels, which has turned into an asymmetric conflict since 2014. Some analysts even claim that a "New Cold War" has emerged between Russia and the West. Yet, for Glebov, the risk of such a new Cold War directly affects the sustainability of the Trans-Atlantic security architecture especially in light of Moscow's efforts to preserve the post-Soviet space as an area of geopolitical turmoil and a target of its aggression and domination. The author argues that by punishing Ukraine for its Western aspirations, Moscow openly expressed its geopolitical will to become a global—although an isolated and hybrid—superpower. In this respect, it should be indicated that Russia continues to portray the West as a "wicked scarecrow" in order to hide its own imperial designs.

Regina Heller argues that the hard power policy of Russia towards Ukraine since 2014 is not only about projecting its regional power but also about reclaiming a principal rank in the social order of the international community in the twenty-first century. This assumption is based on two main observations: (a) Russia has actually been losing its influence over Ukraine as well as the former Soviet space due to its coercive policies to maintain its control over Ukraine, and (b) while Russia has discursively placed the Ukraine issue in the context of global power shifts and renegotiation of the world order and defended traditional international relations principles such as state sovereignty and non-intervention, it has actually neglected the same principles in Ukraine. The chapter argues in this regard that the Russian policy towards Ukraine is closely related with the efforts of the Russian elites in order to deal with their unresolved anger over earlier negative experiences of status deprivation in their relations with the West.

In their chapter (Chap. 11), Victor Jeifets and Nikolay Dobronravin highlight the main dynamics that shape Russia's policy towards aspiring political movements and unrecognized states. Moscow's attitude towards these actors has been traditionally determined by its foreign policy paradigm which favours establishing official links only with sovereign and recognized states. This attitude was quite noticeable even during the Soviet era when Moscow supported the idea of a world revolution and Soviet foreign policy was officially coordinated with the activities of the Communist International all around the world. Between 1991 and 2008, the leadership of the Russian Federation also continued this policy. Yet, Russia's attitude started to change when Kosovo's independence was recognized by many Western states, which has also been one of the main reasons prompting Moscow to recognize the independence of Abkhazia and South Ossetia following the Russian-Georgian war. The authors argue in this regard that since 2008, Russia's policy has gradually drifted towards a wider recognition of the de facto states and aspiring political movements around the world.

In his chapter (Chap. 12), Philipp Casula investigates Russia's foreign policy along with three key types of power that modernity has produced—sovereignty, reason of state and biopolitics—highlighting how their respective instruments are fielded by Russia's current regime. In this sense, his analysis is different from many Western observers who have been quick to declare "a new Cold War" with Russia or to point at the inherently autocratic character of the Russian regime in order to explain the motivations behind Moscow's annexation of Crimea and its military intervention in Syria. The chapter does not simply seek to explain the reasons underlying Russia's foreign policy conduct, but rather aims to analyse its formal mechanisms, which often resemble those of other modern great powers. Casula argues that Russia's military interventions in Crimea and Syria do not represent a break with the previously professed principles of Russian foreign policy. Rather, Russia has adopted the entire repertoire of devices, means or mechanisms available to modern states: all the tools of sovereignty, reason of state and biopolitics remain present both in domestic and foreign policy.

In the final chapter of the volume (Chap. 13), Alexey Khlebnikov focuses on the Middle East and claims that the region has never been a priority area for Russian foreign policy, although in the last few years Moscow visibly boosted its ambitions and enhanced its influence there. The chapter argues that the current Russian leadership is guided by two major factors in the Middle East: (a) security concerns (terrorist threats and destabilization of fragile states) and, (b) economic opportunities (energy, arms sales, etc.) which accompany the improvement of political ties. Furthermore, Moscow's more ambitious policy towards the Middle East can be explained not only by its overall strategy to increase its regional influence, but also by the foreign policy opportunities that are created by the gradual retreat of the US from the region. Thus, for Khlebnikov, Moscow's Middle East policy is basically shaped by the US actions and decisions with regard to this region. As Russia lacks the resources to constantly support its presence in the Middle East and the Russian leaders are well aware of such limitations, the Kremlin pursues a policy which seeks to limit the risks and loss of investments in this region.

In Lieu of Conclusion

Whether Russia should be regarded as a great power or a rising power depends on the perspective through which one looks at the Russian foreign policy. The main motives and policies of Russia as well as the degree of its activism show a striking change depending on the issue Moscow deals with. In various global governance issue areas such as environment, climate change, health and development, Russia engages with the international system in a similar way with the other rising powers. On the other hand, its permanent membership at UNSC and its actorness in the security sphere, which has largely been constructed during the Cold War era, make Russia an indispensable actor for global security governance. In this sense, as also discussed in many chapters of this volume, Russia can be defined as a "hybrid actor" in terms of its identity and role as well as its material and ideational power. At the same time, however, the pursuit of different types of relations with multiple state and non-state actors makes Russia a "complex actor" that needs to be further analysed at the domestic, regional and global levels.

As the chapters of the volume suggest, the gap between motivation and action is very significant in the Russian case and this gap has a large impact on Russia's policies in the global governance architecture. Its economic weaknesses as well as its illiberal policies both at home and abroad turn Russia into a fragile state at the international level (Johnson and Köstem 2016). This also prompts the Russian leaders to pursue status-seeking policies in multiple international organizations and forums. On the other hand, its quest for a higher status in the international system makes Russia a revisionist power in its immediate neighbourhood. Russia's annexation of Crimea and military involvement in Syria clearly demonstrate the pursuit of a "grandeur policy" in this regard.

Yet, as indicated by the developments in the Middle East, despite its bold ambitions, Russia possesses a limited military and diplomatic power capacity to decisively shape the course of events in the Syrian crisis. In fact, the Syrian issue has demonstrated Russia's limitations in regional security governance and put the Russian efforts into test regarding the new order that is taking shape in the Middle East. On the other hand, whether its involvement in the Syrian civil war has really enabled Russia to upgrade its status in the international system still remains an open question (Pieper 2019).

In short, its nuanced understanding of the liberal world order and multilateralism showcase the dual nature of Russia's role in world politics. Russian foreign policy in this sense is often in contradiction with the liberal principles of the Western foreign policy at the normative level. In this era of post-hegemonic world order, which has been marked by continuous power shifts from the Global North to the Global South, Russian efforts to create "safe and peaceful" regional orders clearly show the extent to which Moscow has been pursuing revisionist foreign policy ambitions.

References

Allison, Roy. 2017. Russia and the Post-2014 International Legal Order: Revisionism and Realpolitik. *International Affairs* 93 (3): 519–543. https://doi.org/10.1093/ia/iix061.

Averre, Derek, and Lance Davies. 2015. Russia, Humanitarian Intervention and the Responsibility to Protect: The Case of Syria. *International Affairs* 91 (4): 813–834. https://doi.org/10.1111/1468-2346.12343.

Charap, Samuel, John Drennan, and Pierre Noël. 2017. Russia and China: A New Model of Great-Power Relations. *Survival: Global Politics and Strategy* 59 (1): 25–42. https://doi.org/10.1080/00396338.2017.1282670.

Clunan, Anne L. 2018. Russia and the Liberal World Order. *Ethics & International Affairs* 32 (1): 45–59. https://doi.org/10.1017/S0892679418000096.

Götz, Elias, and Camille-Renaud Merlen. 2019. Russia and the Question of World Order. *European Politics & Society* 20 (2): 133–153. https://doi.org/10.1080/23745118.2018.1545181.

Holm, Minda, and Vibeke Schou Tjalve. 2018. Visions of an Illiberal World Order? The National Right in Europe, Russia and the US. *Norwegian Institute of International Affairs*, November 5. https://www.nupi.no/en/Publications/CRIStin-Pub/Visions-of-an-Illiberal-World-Order-The-National-Right-in-Europe-Russia-and-the-US.

Johnson, Juliet, and Seçkin Köstem. 2016. Frustrated Leadership: Russia's Economic Alternative to the West. *Global Policy* 7 (2): 207–216. https://doi.org/10.1111/1758-5899.12301.

Kaczmarski, Marcin. 2015. *Russia-China Relations in the Post-crisis International Order*. London: Routledge.

Levitsky, Steven, and Lucan A. Way. 2010. *Competitive Authoritarianism: Hybrid Regimes After the Cold War*. New York: Cambridge University Press.

Macfarlane, S. Neil. 2006. The 'R' in BRICs: Is Russia an Emerging Power? *International Affairs* 82 (1): 41–57. https://doi.org/10.1111/j.1468-2346.2006.00514.x.

Ministry of Foreign Affairs. 2018. Foreign Minister Sergey Lavrov's Remarks at BRICS Foreign Ministers Meeting, Pretoria. June 4. http://www.mid.ru.

Miskimmon, Alister, and Ben O'Loughlin. 2017. Russia's Narratives of Global Order: Great Power Legacies in a Polycentric World. *Politics and Governance* 5 (3): 111–120. https://doi.org/10.17645/pag.v5i3.1017.

Oğuzlu, Tarık, and Emel Parlar Dal. 2013. Decoding Turkey's Rise: An Introduction. *Turkish Studies* 14 (4): 617–636. https://doi.org/10.1080/14683849.2013.861112.

Parlar Dal, Emel. 2019. Status Competition and Rising Powers in Global Governance: An Introduction. *Contemporary Politics*. https://doi.org/10.1080/13569775.2019.1627767.

Pieper, Moritz. 2019. Rising Power Status and the Evolution of International Order: Conceptualising Russia's Syria Policies. *Europe-Asia Studies*. https://doi.org/10.1080/09668136.2019.1575950.

Radin, Andrew, and Clint Reach. 2017. *Russian Views of the International Order*. Santa Monica: Rand.

Romanova, Tatiana. 2018. Russia's Neorevisionist Challenge to the Liberal International Order. *The International Spectator* 53 (1): 76–91. https://doi.org/10.1080/03932729.2018.1406761.

Sakwa, Richard. 2017. *Russia Against the Rest: The Post–Cold War Crisis of World Order*. New York: Cambridge University Press.

Tsereteli, Mamuka. 2018. Can Russia's Quest for the New International Order Succeed? *Orbis* 62 (2): 204–219. https://doi.org/10.1016/j.orbis.2018.02.003.

CHAPTER 2

Stasis and Change: Russia and the Emergence of an Anti-hegemonic World Order

Richard Sakwa

INTRODUCTION

After a quarter century of stasis, the pattern of world order is changing. The inter-cold war period of the cold peace is giving way not to a thaw, but to the re-entrenchment of bipolar confrontation. Like the First Cold War, the second is also about the conflicting views of world order, although the language and modalities differ. The US-led liberal international order is challenged by the emergence of a putative anti-hegemonic alignment (Sakwa 2017). This phenomenon is much bigger than simply the re-emergence of China as a global actor or Russia's neo-revisionist stance that challenges the practices of the previously hegemonic world order. Both countries defend the multilateral norms of the international system, but challenge the assumption that the liberal world order is synonymous with order itself. The two countries and to varying degrees their allies in the emerging alternative architecture of world affairs—notably the Shanghai Cooperation Organization (SCO) and the BRICS (Brazil,

R. Sakwa (✉)
University of Kent, Canterbury, UK
e-mail: r.sakwa@kent.ac.uk

© The Author(s) 2020
E. Parlar Dal, E. Erşen (eds.), *Russia in the Changing International System*, https://doi.org/10.1007/978-3-030-21832-4_2

Russia, India, China, South Africa)—have also adopted elements of the neo-revisionist position, and this provides the ideational framework for the emerging anti-hegemonic world order.

Members of this nascent alignment stress that it is not directed against anyone. The stated goal is to restore balance in world affairs within the framework not simply of multipolarity (although polycentrism, as Russians put it, is a key value) but through a positive agenda of a new model of international relations. The alignment is thus not "counter" hegemonic, which would simply replicate the existing pattern of international behaviour, but "anti" hegemonic, questioning the very idea that a single state and its allies can claim "primacy" in world affairs or that their ideology can be considered universal. This position was already implicitly asserted in 1945 in the Yalta system of great power relationships but was then "democratized" through the principles enunciated in the Helsinki Final Act of August 1975. In the First Cold War, the US-led liberal international order was challenged by the Soviet bloc within the framework of a bipolar international order, but in the post-1989 period, the assertion of unipolarity undermined the principles of both Yalta and Helsinki (Ikenberry 2011). Today the aspirations for multipolarity are embedded in the broader emergence of two contesting visions of world order (Smith 2013). The confrontation between the expansive liberal international order and the resistance of a group of states provoked the Second Cold War. The Trump phenomenon then emerged as an intervening variable, challenging both post-war representations of American hegemony and those who were coalescing in resistance to it.

This chapter seeks to explore Russia's perceptions regarding the emergence of an anti-hegemonic world order at a time when the stasis in the international system is being replaced by dynamics of change. The first section discusses the end of stasis in the international system and how Russia responds to it—particularly in terms of its relations with the West. The second section elaborates on the factors shaping Russia's distinct neo-revisionism which has emerged largely as a reaction to the absence of transformation of the European security system at the end of the Cold War. The third section focuses on the dynamics of change in the international system and the way Russia tries to redefine its relations with the West as well as other rising powers like China.

The International System and the End of Stasis

The emergence of a putative alternative model of world order promises to disrupt the long stasis in international affairs that predominated since 1945. Although 1989 brought important changes to the practice of international politics, the international system was not fundamentally transformed (Pouliot 2010). Equally, the current period of dynamic change is not intended by the key subaltern actors to revise the international system but only its practices. This is why Russia and China are not revisionist powers, but neo-revisionist: seeking to change how the existing works rather than changing the system itself. In the quarter century of the inter-Cold War years (1989–2014), otherwise known as the period of the cold peace, the liberal international order became more ambitious (within the framework of the ideology of globalization and the "end of history"), but the post-1945 order prevailed. The main process after 1989 was the "enlargement" of the liberal order accompanied by extensive claims to hegemony. From that perspective, 1989 did not represent such a radical break, other than for the countries directly involved. Only after the expanding liberal order "hit reality" has some rethinking begun (Mearsheimer 2018).

Only now, some 70 years after the end of the Second World War, is a major shift taking place in the international system. Acharya (2017) describes the new system as "multiplex", while Flockhart (2016) describes the phenomenon as a "multi-order" world. The central point is not only that unipolarity has given way to multipolarity, but that the framework for relations between orders marks a qualitative change in international relations, and thus represents a return to the "transformative" agenda outlined by Mikhail Gorbachev at the end of the First Cold War. The inter-Cold War period was characterized by tension between enlargement and transformation, but with the onset of the Second Cold War in 2014, the long period of stasis when the US-led liberal order predominated (although challenged by the Soviet Union and its allies for some of the period) is now giving way to a renewed period of confrontation. While Gorbachev and his successors at the head of the Russian state sought a positive transformation within the framework of the post-Second War international system, the Second Cold War is characterized by a negative transformation in which the logic of confrontation has been restored.

Stasis means more than simply stagnation, but it does suggest a certain inflexibility, immobility and absence of institutional or ideational innovation. It is in the latter sense that the term is used to describe the post-First

Cold War security order in Europe. The foundations of that order were laid after 1945 in conditions of a developing bipolar confrontation between the Soviet bloc on the one hand and the US and its allies on the other. This Atlantic system became the core of the global US-led liberal international order. After 1989, this order—dubbed by Russian scholars the "Historical West"—began a process of enlargement to Eastern Europe, while at the same time under the guise of "globalization", it made claims to be universal. However, from the very beginning, Gorbachev, the Soviet leader who did the main work in bringing the Cold War to an end, believed that instead of enlargement being the governing process, the conduct of international relations should have been transformed to take advantage of the uniquely benign situation of the late 1980 and early 1990s. The idea was that the Soviet Union, and later Russia under its leader Boris Yeltsin, would engage with the Historical West as the co-founders of a new political community, what could putatively be called a "Greater West". The deeper aspiration no doubt was to strip out the elements of American globalism (the power system) from globalization (the convergence of world politics through economic and societal interactions).

This would have required some institutional innovation and ideational creativity, but the project for a positive transcendence of the logic of conflict, Russian political leaders and academics continue to insist, was not only feasible but essential if the Cold War and confrontation were not to return to divide the continent. However, old-style globalism remained and in certain respects was reinforced. Russia refused to accept the role of junior partner in an already established enterprise, but sought to join that enterprise as an equal, believing thereby that the enterprise would be transformed by its membership. In other words, Russia's assertion of its great power status did not entail the reassertion of some sort of imperial project, particularly in its neighbourhood, but sought to be institutionalized through the transformation of the traditional Atlantic community into a pan-European and indeed global community. This would have avoided the tension generated by the merger between democratization and geopolitics that structured the cold peace and then generated the Second Cold War. The "democratic peace theory" in this period assumed that the enlargement of the sphere of liberal democracy would guarantee the security of the Atlantic system. It was thus assumed that joining NATO was the "democratic" thing to do, even if large sections of the relevant populations opposed the idea.

Russia's ideas for an alternative were only slowly formulated, and to this day lack substantive theoretical articulation. This is why Russia is sometimes seen as a "spoiler": unwilling to accept what is posed as universal values, yet unable to formulate an intellectually attractive alternative. Instead, the enlargement agenda, specifically in Europe but globally as well in the form of the agenda of the liberal international order became hegemonic. However, the contradictions in that order, above all the tension between its norms and power system in which it was embedded—the tension between democratization and geopolitics (condemned by Russia as "double standards")—in the end provoked a reaction which gave rise to an anti-hegemonic alignment.

This is not an alliance let alone a bloc, but the alignment is gradually developing a more ramified institutional architecture, while at the same time, formulating a more coherent model of an alternative world order—all within the framework of the existing international system. The clash of orders is accompanied by contending models of international affairs. On the one side, realists assert that structural factors shape international politics, although there is no consensus about what the relevant structures are. Offensive realists stress the importance of anarchy as the primary condition, with international relations determined by the struggle for power and predominance by an international system populated by "billiard ball" states, in which domestic regimes and systems of governance are irrelevant (Mearsheimer 2014a). At the other extreme are constructivists, who argue that identities are shaped by mutual interaction between the "self" and "other" (Wendt 1992). Equally, realists are countered by the partisans of the "liberal world order" who assert that the rules-based system that has become predominant since 1945, and reinforced by Western "victory" over the Soviet Union after the end of the First Cold War in 1989, means that the traditional lexicon of great power politics, along with spheres of influence, balancing and bloc politics, have become anachronistic.

In this conception, the democratic sphere is universal and assumes a monistic ideological and institutional character, whereas Gorbachev's early proposal for a common European home, taken up by his successors in the form of the idea of "greater Europe", assumes a pluralism of ideational and institutional forms. In other words, expansive globalism (although embedded in the putative universalism of globalization) ran into the rocks of Sino-Russian particularism—although this particularism is embedded in a conservative form of internationalism.

This only makes sense in the context of a credible understanding of the international system. Drawing on English School thinkers, I argue that the international system today is a fundamental hybrid, in which realist concerns about state sovereignty, security and autonomy predominate at the horizontal level in relations between states; but at the vertical level neo-revisionist states such as Russia and China are committed to the institutions of multilateral governance (Sakwa 2017). Thus the international system has a binary structure. At the top there is the UN and the ramified "secondary institutions" (as termed by English School theorists) of international legal, economic, environmental and financial regulation. Although the autonomous power of these institutions should not be exaggerated, neither should they be dismissed. The UN remains the main source of legitimacy for international cooperative endeavours. At the lower level we have an increasing number of independent states, but their interactions have also evolved.

The triumphant US after the Second World War embedded its hegemony in the Atlantic alliance system, and on the global level advanced the multilateral and universal practices of the liberal world order. After the First Cold War, this multidimensional alliance system became the core of an enlarging "world order" with universalistic aspirations. One of the distinctive features of the Second Cold War is that the US under President Donald J. Trump has emerged as a genuinely revisionist power, no longer willing to be constrained either by the liberal international order of which it was once the core, or by the structures of multilateral governance that it had done so much to foster in the years after 1945. At a time when the traditional liberal world order is beginning to unravel (although the extent of this should not be exaggerated), the alternative "anti-hegemonic" (or post-Western) world order is beginning to take shape, intended not to challenge the norms of the international system as they have developed since the Second World War, and codified in the institutions of global governance, but to question the hegemonic role of the states comprising the liberal world order. The challenge is to the practices of international affairs as conducted by the US and its allies, and not the norms on which the international system today is governed. This is why Russia, China and their allies are neo-revisionist, and not out-and-out revisionist.

For various reasons Russia was not incorporated into the "Historical West", despite its earlier aspirations to join, and for more obvious reasons neither ultimately was China, although both took advantage of what the liberal world order had to offer. For status and a variety of historical and security reasons, neither could join the US-led liberal international order as subaltern powers. Their fundamental argument is that the liberal world order is not synonymous with order itself. Washington and its allies represent one power system, and although this system has done much to advance the public goods associated with rules-based multilateral development, it also remains a particularistic system, despite its pretensions to universality. The "secondary institutions" of international society have now come to represent an autonomous level of universal order, based on principles and ideas that are far from the proprietary invention of the US-led liberal international order (Dunne and Reut-Smith 2017). The ideas and principles underlying this universal order have long been debated in most civilizations, and although their normative formulation was greatly advanced after the Second World War, notably in the UN's Universal Declaration of Human Rights of December 1948, even this Declaration was formulated with the participation of all the major powers of the time.

In this context, the fundamental cleavage in international politics today is between the partisans of the *enlargement* of the liberal international order (even if the baton of leadership may be passing from the US to European states) and those who defend an *anti-hegemonic* view. The process of enlargement inevitability has an imperial element, if not conducted in a classically imperial manner (this is the fundamental source of "double standards" in international affairs). And imperial aggrandizement inevitably provokes a reaction. Russia, China and other powers are beginning to shape the lineaments of an alternative world order, based not on "anti-Westernism" let alone opposition to "globalization", but for the defence of pluralism in the international system. Thus an anti-hegemonic alignment is gradually taking shape, with such institutions as the SCO, BRICS and other informal ties at its core. This is post-Western rather than anti-Western (Stuenkel 2016). It betokens the onset of Flockhart's "multi-order" world and the multiplex arrangements described by Acharya. The nascent anti-hegemonic alignment defends not so much globalization as the deepening integration of global markets and development strategies through intensified internationalism, in which states retain the power to shape their industrial strategies and social policies, and to resist the supra-nationalism of investor-state adjudication mechanisms. Because of the continued vertical commitment to multilateral institutions of global governance, this is more than a reversion to traditional Westphalian internationalism. Classic definitions of globalization were understood to represent an ideological project for the enlargement of a specific model of economic relations, with US power at its core (Panarin 1998), whereas the anti-hegemonism of the rising powers insists on a modified model of multilateral globalism.

RUSSIA AND NEO-REVISIONISM

How does Russia fit into all of this? At the end of the Cold War, Russia advanced a programme to transform the European security system, and by implication, the pattern of global politics entrenched in Cold War institutions and ideologies. Gorbachev talked of a "common European home", which fitted into the classic Gaullist discourse of "Europe from the Atlantic to the Urals" and François Mitterrand's idea of a "confederation of Europe". Moscow insisted that it was the instigator of the end of the Cold War, and had thus won the right to be the co-author of a transformed post–Cold War world. With Russia's inclusion, the "Historical West" would become a "Greater West", and the structures of the Cold War would be dismantled as a common developmental programme was devised. Fearing normative dilution, institutional incoherence and, perhaps above all, the weakening of American leadership (globalism), this programme of radical transformation was rejected in favour of an enlargement agenda of the existing structures, those that had apparently achieved "victory" over the Soviet Union.

Wohlforth and Zubok (2017, 416) argue that "There were no easy 'missed opportunities' to integrate the USSR or post-Soviet Russia seamlessly into the West. To have achieved that outcome would have taken statesmanship of the sort rarely if ever witnessed in international politics". Equally, there was not much, in their view, that Russia could have done to avoid the effects of disintegration and the collapse of the Soviet bloc. There was, they rightly argue, no "vast conspiracy" to keep the country down, and instead "Russia is not an abiding preoccupation but rather an inconvenience for the West, which has strong reasons not to put its core approach to security at risk to accommodate Moscow". This is true as far as it goes but neglects the quite practical ideas put forward by the Soviet leadership at the time that provided a route out of Europe's endemic conflicts. In other words, their argument makes sense as seen from Washington, but not from the continental European capitals. The failure to seize the opportunity to build a pan-European peace order gave rise to the 25 years of the cold peace, provoking in the end the Second Cold War. In other words, no exceptional statesmanship was required, but just openness to exploit an opportunity to bring Russia and its neighbours into an inclusive and indivisible security system, thus precluding the onset of an intensifying security dilemma that provoked the 2008 Georgian war and the 2014 Ukraine conflict. While the Congress of Vienna quickly found a way to incorporate defeated France into the post-war order, the Treaty of Versailles failed to do so for Germany and thus contributed to creating the conditions for the Second World War (Kissinger 2014). The post-1991 settlement has elements of the second approach, although couched in the language of friendship and support, and thus after a "25 years' crisis" (Sakwa 2008), the First Cold War gave way to the Second.

Given that the Soviet system had dissolved and the country disintegrated, the victory discourse seemed plausible. However, politics of transformation is something that Russia would not give up so easily, along with those aligned with it outside of the liberal world order, and even within. As the radicalism of Bernie Sanders and Jeremy Corbyn suggests, the programme of transformation has deep roots in the heartlands of the liberal international order, accompanied by resurgent peace and non-aligned movements worried by the renewed drift towards militarism and confrontation. New political thinking is not a purely Russian phenomenon. The transformation agenda in international politics is accompanied by the desire for change domestically. The two are connected, and the frozen character of international relations intensified certain governing practices that introduced policy stasis into domestic politics, which in the end exploded in a wave of populist nationalism. It is hardly surprising that the right and left "populism" of today is provoked by hostility to what are perceived as global elites concerned only with the mobility of capital, labour, goods and services, while neglecting the concerns of domestic populations, who increasingly perceive themselves as the victims of globalization. Post-First Cold War elites failed in addition to create a viable European security order, provoking the Second Cold War.

While 1989 may well have been a "masterpiece of history" (Savranskaya et al. 2010), the absence of institutional and ideational innovation at the end of the Cold War is striking. Everything in Russia's history militated against it becoming simply a subordinate element of an expanding "Historical West". At first, Russia sought to devise a fundamental partnership with the enlarging EU, but even that faltered by the mid-2000s, as a wave of traditionally anti-Russian, post-communist countries joined (Maas 2016; Forsberg and Haukkala 2016). Even more disruptive was NATO enlargement, something that realists, such as George Kennan, warned would ultimately provoke a Russian counter-reaction. Equally portentous was the way that the enlargement agenda incorporated the structures of the Cold War into the expanding system. Although there was no deliberate attempt to exclude Russia, institutions such as the NATO-Russia Council were clearly devised within the framework of mitigation rather than transformational strategies. The structural condition of the cold peace was the merger of democratization and geopolitical agendas in the expanding West, in which normative concerns fused with the enlargement of the Atlantic security system. The result was "trans-democracy", based theoretically on liberal peace theory, but with enormous practical consequences (Sakwa 2017, 98–104).

As far as Russia was concerned, the 25 years of the cold peace failed to resolve any of the fundamental problems of European and global security. For Russia, NATO enlargement represented not only a betrayal of the verbal assurances apparently given at the time of German unification that the alliance would not move "one inch to the East" of the former East German territory (Savranskaya and Blanton 2017) but a provocation that only intensified the security dilemma that the alliance was intended to avert. At the end of the Cold War, Russia was offered associate membership of an existing enterprise, the "Historic West", but Russia's enduring aspiration was to become a founder member of a transformed "Greater West". Membership of the transformed community would have provided a benign framework for Russia's domestic transformation, while removing the institutional and ideational structures of the Cold War. By contrast, joining an untransformed "Historic West" entailed status demotion, since it would have been a subaltern element in a US-dominated system (Larson and Shevchenko 2003). Even under Yeltsin in the 1990s this was hard to swallow, and under Putin in the 2000s there were attempts to find a new balance between Russian adaptation and foreign policy and developmental autonomy. By the time Putin returned to presidency in 2012 for his third term, Russia had shifted to a policy of neo-revisionism: maintaining a commitment to the norms of international society, but resisting the practices of US primacy and globalism.

Neo-revisionism is the product of frustration that none of the three earlier phases of post-communist Russian foreign policy had delivered the anticipated benefits. In the first phase, that of *liberal internationalism* accompanied by a nascent Atlanticism to temper Russia's traditional Eurocentric continentalism, all sides believed that a new international community could be established. It soon became clear that the West and Russia had very different ideas of how this could be achieved, with Russia still insisting on elements of transformation and co-constitution, and the West beginning the process of enlargement that would see NATO and the EU expand to Russia's borders. This helped provoke the second stage, the era of *competitive coexistence*, from the mid-1990s under the leadership of Yevgeny Primakov, first as foreign minister from January 1996 to September 1998, and thereafter as prime minister to May 1999. Policy shifted away from what was condemned as uncritical Atlanticism towards multipolarity, strategic competition with the West, and the emphasis on what at the time was called the RIC (Russia, India, China) combination. This did not preclude cooperation, but the nascent post-communist ideology of anti-hegemonism was now clearly articulated at the highest levels of Russian policy-making.

On coming to power in 2000, Putin inaugurated the third phase—the policy of *new realism*—which tried to find a new framework for relations with the expanding West. It was *realist* to the degree that Putin defended elements of traditional Westphalian sovereignty, but it was *new* because it remained committed to the fundamental precepts of Gorbachev's "New Political Thinking" of the perestroika years, and sought to find new ways of overcoming the contradictions of the cold peace. Contrary to the standard image of Putin, he tried to find a "third way" in which Russia could integrate into the liberal international order while maintaining its strategic autonomy. In the end, no such formula could be found, precipitating the slide into neo-revisionism, which became the dominant paradigm of Russian foreign policy on Putin's return to the presidency in 2012. Putin was thoroughly disillusioned and disappointed in the West, especially after the intervention in Libya in 2011, and now sought to accelerate integrative endeavours in the post-Soviet space accompanied by the development of deeper ties with China. All this preceded the Ukraine crisis while at the same time helping shape Russia's response to that crisis following the overthrow of Viktor Yanukovych in February 2014. In other words, well before the onset of the Second Cold War in 2014, Putin had come to the conclusion that it was impossible to deal with the "Historical West", and accelerated moves towards Eurasian integration, the "pivot to the East", and insulating the Russian economy from dependence on the West.

Russia's neo-revisionism is a response to the dilemmas provoked by the absence of transformation of the European security system at the end of the Cold War. Wohlforth and Zubok (2017) rightly stress the impediments to such a transformation but fail to take into account the specifically European context of the transformation. In global terms their realist paradigm is convincing, but the dynamics in Europe were potentially different. It is here that the normative impetus for transformation was highest, including domestic constituencies, as well as the institutional framework for a specific European international society, instantiated not only in the EU but also in the Council of Europe (CoE) and Organization for Security and Cooperation in Europe (OSCE). There were powerful countervailing trends, notably the US-dominated security system that was extrinsic to the transformative processes on the continent. The potential was there. After all, the EU would not exist were it not for the desire for a new type of peace order after the devastation of the Second World War. It did indeed take some visionary leadership to make it a reality, but mostly it emerged out of a recognition of mutual necessity (Milward 2000). However, the EU from the beginning was part of an Atlantic system, and after the Cold War it became the spearhead for the enlargement of that system (Mearsheimer 2014b).

On the other side, Russia since the end of the Cold War has been engaged in what Suzuki calls the "recognition game", the attempt by "frustrated great powers" to convince their peers that they are worthy members of the international system. It is important, as Suzuki argues, to understand the intentions of these putative great powers. Rather than subverting the norms of international society, Russia has in fact, along with China, been strengthening the normative structures of international society as they seek to gain legitimation for their desired status (Suzuki 2008). Thus, Russia has repeatedly called for the UN to remain the only legitimate arbiter for international interventions, and China has stepped in to defend the rules-based globalized economic order against Trumpian protectionism. However, because of the structure of hegemonic power in the international system, expressed above all in America's intention to maintain primacy, there is no path towards acceptance as a legitimate peer. This is why both Russia and China have moved towards the stance of neo-revisionism in which they no longer believe that it is in the gift of the hegemonic power to grant or withhold their respective status as great powers.

The realist paradigm considers Russia as no more and no less than a normal power, pursuing a rational (although that does not mean uncontested) foreign policy to maintain its position in the world and its neighbourhood. In that context, Moscow welcomed the conciliatory comments from Trump that it made sense to "get along" with Russia, and to that degree Moscow saw Trump's election in November 2016 as an opportunity genuinely to "reset" the relationship based on mutual respect for the interests of the other. Although Trump was committed to the maintenance of US primacy (as evidenced in the sharp rise in defence spending), this would be achieved less through the multilateralism of the Obama-style "leadership" agenda, and instead a more muscular nationalism would be expressed through the assertion of "greatness" and transactional relations between the great powers. Geopolitics would be decoupled from democratization. In other words, the plan was to normalize US globalism and to decouple it from messianic ambitions to reshape the world in America's image. This suited Russia just fine. It meant the end of the "enlargement" agenda, in which democratization was mixed with geopolitical concerns. Democracy promotion was curtailed and regime change was declared no longer on the agenda, much to the chagrin of those who considered Russia an "autocracy" (Carothers and Brown 2018). However, it offered little in the way of system transformation of the sort desired by Russia, and to that degree Trump for Moscow represented little more than the opportunity for a more transactional relationship.

In the event, "Russiagate" served to constrain Trump's freedom of manoeuvre, and a more traditional US foreign policy was reasserted. Even modest moves towards a more pragmatic relationship were stymied, although there was some cooperation on the ground in Syria and other global issues. The big picture was one of a continued impasse in Russia's relations with the West. Angela Merkel's re-election in Germany in September 2017 meant that the fragile status quo looked to be maintained in Europe, with the constant danger of a sharp deterioration. The post–Cold War attempt to maintain the Atlantic system and blunt the emergence of a more pluralistic international system looked set to continue, and with it the neo-containment policy. The US sanctions are unlikely to be rescinded any time soon, and with Merkel's election, the EU-sponsored ones look set to endure. However, history suggests that stasis in the international system generates disorder. The new inter-order balance between the US-led liberal international order (although threatened from within by a potential US defection) and the nascent anti-hegemonic alignment became constitutive of international relations. The Second Cold War may well endure as long as the first. Thus, the scene is set for prolonged confrontation and conflict, mitigated only by the UN and other secondary institutions of international society.

THE DYNAMICS OF CHANGE

The West sees in Russia a heuristic image of itself, when in fact Russia has broken out of the traditional hermeneutics of European international relations. The starkest manifestation of this is the intensification of the continuing "pivot to the East", and in particular the close alignment with China accompanied by the strengthening of a "post-Western" world order encompassing such bodies as the SCO and BRICS, the heart of what is emerging as an anti-hegemonic alignment. Even Europe is shaken by the new dynamic of change, undermining the stasis in its affairs. The Atlantic enlargement strategy did not represent the resolution of the European security dilemma but the intensification of that problem. Relations between Russia and Europe, and with the West more generally, entered a deep impasse. The resolution of the problem it appeared could not be found from within the hermeneutics of the system itself, in which the liberal international order is faced by a number of rising powers loosely aligned in an anti-hegemonic bloc. There is a clash of orders, but at the same time some profound changes are taking place in international relations. In the framework of my two-level model of the international system, there are changes in the vertical axis—relations between states and orders and the institutions of global governance, above all the UN; and at the horizontal level, where the universalistic ambitions of the liberal international order are challenged by the emergence of the anti-hegemonic alignment as well as by non-systemic forces that seek to destroy the entirety of the international system to create, in particular, a new militant form of the Islamic *ummah*.

The clash between Russia and the West is only an early version, and ultimately perhaps not the most significant, of the challenges now challenging the long-term stasis in international affairs. International relations are now being reshaped, above all by the putative defection of the US from the core of the liberal international order that it has so assiduously developed over the last 70 years. Many of the themes sounded by Trump were advanced in one form or another by American leaders before him, but none with such intensity or generated by ideas that are so fundamentally at odds with the multilateral normative Atlanticism that took shape after 1945. Trump is the consummate national realist, having little respect for international institutions or multilateral processes. By contrast, Russia's continuing commitment to international society as expressed in the UN and other "secondary institutions" means that Putin is a "conservative institutionalist", defending international law and the traditional rules of global governance (the intervention in Ukraine in 2014 was a revisionist act, but not part of a revisionist strategy). By contrast, after 1989 "democratic institutionalists" sought to use international society to "remedy drawbacks of traditional international law and develop new institutions by using the rule of the majority in roughly the same way it works in domestic politics" (Sokov 2018). There has long been a national realist strain in US foreign policy, and it was this tendency which defeated Woodrow Wilson's attempts to create a multilateral world order in the wake of the First World War, and which kept the US out of the League of Nations. Although Putin's policy is pragmatic and broadly realist, it is not realist in the strict definition of the term because of its willingness to share sovereignty with international institutions (notably the UN, Council of Europe and World Trade Organization), irrespective of its chequered relations with these bodies.

At the same time, Russia challenges the attempt by democracy promotion activists and others to extend the scope of global governance bodies to disrupt the balance between sharing and maintaining sovereignty. The Responsibility to Protect (R2P) mechanism adopted in 2005 alarmed Russia and other states who considered it as an unwonted increase in the power of an international community dominated by the hegemonic powers, although in practice Russia engaged with R2P, despite the conservatism of its institutionalism (Averre and Davies 2015). In the inter–Cold War years, the main tension between Russia and the US was between the two forms of institutionalism, although both camps evolved under different leaders. Even though Putin pursued a "new realist" policy, this represented an attempt to find some mode of integration and reconciliation with the democratic institutionalist agenda, but in the end this was doomed to fail. Nevertheless, even as neo-revisionism came to predominate in Russian foreign policy, this did not make Putin a realist of the old school. It is for this reason "any cooperation between them [Putin and Trump] can only be temporary and tactical". For Trump power is the key asset, deployed as finite asset, in a context where the balance of power is perceived to be moving away from the US (Sokov 2018). Hence Trump insists that allies contribute more to their own defence, a long-term stance of US leaders but now couched in terms of a transactional relationship rather than the traditional common commitment to multilateral institutions. It is in this light that Trump while campaigning in 2016 argued that NATO was "obsolete", and in power he made little effort to hide his distaste for the EU. He appeared to make NATO's Article 5 security guarantee dependent on whether a state met the 2 per cent defence spending target set in Wales in

September 2014. This represents a shift from collective to transactional defence, where security guarantees apply only if the appropriate contribution has been made.

Trump's approach to Russia is in line with his national realist view of international relations. He consistently stressed the importance of good relations with Russia (provoking the fears of the defenders of the traditional order in Washington), and pushed for the Helsinki summit with Putin in July 2018. However, this did not prevent him from taking numerous measures against Russia, including the sale of lethal arms to Ukraine, ramping up funding for the European Reassurance Initiative and reinforcing the US troop presence in Europe, condemning the building of Nord Stream 2 as making Germany subservient to Russia, imposing harsh sanctions, expelling Russian diplomats and closing down Russian diplomatic facilities in the US. His overall strategy was in the Henry Kissinger mode (and he appears to have been advised by Kissinger), namely to try to recruit Russia to align with the US against what was perceived as the greatest long-term threat, China. In practice, the sum of US actions only reinforced the Russo-Chinese alignment, and there was zero chance of Russia defecting. At the best of times, the two countries saw the US as an unreliable protagonist, and although there are plenty of voices in Moscow warning of the dangers of a too-close embrace with China, their alignment is far more than one built on the truly extraordinary relationship between Putin and Xi Jinping. The two share not only a strong personal relationship but also the conservative institutionalist position. Thus Russia condemned Trump's withdrawal from the Joint Comprehensive Plan of Action (JCPOA, Iran nuclear deal) in May 2018 while emphasizing the crucial role of the UN, while China emerged as the great defender of open markets and global economic governance.

The struggle for recognition as an equal in the management of international affairs is now a more credible proposition, as evidenced in Russia's remarkably effective intervention in Syria from September 2015 (even though the end game of the Syrian civil war may entail intensified great power conflict). At the tenth BRICS summit, held in South Africa in July 2018, Putin noted that the group had developed into "a full-scale organization with new spheres of activity and broader common interests". The main topics discussed were "resistance to unilateral approaches in global affairs, the protection of multilateralism", and the condemnation of economic sanctions and the use of force in violation of the UN Charter (Kremlin.ru 2018). BRICS established its New Development Bank in July

2014, based in Shanghai but with plans to open regional branches in all the BRICS members. At that time the BRICS accounted for 26.5 per cent of the world's land area, 42.6 per cent of world population, and according to the IMF in 2015 generated almost a quarter of the world's GDP and contributed more than half of global economic growth in the previous decade (*RT* 2018). George Toloraya (2018), executive director of the Russian National Committee on BRICS research, argued that "BRICS is about world order", creating its own structure of global governance "to create a world order that will be more just and balanced than what we see now".

Russia and China are not the harbingers of a new nationalism but of a new internationalism. Both insist on the equal status of all countries under international law. Under the flag of this principle, they contested the slide towards democratic majoritarian rule in international politics, and thus opposed humanitarian intervention unless sanctioned by the UN Security Council. They opposed attempts by the West to impose rules through majority decisions or the use of multilateral institutions for political purposes. This was the case when in July 2018 the majority of members of the Organization for the Prevention of Chemical Weapons (OPCW) voted on the right to draw on outside expertise to assign responsibility for the use of chemical weapons, which Russia argued gave it a political role that it feared could be used by the West to pursue broader unrelated political objectives. Moscow's concern at the perceived politicization of the organization opened up the possibility that Russia could even leave the Chemical Weapons Convention.

Overall, if the twentieth century was the century of ideology, then the twenty-first in its Trumpian version is beginning to look rather more like the nineteenth, that is, nationalistic and mercantilist. For the commentators who in 2014 condemned Russia's actions in Ukraine as a throwback to the nineteenth century, this would confirm a natural convergence between Putinite Russia and Trumpian America. However, this would be wrong for the reasons outlined earlier. Paradoxically, it is now Russia and China that are defending multilateralism and the governance institutions of international society. Both defend the traditional view of state sovereignty, but as noted this does not represent a simple reversion to Westphalian internationalism. Their conservative institutionalism is ranged as much against the Trumpian sovereignty discourse as it is against the expansive interventionism of the democratic institutionalists.

One of the more striking manifestations of the shift from stasis to change is that the very concept of "the West" is being challenged. It is not that Russia is looking to the East to build alliances with other illiberal states, the way that recent developments are categorized by defenders of the old liberal hegemony, but an expression of the changing realities of global politics. The West is no longer the centre of the world in economic and even normative terms. Values of good governance, defensible property rights, rule of law, free and fair elections remain embedded as the core values of international society, although tempered by developmental and security considerations in countries like Russia and China. In fact, if decoupled from the Western power system and its inexorably hegemonic demands, there is a greater chance for them to be achieved. NATO enlargement effectively militarized the democracy promotion efforts of the West, while unmediated EU enlargement and power projection into the contested "common neighbourhood" reinforced the view of critics in Moscow that "democratic institutionalism" represented a fundamental threat to Russia's security and national interests (Hahn 2018).

Not surprisingly, some Russian analysts take great glee in describing the travails of the disintegrating West. In their view, Trump's policy called into question the common interests and common values of some of the fundamental institutions of the old order. The G7 summit in Taormina, Italy, in May 2017 was considered a failure, while the one in La Malbaie, Canada, in June 2018 proved a veritable disaster. Trump's application of the transactional business model to his allies raised the question of whether the West would survive in its traditional form at all. This would provide an opportunity for the anti-hegemonic alignment to assume a greater share of the burden of global leadership, but only if the end of stasis in international affairs was accompanied by the positive transcendence of immobilism. However, just as after the end of the First Cold War, a negative transcendence is possible, intensifying the conflicts and deepening the Second Cold War. The inertia associated with the post-war stasis has deep roots, but its unravelling can have both positive and negative outcomes.

Conclusion

Is an alternative possible? Some years ago Andrew Hurrell (2006, 1) noted that the four BRIC countries had a certain "capacity to contribute to the production of international order, regionally or globally". At that time Russia was considered the outlier, since "the reality of the past two decades here has been one of decline and the dissolution of power" (Hurrell 2006, 2; MacFarlane 2006). Hurrell (2006, 2) noted that while a central theme of the twentieth century was the struggle of revisionist states to achieve equal rights, "the recognition of regional spheres of influence, and the drive for equality of status within formal and informal international institutions", and although in the recent period "the currency of power" may have changed, the issue of recognition "has been sharpened by the growth of the idea that international society should aim to promote shared values and purposes rather than simply underpin coexistence and help to keep conflict to a minimum". In the second decade of the twenty-first century, Russia re-emerged as an active player in international affairs, and although still only barely in the top dozen countries economically, its impressive military reform and re-equipment since the 2008 Russo-Georgian war allowed it to "punch above its weight". Stasis and change now balance each other, and although the post-First Cold War order is unravelling, this has given rise to both a Second Cold War and the emergence of an anti-hegemonic alignment. The question today is whether the latter can help transcend the former.

Although the sinews of a post-Western world are emerging, notably in the form of SCO and BRICS, it remains to be seen whether these bodies and countries behind them will be able to sustain the multilateralism of the past seven decades in the absence of the hegemon that had provided the security and support for such multilateralism to thrive. The post-Western world may well assume the characteristics of the pre-Western international system, dominated by vast competing empires. Nevertheless, Trumpian realism entails partial de-globalization, and it would be the supreme irony if liberal internationalism and open markets were to be saved by the leaders of the anti-hegemonic alignment. This could herald a new age of post-hegemonic internationalism, but it could equally inaugurate a new era of zero-sum conflict, protectionism, a drive to the bottom in regulatory standards and another three-decade-long Cold War.

REFERENCES

Acharya, Amitav. 2017. After Liberal Hegemony: The Advent of a Multiplex World Order. *Ethics and International Affairs*, September 8. https://www.ethicsandinternationalaffairs.org/2017/multiplex-world-order

Averre, Derek, and Lance Davies. 2015. Russia, Humanitarian Intervention and the Responsibility to Protect: The Case of Syria. *International Affairs* 91 (4): 813–834. https://doi.org/10.1111/1468-2346.12343.

Carothers, Thomas, and Frances Z. Brown. 2018. Can U.S. Democracy Policy Survive Trump? *Carnegie Endowment for International Peace*, October 1.

https://carnegieendowment.org/2018/10/01/can-u.s.-democracy-policy-survive-trump-pub-77381

Dunne, Tim, and Christian Reut-Smith, eds. 2017. *The Globalization of International Society*. Oxford: Oxford University Press.

Flockhart, Trine. 2016. The Coming Multi-Order World. *Contemporary Security Policy* 37 (1): 3–30. https://doi.org/10.1080/13523260.2016.1150053.

Forsberg, Tuomas, and Hiski Haukkala. 2016. *The European Union and Russia*. London: Palgrave Macmillan.

Hahn, Gordon. 2018. Trump-Putin Summit. *Russian and Eurasian Politics*, July 5. https://gordonhahn.com/2018/07/05/trump-putin-summit.

Hurrell, Andrew. 2006. Hegemony, Liberalism and Global Order: What Space for Would-be Great Powers? *International Affairs* 82 (1): 1–19. https://doi.org/10.1111/j.1468-2346.2006.00512.x.

Ikenberry, G. John, ed. 2011. *International Relations Theory and the Consequences of Unipolarity*. Cambridge: Cambridge University Press.

Kissinger, Henry. 2014. *World Order: Reflections on the Character of Nations and the Course of History*. London: Allen Lane.

Kremlin.ru. 2018. News Conference Following the BRICS Summit. July 27. http://en.kremlin.ru/events/president/transcripts/58119

Larson, Deborah Welch, and Alexei Shevchenko. 2003. Shortcut to Greatness: The New Thinking and the Revolution in Soviet Foreign Policy. *International Organization* 57 (1): 77–109. https://doi.org/10.1017/S0020818303571028.

Maas, Anne-Sophie. 2016. *EU-Russia Relations, 1999–2015: From Courtship to Confrontation*. London: Routledge.

MacFarlane, S. Neil. 2006. The 'R' in BRICs: Is Russia an Emerging Power? *International Affairs* 82 (1): 41–57. https://doi.org/10.1111/j.1468-2346.2006.00514.x.

Mearsheimer, John J. 2014a. *The Tragedy of Great Power Politics*. New York: W.W. Norton.

———. 2014b. Why the Ukraine Crisis Is the West's Fault: The Liberal Delusions That Provoked Putin. *Foreign Affairs* 93 (5): 77–89. https://doi.org/10.1080/21598282.2017.1316436.

———. 2018. *The Great Delusion: Liberal Dreams and International Realities*. London/New Haven: Yale University Press.

Milward, Alan. 2000. *The European Rescue of the Nation State*. London/New York: Routledge.

Panarin, Alexander. 1998. *Revansh istorii: Rossiyskaya strategicheskaya initsiativa v XXI veke*. Moscow: Logos.

Pouliot, Vincent. 2010. *International Security in Practice: The Politics of NATO-Russia Diplomacy*. Cambridge: Cambridge University Press.

RT. 2018. BRICS Trade Surges by 30% as Global Market Influence of Developing Economies Grows – Putin. July 26. https://www.rt.com/business/434330-russia-brics-trade-economy

Sakwa, Richard. 2008. 'New Cold War' or Twenty Years' Crisis? Russia and International Politics. *International Affairs* 84 (2): 241–267. https://doi.org/10.1111/j.1468-2346.2008.00702.x.

———. 2017. *Russia Against the Rest: The Post–Cold War Crisis of World Order.* Cambridge: Cambridge University Press.

Savranskaya, Svetlana, and Tom Blanton. 2017. NATO Expansion: What Gorbachev Heard. *National Security Archive of George Washington University,* December 12. https://nsarchive.gwu.edu/briefing-book/russia-programs/2017-12-12/nato-expansion-what-gorbachev-heard-western-leaders-early

Savranskaya, Svetlana, Thomas Blanton, and Vladislav Zubok, eds. 2010. *Masterpieces of History: The Peaceful End of the Cold War in Europe, 1989.* Budapest/New York: Central European University Press.

Smith, Martin A. 2013. Russia and Multipolarity since the End of the Cold War. *East European Politics* 29 (1): 36–51. https://doi.org/10.1080/21599165.2013.764481.

Sokov, Nikolai. 2018. The Putin-Trump Summit: In Helsinki, Three Worldviews Will Clash. *The National Interest,* July 15. https://nationalinterest.org/feature/putin-trump-summit-helsinki-three-worldviews-will-clash-25766

Stuenkel, Oliver. 2016. *Post-Western World: How Emerging Powers Are Remaking Global Order.* Cambridge: Polity.

Suzuki, Shoigu. 2008. Seeking 'Legitimate' Great Power Status in Post–Cold War International Society: China's and Japan's Participation in UNPKO. *International Relations* 22 (1): 45–63. https://doi.org/10.1177%2F0047117807087242.

Toloraya, George. 2018. BRICS and the World Order. *Valdai Club,* July 25. http://valdaiclub.com/a/highlights/brics-and-the-world-order

Wendt, Alexander. 1992. Anarchy Is What States Make of It: The Social Construction of Power Politics. *International Organization* 46 (2): 391–425. https://doi.org/10.1017/S0020818300027764.

Wohlforth, William C., and Vladislav Zubok. 2017. An Abiding Antagonism: Realism, Idealism, and the Mirage of Western-Russian Partnership After the Cold War. *International Politics* 54 (4): 405–419. https://doi.org/10.1057/s41311-017-0046-8.

CHAPTER 3

Russia's European Policies in a Post-liberal World

Andrey Makarychev

Introduction

Thirty years after the commencement of tectonic changes in Europe's east, including the demolition of the Berlin Wall, the disintegration of the socialist community, the fall of the Soviet Union and the end of the Cold War, Moscow's policies towards the EU are marred by deep controversies, and Russia's role in Europe looks highly uncertain. Russia's discord with the EU's liberal international philosophy ultimately grew in a serious challenge, which is part of a wider set of external contestations the EU has to face and deal with.

The annexation of Crimea in 2014 was widely considered in the West as the most serious blow to the post–Cold War international order, which triggered economic and personal sanctions, discontinuation of previous diplomatic tracks, freezing of the whole structure of Russia's relations with the West, and securitization and militarization of the political agenda. In response, Russia put a premium on contacts with anti-establishment forces within EU member states, foreign propaganda became an issue again as it was during the Cold War, and the importance of cultural differences between

A. Makarychev (✉)
Johan Skytte Institute of Political Science, Tartu, Estonia

© The Author(s) 2020
E. Parlar Dal, E. Erşen (eds.), *Russia in the Changing International System*, https://doi.org/10.1007/978-3-030-21832-4_3

Russia and European liberal mainstream is on the rise as well. The main features of the post-2014 Russia's discourse of self-assertion is its imperial content manifested through the "Russian World" doctrine, Eurasianism, moral/religious conservatism (the idea of a "holy Russia") and de facto rehabilitation of the Soviet project in popular and media discourses.

Major factors defining dynamics of Russian foreign policy are escalating alienation of Putin's Russia from the EU as a liberal "normative power" and Moscow's alliance with right-wing parties in some EU member states. The Kremlin might have strong political arguments and trump cards, but it is apparently weak and vulnerable economically. The EU, vice versa, might perform badly in political terms (since from the outset it was designed/conceived to function as an institutional rather than a full-fledged political actor), but economically it has an upper hand in dealing with Russia, mainly through policies of sanctions. For the West, sanctions are a terrain for negotiations and bargaining with Russia, where threats of even stronger measures (incremental pressure) are a part of the process. Obviously, sanctions have serious repercussions for Russia's leadership in the Eurasian Economic Union (EAEU), as well as for Russia's budget.

Yet despite the current conflict, the EU remains a key reference point in a plethora of Russian discourses that are Europe-centric in the sense of playing with different arguments aimed at vindicating Russia's belonging to Europe through loosely defined history, geography and culture, but also through accentuating Russia's military presence and ability to interfere in European domestic processes. What is completely missing in the repertoire of Russia's policies are attempts to implement European norms that would allow Russia to become a recognized member of European normative order.

In this chapter I trace the trajectory of Russia's EU policies since the beginning of the 1990s till present, compare Russian and European approaches to international relations and discuss Russia's rhetorical manoeuvring under the conditions of drastic deterioration of relations with the West after 2014. Then I will look at the subject of my analysis from the viewpoint of broader debates on post-liberal international order, and share some critical insights on the state of communication between Russia and Europe.

From the Fall of the Soviet Union to the Crisis of Liberal International Order

The dominant narrative in the times of Mikhail Gorbachev's *perestroika* consisted of a number of nodal points. The Soviet system was sharply criticized for its social inefficiency, autocratic nature and a "black-and-white" type of thinking. It became obvious that the Soviet regime could not prevent environmental decay, which was made clear by the 1986 catastrophe in Chernobyl. The Soviet rule was also inimical to *intelligentsia* who pioneered in claiming that the imperial overstretch and the flexing of muscles in foreign policy did not bring benefits to the country.

In the meantime, the transition from the Soviet Union to post-Soviet Russia was marked by a sense of frustration, confusion and loss of direction and coordinates. Militant separatism in Nagorno-Karabakh, Transnistria, South Ossetia and Abkhazia was believed to be the direct result of the fall of the Soviet empire, thus creating a fertile ground for multiple risks of nationalism and new divisions within a formerly common (imperial) space.

The years of transition—end of the 1980s and beginning of the 1990s—produced two major foreign policy discourses, both borrowed from the West and adopted to the post-Soviet condition. One was grounded in *liberal idealism*, with transition to democracy, Europeanization and cross-border regionalism at its core. Widely circulated ideas of a "common European home" (enthusiastically supported by Gorbachev) and a "wider Europe" (promoted by the EU) were constitutive elements of the liberal platform advocating for softening of international relations, exemplified by concepts of "soft power" and "soft security". For quite a while, a bunch of post-modernist versions of globalization (a "borderless world", multiple/hybrid identities, de-territorialization, etc.) were quite popular among the Russian foreign policy experts.

The second platform consisted of *de-politicized technocratic discourses*, with the prevalence of managerial agenda and technical/procedural convergence with international rules and standards. This discourse referred to European traditions of modernity with central notions of effective state and good governance.

Both platforms envisioned positive engagement with Russia's European counterparts and interlocutors who were, from their part, eager not only to cooperate with Russia, but even grant Russia a privileged position among all post-Soviet countries (a "Russia first" policy). Both liberal idealist and technocratic approaches were constituted by discourses accepting—though in different ways—the idea of universal applicability of European policy models. In the first years after regaining independence, Russia positioned itself as a natural part of Europe and did not claim its extraordinary uniqueness. Moscow clearly displayed disinterest in ideologically framing its relations with the West and accepted major European political concepts (democracy, human rights and modernization), although interpreting some of them in its own way.

Russian foreign policy in the 1990s was an attempt to adjust to profound structural changes in the entire system of international relations. It drifted away from geopolitics to normative commitments and—potentially—a value-based international order. In the categories of the English school of international relations, this trajectory could be described as a transition from international system to international society and then—in a long run—to international community. The "old" world order (with bipolarity, spheres of influence, military force as the key source of power and a resource-based equality of power holders) has evolved into a "new" world order, where spheres of influence would be substituted by adherence to common norms and values, with the ensuing de-legitimation of autocracies as deviations from the norm. In the security sphere, "old" dichotomies (East versus West) were acknowledged obsolete and a new bunch of concepts—such as "asecurity" and de-securitization (thinking beyond the obsession with security arguments), non-offensive defence and human security—appeared.

The EU was duly considered as a harbinger of a new type of normative foreign policy. EU's self-attributed brand of normative power implied the definition of the normal and—ideally—presupposed that normative ends should meet normative means. The EU-produced liberal norms were expected to define material interests of countries belonging to Europe as a normatively dense space. These norms were supposed to geographically expand, while the EU saw itself as a norm-projector that incited its neighbours to make normative choices. The EU as a post-modern actor refused to consider military force as the central foreign policy tool. In the spirit of globalization, these developments implied a transition from the world of conflicting particularities to a normatively "universal" world, from fragmentation to coherence.

Post- Versus Multi-

In the aftermath of the end of the Cold War and fall of the Berlin Wall, the hegemonic expectation in Europe was that this new world would move in the direction of post-modernity and eventually become post-ideological, post-national and post-political. The alleged end of modernity was largely associated with decline of centralized structures, reversal of hierarchical relations between centres and peripheries and appearance of a more variegated system of governance based on multiplicity of identities. Numerous scholars were quick to conceptualize these changes as the end of dichotomies and the emergence of non-binary/inclusive logics that—allegedly—would repair the disjunctions of the international system through more elasticity, connectivity, accessibility and networking.

In this context, post-nationalism was conceptualized through the lens of the crisis of the nation-state system, a greater role for supranational and cross-border institutions and practices that skip nation state, and full recognition of non-state-based actorness. Post-political strategies were seen as aimed at reaching societal consensus on the basis of policy approaches publicly presented as presumably self-evident and necessitating no debate on substantial issues. Post-politics incorporates strong elements of security and police functions, implying control, surveillance and supervision for the sake of public safety, but in the meantime it also includes a merger of consumerism, branding and the neoliberal/market-driven entertainment industry.

This explains why the neoliberal idea of good governance was central to the post-1991 changes: to put it in Michel Foucault's vocabulary, unlike the "old" sovereign power, governmentality is grounded in the understanding of power as a means to achieve greater freedom and stimulate self-awareness of individuals who are incited to act consciously and responsibly. Within this philosophy, the EU constructed its subjectivity not on the ability to impose its political power, but on a capacity to help other members of the international community-in-the-making to act rationally and optimize their limited resources.

Yet the implementation of this scenario was conditioned by its acceptance by EU's immediate neighbours, which presupposed drastic transformation within Russian identity towards de-imperialization. However, even in the most cooperative times, Russian mainstream discourse remained relatively indifferent to conceptualizations of politics starting with the "post-" prefix and instead displayed sympathy to a different optics grounded in the idea of multiplicity and plurality. The concepts of multipolar world with spheres of influence and the concomitant dialogue of civilizations seem to be the best illustration of Russian foreign policy philosophy starting from the mid-1990s.

The distinction between "post-" and "multi-" is crucial for understanding the basic perception gaps between Moscow and Brussels. "Post-" implies some sense of transition from what is considered as obsolete and needs a drastic reshuffle, although the destination point of this transformation might remain unclear. Yet "multi-" does not necessarily presuppose acceptance of meaningful societal changes at all. Instead, it simply calls for a fragmentation of the field of the international into a number of areas—each supervised by a certain power holder. Seen through this lens, Russia's European orientation was not a normative choice, but a combination of technocratic pragmatism of the ruling elite and a feeling of non-self-sufficiency of Russian identity, which implies indispensability of Europe as its key signifier.

FROM CONCEPTUAL DISAGREEMENT TO POLITICAL REBUFF

Institutional legacies of Russia's cooperation with the EU during the first decade and a half after the end of the Cold War were quite significant: Partnership and Cooperation Agreement, Four Common Spaces and the roadmaps to them, and Partnership for Modernization, which created preconditions for Russia's "strategic partnership" with the EU. Despite conceptual disagreements, there were many attempts to find compromises on specific issues. Thus, Russia accepted French mediation during the conflict with Georgia in 2008, did not veto the UN Security Council resolution on Libya in 2011 and withdrew its military units from Georgia and Azerbaijan. The Bucharest summit of NATO in 2008 which put on hold the prospects of Ukraine and Georgia's membership, yet formally left the doors open in a long-run perspective, could be considered as a compromise that could help avoiding a further confrontation.

Nevertheless, the feeling of existential insecurity continued shaping Russian foreign policy. In general terms, this sense of external danger was grounded in EU's normative expansion and the inability of Russia to meet the EU-set standards of democratic governance, which created a traumatic feeling of inevitable normative inferiority. The EU's self-redefinition through democracy led to normative marginalization of Russia and ultimately was conducive to the conflict in which Ukraine was a trigger.

Russia's sense of insecurity was strongly shaped by other presumptions, too. The most important among them was Putin's characterization of the fall of the Soviet Union as a major geopolitical catastrophe of the twentieth century, which implied that Russians are divided people. The Kremlin assumed that the USSR did not lose the Cold War as it has started transforming itself and thus did not deserve being treated as a defeated party. Moreover, there exists a feeling of "betrayal" in the Russian security thinking: Moscow started the reforms of socialism, gave independence to satellite states and then to Soviet republics, yet did not get ultimately any rewards or even appreciation in exchange.

Not surprisingly, Russia's international self-assertion commenced in the so called near abroad. Russia's policies in the post-Soviet area were driven by two interrelated dynamics: the transformation of the legal status of the Soviet successor to a political claim of Russia's "special rights" in its "near abroad" and the concomitant transformation of cultural concerns about Russian language in neighbouring countries into a "compatriot policy" of "protecting" Russians living beyond the country's borders. Russian hegemonic claims were grounded in a number of structural underpinnings. Security-wise, in the beginning of the 1990s, Russia filled the security vacuum in such conflict spots as Transnistria, Abkhazia, South Ossetia and Tajikistan, since no other international actor wished to get involved militarily on the ground. Russian peacekeeping operations initially included interactions with host countries (in particular, Moldova and Georgia) and post-Soviet organizations (Commonwealth of Independent States or CIS and Collective Security Treaty Organization or CSTO), which provided some legitimacy for Russia's neighbourhood policies.

Eventually, the changes in Russian foreign policy in the 2000s drove the country away from post-political/managerial pragmatism to ideologization, and from mimicking the EU to challenging the liberal West. The short-lived post-political structure of international relations evolved into a system where political contestations and conflicts prevailed. The Russian government was gradually getting rid of the illusions of politically neutral and ideologically sterile international community and returning to a world of political contestations. The whole revisionist strategy of Moscow is based on the presumption of diminution of Western power, which justifies Kremlin's militaristic policies and a strong sense of war-time mentality.

Of course, there might be liberal answers to Moscow's grievances. One of them would be a supposition that the fall of the Soviet Union gave all the new states a chance for national revival and an opportunity to (re)build nation states, as opposed to an empire. Russia secured politically beneficial membership in many international organizations (Council of Europe, G8, WTO) and strategic partnership with other institutions (NATO, EU), received generous financial and technical assistance and was able to integrate with regional institutional frameworks (Baltic, Black Sea, Barents-Euroarctic regions). Yet Russia preferred to stick with a set of illiberal interpretations, focusing on NATO expansion to the Russian borders, on the alleged domination of anti-Russian elites in many post-Soviet countries, on the lack of NATO and EU membership prospects for Russia itself and on Western policies of what Moscow viewed as disregard of both international law and Russia's interests (e.g. the West's military support for Kosovo and the war against Serbia in 1999 as well as the military interventions in Iraq and Afghanistan). From two options—to remain a consistent defender of global normative principles (sovereignty and territorial integrity, primacy of international law over interests of major states) or to replicate the type of behaviour that Russia itself considered inappropriate—Russia opted for the second and this is this choice that predetermined the consequent conflict between the EU and Russia.

REALIST CONSERVATISM: A TOXIC BLEND

Russia's illiberal EU-scepticism was grounded in two platforms. One can be dubbed normative counter-offensive, exemplified by promoting a conservative agenda Europe-wide. Another platform is anormative, being geared towards a spheres of influence type of policy and implying autocracy promotion and flexing military muscles.

For Russian conservatism, the central normative concept is sovereignty interpreted as equality of power holders and non-intervention in domestic affairs, traditional understanding of social and political actorness, vision of the nation as a big family, accentuation of "spirituality", messianic appeals based on Russia's self-proclaimed "moral superiority" over the West, strong emphasis on civilizational underpinnings of international relations and tacit re-actualization of the Soviet legacy. Social conservatism (traditions, family values, respect to national history and its key figures, religion) from Russian domestic politics gradually migrated to foreign policy. Arguably, Russia develops a conservative version of soft power. For example, Russian Orthodox Church is eager to associate itself with a Christian Europe and dissociate with the liberal emancipatory EU institutions. By the same token, the Kremlin is sympathetic with national conservative parties in some European countries (France, Italy, Germany, Austria—but not in the Baltic/Nordic Europe). The Russia-promoted conservatism is an antithesis of EU's liberal project that is portrayed in the Kremlin discourse as disrespectful to national sovereignties ("democracy promotion" and "regime change") and conducive to radicalization in affected countries (instead of "democratic peace"), such as Libya and Egypt. Russia attacks liberalism basically by teaming up with far-right parties in Europe and playing a conservative card, which obviously has its limitations.

The conservative turn is complemented by a new Russian realism that manifests itself in the rhetoric of defence of Russia's—usually unspecified—interests, struggle for recognition of Russia as a great power with its own sphere of influence, challenging the existing political conventions (inviolability of borders and respect to national jurisdictions), disdain to international institutions (G8, WTO, EU, NATO, etc.) and international law. Under Vladimir Putin's presidency, Russia started more intensely using realist vocabulary to attack the validity of EU normative project, claiming that conflictual competition and rivalry are inevitable, as are securitization and bordering. Drawing on realist reasoning, Russian mainstream discourse exposed strong scepticism towards the idea of a peaceful Europe without divides, referring to new security threats (like terrorism and refugee crisis) and the dysfunctionality of EU's policy of democracy promotion. Russian discourse de facto was conducive to legitimation of autocracy and reinstalling Russia's *droit de regard*, as opposed to the logic of inclusion into the EU-constructed space of liberal normativity. A particular ramification of a new Russian realism is a cynically transactional attitude to the West: "We have received from Europe that we could and should….Technologies, military organization, culture….But we have exhausted their storehouse" (Karaganov 2018). All together these policies are conducive to a more anarchic structure of international relations that Russia seems to favour.

The return of realist and geopolitical thinking implied traditional distinctions between "big" and "small" powers, yet also evoked more nuanced concepts such as state-diaspora relations (the "Russian World"), soft power techniques, information management, religious diplomacy (the use of Russian Orthodox Church as a foreign policy tool), along with biopolitical tools of targeting/taking care of population rather than territories. The structure of Russia's soft power influence includes think tanks (such as the European Institute of Democracy and Cooperation, Dialogue of Civilization Forum or Valdai Club), practices of cultural diplomacy (Russian Centres for International Scientific Cooperation, Pushkin Institute, etc.), and GONGOs ("Night Wolves" bikers club). Another instrument is mega sport events (Sochi Winter Olympics in 2014, FIFA World Cup in 2018) that Moscow sees as important playgrounds for demonstrating the fruits of "raising from the knees".

Conservative and realist platforms in Russian foreign policy can merge, exemplified in particular by the Kremlin's usage of the Russian World concept as a cultural vindication for the geopolitics of spheres of influence. In the meantime, there are meaningful differences between the two platforms: realism is a norm-rejector and prioritizes material interests and a rational calculus, while conservatism, in its turn, looks more as a norm-projector and appreciates identities, norms and ideological arguments more than materials ones.

Russia's realist conservatism appears to be a revisionist (anti-status quo), anti-liberal, anti-universalist and reactive type of thinking. The problems with this realist-conservative blend are multiple: conflictuality inherent in this double-edged philosophy, limited rationality and international socialization, and inevitable re-actualization of the Soviet practices conducive to a new Cold War. Russia cannot seriously rely upon direct political support from organizations that it created or contributed to, including CSTO and Shanghai Cooperation Organization (SCO). Besides, Russia's agenda provokes counter-reactions: from pro-NATO debates in Sweden and Finland to the revival of an old idea of *Intermarium* to contain Russia in Central Europe.

Russia's appropriation of conservative vocabulary opened up a pathway to informal and formal alliances with a group of right-wing populist and nationalist parties in some European countries that look at the world from similar vantage points. The realist approach, in its turn, facilitated Russia's communication with like-minded adherents of *Realpolitik* and geopolitics in the West—such as John Mearsheimer, Henry Kissinger or Richard Sakwa—who see international politics as a series of recurrent patterns of domination of great power over their spheres of influence with little room left for smaller actors, along with institutions or normative commitments. Many of the new concepts coined by European experts who are convinced that security in Europe is unachievable without Russia have a realist pedigree: examples are ideas of "plural peace" (Dembinski and Spanger 2017) and calls for accommodation with Putin's Russia through "offering Moscow a more comprehensive set of topics for negotiations, for example on EU/EAEU economic cooperation and climate change, in the hope of making it easier to find some common ground with Moscow" (Orsini 2018, 20).

Discursive Manoeuvres

The escalating sanctions and growing political gaps with the West made Russia manoeuvring in search for avoiding even further marginalization vis-à-vis the West. Many speakers close to the Kremlin argue that Ukraine is not the central issue for Russia's relations with the West and therefore a broader perspective is needed to understand the nature of the current crisis. According to the Kremlin's logic, both Russia and the West should be ready for a Cold-War-like peaceful co-existence and spheres of influence to avoid direct conflicts. Ironically, Russia even claimed to offer "protecting Europe" from excessive dependence on the US (Rambler.ru 2018).

In the security sphere, Russia expected that the global war on terror could become a unifying platform allowing the West to accept Russia as an equal partner. However, this strategy did not work, because Russia's Western partners had all reasons to deem that for Russia the global anti-terror coalition is a tool to legitimize the regime and its impunity. Particularly in Ukraine, Russia with its hybrid war tactics is the problem rather than a solution.

Politically, Russia considers itself "real" Europe, that is, nation-state based, conservative/Christian and sovereign. In radical versions, it amounts to claiming that Russia is even the "better Europe". Russia's understanding of democracy equates it with majority rule, with very little attention paid to minority protection. The concept of democracy is externalized, that is, used as a foreign policy tool (e.g. Russian minorities in the Baltic States) rather than as a platform for building a national community at home. In the meantime, many Russian experts draw a caricature picture of the EU as an entity allegedly being unable to reconcile its policy with "a pluralist framework between states with different interests and values", and Western leaders as refusing "to show any regard for the interests of other countries" (Titov 2016). The EU is accused of being unwilling to compromise its principles and even failing to indicate where the "red lines" that Putin ultimately crossed are (Shevtsova 2015). Even those experts who are considered in Europe as relatively independent deem that Moscow feels more comfortable to interact with leaders of China or Kazakhstan than with Brussels, and that "the EU is getting older, while Russia and its Eurasian partners might bring a 'new blood' in the European body" (Kortunov 2018). The following statement seems to be quite typical for the Kremlin analysts: "While enjoying its successes, Europe made numerous strategic mistakes and became embroiled in a series of crises….The "strategic frivolity," or readiness to create dangerous international situations in order to achieve insignificant goals, was highly characteristic of the European politicians" (Bordachev 2018).

An important component of Russian mainstream discourse is a strong emphasis on structural factors shaping international politics, as opposed to Russia's own policies. In particular, this is the case of Ivan Timofeev (2018), who—quite correctly—claimed that the whole fabric of the Helsinki process faces deep challenges rooted in the changing nature of nation-states and their sovereignties. This pretty post-modernist argument is used to relegate responsibility for what provoked the crisis in 2014—the annexation of Crimea and the Russia-instigated war in Donbas—from the

Kremlin to "global trends". As a follow-up to this logic, Russian experts ascribe the "chaos in Ukraine and Iraq" to the effects of EU policies (Lukin 2016), which—according to the plethora of pro-Kremlin interpretations—justifies Russia's interference in Ukraine where "Russia is fighting for its survival as a truly independent state. It simply wants to avoid being encircled and subjected to the political control of the United States and its allies, and for its neighbours to remain friendly, or at least neutral" (Lukin 2016). Former Foreign Minister Igor Ivanov referred to both Russia and the EU as victims of the Ukraine crisis (Ivanov 2018), which de facto serves to ignore the role Russia played in annexing Crimea and instigating military insurgency in Donbas.

What is missing in Russian discourse is a critical reassessment of Moscow's policies that were conducive to the crisis of relations with the EU. Consequently, the changes needed from the Russian side are beyond the Russian debate. EU-Russia relations are believed to depend first of all on "what kind of Europe we are going to see in" the future, while Russia itself might behave from the vantage point of "strategic patience". In other words, Moscow can afford waiting "until the EU realizes that for a whole range of historical, economic, cultural and civilizational reasons Russia and the EU need each other" (Permanent Mission 2017). These expectations are accompanied by the traditional self-portrayal of Russia as a "more European" identity than the EU where a "Soviet-style mentality" persists (Kantor 2015). The EU allegedly tends to forget that Russia several times saved Europe from dictatorial regimes (Napoleon, Hitler), yet it is still treated as an Oriental/barbaric country. But nowadays "Russia could have been contributing to a positive transformation of the EU" (Kortunov 2017) without making any concessions that might be considered as "capitulation" and thus unleash detrimental consequences for the Kremlin (Trenin 2018).

The refusal to seriously discuss Russia's policy towards Ukraine as a trigger for the crisis in relations with the West leads to underestimation of the depth of the resulting ruptures, and then to excessively optimistic expectations for the nearest future. Some Russian experts anticipate a "dialogue between Russia and Western countries about the problems of migrants and refugees, and exchanging experience on related topics, for example with a summit on migration problems" (Nikitin 2016). Reviving the NATO-Russia Council is also on the agenda of some pro-Kremlin analysts, along with fostering trilateral discussions—that have previously failed—involving the EU, Russia and Ukraine on economic issues. Many voices in Moscow expect Russia to return to Europe through its growing engagement with Asia (Kortunov 2018) and encourage steps towards opening a communication track between the EU and EAEU where Russia accords major roles to Belarus and Kazakhstan (Bordachev 2017).

Being extremely critical to the EU modus operandi, most Russian experts, however, agree that a probability of EU disintegration will not serve the Russian interests (Moskovskiy Komsomolets 2016), potentially bringing "gigantic risks, and scarce advantages" (Bordachev 2017). Realistically, Russian experts do not predict new cases similar to *Brexit* (Gromyko 2017) to happen and—much less realistically—fantasize about a possible role for Russia in the EU-UK post-*Brexit* negotiations (Bordachev 2017). A hypothetical fragmentation of the EU might shed doubts on regional integration as such (Busygina 2017), which can affect Russia's plans for Eurasian integration. From a geopolitical perspective, a "strong" EU is a counter-balance to the US. Besides, Russia is not sure what individual member states' policies would be. For the sake of fostering cooperation, Vladimir Chizhov, the head of Russian mission at the EU, suggested that "we don't rule out joint EU-Russia military operations under the EU command" (Novostipmr.com 2016), which however did not resonate on the EU side.

RUSSIA AND THE EU IN A POST-LIBERAL WORLD: RESIDUAL COMMUNICATION

Russian mature EU-scepticism is just one of the multiple examples of the rise of illiberal forms of governance that intend to rebut the key premises of liberal international politics. The EU formulated five principles of future relations with Russia: full implementation of the Minsk agreements on Ukraine, strengthening relations with the Eastern Partnership countries plus Central Asia, enhancing EU resilience in hybrid threats and energy security, selective communication with Russia on global issues and support for civil society in Russia (European Union External Action 2016). Besides, based on the report on the Malaysian Airlines Flight 370 investigation, the EU called upon Russia to acknowledge responsibility for the downing of the passenger plane on Ukraine and fully cooperate with international experts (Council of the EU 2018).

In response, the Valdai Club came up with its own principles on relations with the EU that include, first, bringing more interest groups in dialogue as a measure against "backroom dealing". Second, Russia should accept pro-EU policies of some members of the EAEU. Third, Russia should attach equal importance to relations with both the EU and its member states.

Fourth, Russia and the EU should develop different levels of dialogue. Fifth, Russia can facilitate EU's contacts with its Eurasian economic partners. Sixth, EU should lift sanctions against Crimea (Bordachev 2016). The Russian International Affairs Council (RIAC) added to this list recognition of mutual mistakes, more dialogue between expert groups and the need for Russia's special presidential representative on relations with the EU (Zagorski and Zellner 2016). Council on Foreign and Defence Policy (SVOP) came up with the least pro-EU narrative, proposing the concept of "big Eurasia" (from Lisbon to Vladivostok) instead of "Big Europe".

In a more general sense, these debates revolve around the question of how relations of co-existence with Russia might be incorporated into the emerging post-liberal—more diverse/multi-order(ed) and less Western-centric—world. Within these discussions, two issues deserve attention. Apparently, Russia does have several advantages over the EU. It can mobilize a wider set of resources: military power, energy power, information power, including mimicry and manipulation (with false analogies) and bio-power (a policy of "taking care of our people"). However, there are multiple drawbacks and flipsides for the Kremlin as well: relative isolation, high political cost and inefficiency of the "turn to the east" and a strong sense of solidarity among EU member states in spite of obvious differences between them.

Thus, Russia's influence has its limits and—unlike colleagues from the Higher School of Economics—I cannot find compelling evidences supporting the claim that "Russia's actions in Ukraine have reasserted its dominance in the post-Soviet space" (Krikovic and Weber 2018, 296). So far, Russia did not achieve evident strategic successes. It supported *Brexit*, yet relations with London are not any better than before; it supported Marine Le Pen, but has to deal with Emmanuel Macron as the French President; it celebrated Donald Trump's presidency, but relations with the US are far away from initial expectations; it created fake stories about "our Lisa" affair in Germany, yet the German government took it very seriously and qualified as a coordinated unfriendly interference in domestic affairs. Propaganda and manipulation with information often trigger counter-effects, especially when it comes to direct interference in the domestic affairs of foreign countries. In the communication domain, Russia usually plays the role of a spoiler, helping to hack sensitive information and "sell" it in political markets, spreading fake news and biased (mis)information, indirectly and tacitly supporting the "army of Internet trolls" and investing resources in creating Moscow-controlled cyber-space inside Russia.

Russia's institutional power also remains rather weak. It does invest a lot of effort in the EAEU, SCO and CSTO, but in cases of crises, it remains a solitary actor, with an implicit mistrust to international institutions. Economically, sanctions do work, especially when they are incremental and consistent (Gould-David 2018). The Kremlin itself confirmed this with a law passed in 2018 that criminalizes public support for sanctions. The West cannot prevent Russia from misconduct, yet it can effectively raise the price for misbehaviour, which is happening on a step-by-step basis. Sanctions diminish Russia's ability to control its near abroad, which was in particular illustrated by the change of government in Armenia in 2018 and the new and more critical tones in the public attitudes towards Russia. On a more general note, one should not underestimate the scope of difficulties that Russia faces in promoting its Eurasian integration project: Kazakhstan signed a far-reaching agreement with the EU, Azerbaijan is interested to keep the negotiation track with Brussels open, and with all Russia's hard and soft power, the most Moscow could achieve in Moldova was to make it an observer in the EAEU.

Against this backdrop, Russia's contestation of the liberal international order looks only partial and limited. It is the value-based liberalism that Russia staunchly opposes, with humanitarian interventionism and expansion of liberal norms at its core. Russia wants to be a counter-normative power to challenge the dominance of the Western institutions by supporting social conservative and status quo groups, which is in contrast to EU's soft power philosophy aimed at changes and liberation from the existing dependencies. Yet, as Russia's engagement with international sports associations demonstrates, Moscow can feel quite comfortable with the global political economy of entertainment, tourism and advertisement.

Moreover, even contesting the West, Russia uses Western concepts (multipolarity, concert of great powers, spheres of influence, etc.). It also uses the West as a key reference point for justifying its policies, tries to portray itself as an indispensable partner (e.g. Syria, war on terror) and leaves the doors open to technical cooperation. Parts of Russia's discursive mimicry are concepts borrowed from globalist vocabulary, including interdependence (when it comes to finding a counter-sanction argument) and open/soft borders (as a means to infiltrate Ukraine). Modernization as a concept is understood in Russia mostly as technical adjustment/ upgrade of industry and finances, but not institutions, the legal system or social relations because all this can ultimately bring the regime to collapse.

Thus, Russia's challenge to the liberal order does not seek to destroy it so much as to gain additional influence in its operation. Russia seeks to exploit contradictions inherent in the extant normative order (Romanova 2018, 77). In pursuing this strategy, the major problem for Moscow is that

Putin's revolt against the post-1991 status quo is part of a larger contestation of the extant international order which is best conceptualized in the categories of the European left. Putin's crusade for equality and inclusion, his claims of injustices and anti-American invectives are therefore well dovetailed with the leftist rhetoric of protest. By and large, Putin's radical counter-hegemony is genealogically connected to anti-Western discourses pertaining to the Cold War's non-alignment movement with its anti-colonial and anti-imperialist pathos directed against the capitalist core. Not incidentally, some Russian authors resort to the post-colonial language accusing the EU in exporting its norms to neighbouring countries: "The EU policies are colonial: A drive to spread the Christian faith worldwide during the Crusades eventually gave way to the 'civilizing' mission of the colonial era, which, in turn, has been replaced by the pursuit of 'democracy' and 'human rights' " (Titov 2016). Portrayal of the EU as a "self-loving, sitting on a bag of money, and listening only to itself" (Bordachev 2018) resonates well with the leftist critique of the West. Constant references to the Russian multiculturalism that transcends ethnicity and religion also look harmonious with the leftist mind-set in Europe.

Paradoxically, this structural affinity with a variety of contemporary left-wing discourses remains largely unnoticed in Russian political mainstream that prefers to put itself in an awkward position of instrumentalizing and amplifying the leftist momentum through conservative means. The logical trap in which the Kremlin may find itself is clear at this juncture. On the one hand, the Russian officialdom is scared of—and thus feels itself uncomfortable with—the rhetoric of revolution that stands behind the leftist/neo-Marxist/socialist ideologies. Yet on the other hand, its opposite—conservative nationalism——in many European countries evolved in the direction of de facto reproducing (some of) neo-Nazi appeals to racial purification and cultural homogeneity, which makes too close interaction with right-wing parties highly problematic and hardly compatible with Russia's image as a country that defeated fascism in 1945.

Conclusion

In conclusion, let me discuss three analytical implications resulted from this chapter. First, research in EU-Russia relations elucidates the importance of finding a balance between structural and agential drivers for change. Despite a heavy accent on structural factors in the Russian mainstream discourse that seeks to legitimize Russian foreign policy, one should not discard the Kremlin's sovereign agency that in each specific situation of reaction to external developments (be it relations between Georgia and Abkhazia in 2008 or the Euromaidan revolt in Kyiv in 2013–2014) opted for a more self-assertive and less cooperative policy towards its neighbours, the EU and NATO.

Second, we need to look at Russia more as a part of material and physical reality, and less as an object of normative and ideational investments. In political theory, there is a debate on "new materialism" (Lundborg and Vaughan-Williams 2015) that might be extrapolated into the field of Russian studies in the sense of striking a balance between allegiance to ideational factors (norms and values) and attention to the materiality of Russia's international agency as a hotbed of energy resources and military force.

Third, a nuanced difference between understanding Russia's motives of behaviour and legitimizing Kremlin's discourses becomes crucial when it comes to different combinations of political and academic discourses. The problem for Europe is not only how to convince Russia to return to a cooperative track (which is the core of political debate) but also how to professionally study Russia without engaging in contacts that would ultimately compromise Europe's normative integrity and legitimize the Kremlin's discourse. In other words, studying Russia implies avoiding situations in which the very process of cognition comes at a price of normalizing (if not promoting) Russian mainstream discourses in the West. The transnational political think-tank industry creates multiple opportunities for objects of study (in our case Russia) to influence researchers in a variety of ways and contaminate Western discourses with direct apologetics of pro-Kremlin policies. Perhaps Russian students should learn from such disciplines as cultural anthropology or religious studies where the precondition for a good research is a clear distance between the analyst and the object of analysis and it is these standards that need to be strictly observed in Russian—and post-Soviet in a wider sense—studies.

References

Bordachev, Timofei. 2016. Russia and the European Union: Three Questions Concerning New Principles in Bilateral Relations. *Valdai Discussion Club*, May 12. http://valdaiclub.com/files/10754
———. 2017. Krizis i neopredelennoye budushcheye Yevropy: chto dolzhna delat' Rossiya? *Valdai Discussion Club*, January 18. http://ru.valdaiclub.com/a/highlights/krizis-budushchee-evropy/

———. 2018. Europe: Countdown to the Point? *Valdai Discussion Club*, February 1. http://valdaiclub.com/a/highlights/europe-countdown-to-the-point

Busygina, Irina. 2017. Razvorot k malym: Chto Rossii sleduyet peresmotret' v svoyom podkhode k ES. *Moscow Carnegie Center*, September 20. http://carnegie.ru/commentary/73156

Council of the EU. 2018. Declaration by the High Representative on Behalf of the EU on the Findings of the Joint Investigation Team on the Downing of Flight MH17. May 25. http://www.consilium.europa.eu/en/press/press-releases/2018/05/25/declaration-by-the-high-representative-on-behalf-of-the-eu-on-the-findings-of-the-joint-investigation-team-on-the-downing-of-flight-mh17/pdf

Dembinski, Matthias, and Joachim Spanger. 2017. "Plural Peace": Principles of a New Russia Policy. *PRIF Report*, no. 145. https://www.hsfk.de/fileadmin/HSFK/hsfk_publikationen/prif145.pdf

European Union External Action. 2016. Remarks by High Representative/Vice-President Federica Mogherini at the Press Conference Following the Foreign Affairs Council. March 14. https://eeas.europa.eu/headquarters/headquarters-homepage/5490/remarks-by-high-representativevice-president-federica-mogherini-at-the-press-conference-following-the-foreign-affairs-council_en

Gould-David, Nigel. 2018. Economic Effects and Political Impacts: Assessing Western Sanctions on Russia. *BOFIT Policy Brief*, no. 8. https://helda.helsinki.fi/bof/bitstream/handle/123456789/15832/bpb0818.pdf?sequence=1

Gromyko, Alexei. 2017. Yevrosoyuz dolzhen proyti po lezviyu britvy, chtoby vyzhit'. *Evrazia Ekspert*, October 4. http://eurasia.expert/evrosoyuz-dolzhen-proyti-po-lezviyu-britvy-chtoby-vyzhit

Ivanov, Igor. 2018. RF i Yevropa: ot romantiki k pragmatike. *RIAC*, January 29. http://russiancouncil.ru/analytics-and-comments/analytics/rf-i-evropa-ot-romantiki-k-pragmatike

Kantor, Vladimir. 2015. Myslima li Yevropa bez Rossii? *Gefter*, November 25. http://gefter.ru/archive/16725

Karaganov, Sergei. 2018. My ischerpali yevropeyskuyu kladovuyu. *Kommersant – Ogoniok*, September 10. https://www.kommersant.ru/doc/3719327

Kortunov, Andrey. 2017. Gibridnoe sotrudnichestvo: Kak vyiti iz krizisa v otnosheniyakh Rossii s EC. *Moscow Carnegie Center*, August 28. http://carnegie.ru/commentary/72922

———. 2018. Verniotsya li Rossiya v Yevropu? *RIAC*, August 28. http://russiancouncil.ru/analytics-and-comments/analytics/vernetsya-li-rossiya-v-evropu

Krikovic, Andrej, and Yuval Weber. 2018. What Can Russia Teach Us About Change? Status-Seeking as a Catalyst for Transformation in International Politics. *International Studies Review* 20 (2): 292–300. https://doi.org/10.1093/isr/viy024.

Lukin, Alexander. 2016. Russia in a Post-bipolar World. *Survival* 58 (1): 91–112. https://doi.org/10.1080/00396338.2016.1142141.

Lundborg, Tom, and Nick Vaughan-Williams. 2015. New Materialism, Discourse Analysis, and International Relations: A Radical Intertextual Approach. *Review of International Studies* 41 (1): 3–25. https://doi.org/10.1017/S0260210514000163.

Moskovskiy Komsomolets. 2016. Eksperty: pochemu Rossii nevygoden raspad Yevrosoyuza. December 7. https://www.mk.ru/politics/2016/12/07/eksperty-pochemu-rossii-nevygoden-raspad-evrosoyuza.html

Nikitin, Alexander. 2016. New Helsinki Needed? A View from Russia. *DGAP Analyze*, no. 3, April. https://dgap.org/en/article/getFullPDF/27838

Novostipmr.com. 2016. Rossiyskaya armiya gotova uchastvovat' v operatsiyakh pod egidoi Yevrosoyuza. December 14. https://novostipmr.com/ru/news/16-12-14/rossiyskaya-armiya-gotova-uchastvovat-v-operaciyah-pod-egidoy

Orsini, Dominique. 2018. The Future of Peace and Security in Europe. Ukrainian-Russian-Polish-German Quadrilateral Discussions. *Heinrich Böll Stiftung E-Paper*, June. https://www.boell.de/sites/default/files/e-paper_the-future-of-peace-and-security-in-europe.pdf

Permanent Mission of the Russian Federation to the European Union. 2017. Ambassador Vladimir Chizhov Addresses the EU-Eurasia-China Business Summit. October 9. https://russiaeu.ru/en/news/ambassador-vladimir-chizhov-addresses-eu-eurasia-china-business-summit

Rambler.ru. 2018. Putin poobeschal zaschitit' Yevropu. May 24. https://news.rambler.ru/politics/39933960-putin-poobeschal-zaschitit-evropu

Romanova, Tatiana. 2018. Russia's Neorevisionist Challenge to the Liberal International Order. *The International Spectator* 53 (1): 76–91. https://doi.org/10.1080/03932729.2018.1406761.

Shevtsova, Lilia. 2015. Pochemu vse ne tak? O nesostoyavsheysya lyubvi Yevropy i Rossii. *Novaya Gazeta*, November 21. https://www.novayagazeta.ru/articles/2015/11/21/66461-pochemu-vse-ne-tak

Timofeev, Ivan. 2018. Unbalanced Europe and the New Order in the OSCE Space. *RIAC*, May 3. http://russiancouncil.ru/en/analytics-and-comments/analytics/unbalanced-europe-and-the-new-order-in-the-osce-space

Titov, Andrey. 2016. Russia and the EU: The Global Cooperation Agenda. In *Avoiding a New 'Cold War': The Future of EU-Russia Relations in the Context of the Ukraine Crisis*, ed. Cristian Nitoiu, 81–85. London: LSE Ideas.

Trenin, Dmitrii. 2018. Rossiya i Yevropa: k chemu stremit'sa i chto delat'? *Moscow Carnegie Center*, March 29. https://carnegie.ru/2018/03/29/ru-pub-75938

Zagorski, Andrei, and Wolfgang Zellner. 2016. *Renewing Mechanisms for Russia-EU Cooperation*. Moscow: RIAC. http://russiancouncil.ru/upload/RIAC-DGAP-Report27-en.pdf

CHAPTER 4

Russia as a Regional Actor: Goals and Motivations

Jeanne L. Wilson

INTRODUCTION

Scholars of the Russian political system are close to unanimous in stressing the importance to the Kremlin that Russia be perceived as a great power. A key question, however, has been the credentials that Russia possesses to lay claim to this status. In this context, Russia has increasingly linked its presumed predominance as a regional hegemon to the claim to great power status. The Kremlin places an overwhelming emphasis on the concept of multipolarity—as opposed to a US-dominated unilateralism—as an operative component of the international system. According to the 2016 Foreign Policy Concept, globalization has accentuated the trend towards multipolarity and the "formation of new centres of economic and political power" (Ministry of Foreign Affairs 2016).

This chapter draws on Jeanne L. Wilson, "The Russian Pursuit of Regional Hegemony," *Rising Powers Quarterly* 2, no. 1 (2017): 7–25. http://risingpowersproject.com/quarterly/russian-pursuit-regional-hegemony/.

J. L. Wilson (✉)
Wheaton College, Norton, MA, USA
e-mail: wilson_jeanne@wheatoncollege.edu

© The Author(s) 2020
E. Parlar Dal, E. Erşen (eds.), *Russia in the Changing International System*, https://doi.org/10.1007/978-3-030-21832-4_4

In the post-Soviet era, the Russian government has sought to strengthen and expand the role of regional structures. In the view of the Kremlin, there is a correspondence between leadership of multilateral institutions and multipolarity, such that multilateral structures represent a pole, or vector of power in a multipolar world (Makarychev and Morozov 2011; Kuhrt 2014). These structures include the Collective Security Treaty Organization (CSTO), the Shanghai Cooperation Organization (SCO), and the Eurasian Economic Union (EAEU). In the past several years, the Kremlin has also begun to promote the concept of the Eurasian Comprehensive Partnership (variously known as the Eurasian Partnership, the Greater Eurasian Partnership, or Greater Eurasia) that extends beyond the boundaries of the post-Soviet space. The CSTO, SCO, and EAEU serve multiple goals, both for Russia and for its partners. Nonetheless, I argue in this chapter that Russia's primary orientation towards its regional integration projects is political. As is typically the case in Russia, politics trumps economics, and also influences the Kremlin's calculus of its security interests. This leads at times to a virtual quality, which has also been noted by other observers, in Russian policy (Wilson 2005; Allison 2008). In short, the Kremlin can be observed to be more invested in employing regional structures as a symbol of Russia's great power status than in exhibiting a commitment to their successful operation and institutionalization.

The maintenance of Russia's image as a great power not only drives Russia's foreign policy but serves as a means of domestic legitimation. In this sense, realpolitik coincides with identity issues. Russia's great power status is an integral component of Russia's still evolving national identity. Russian cultivation of regionalism incorporates a defensive component inasmuch as it is meant to form a perimeter that shields Russia from the intrusion of external, most notably Western, influences. Moreover, Russia's efforts to construct a Eurasian Comprehensive Partnership places it at the centre of what it envisions as an integrative order that would simultaneously counterbalance against China and the West. At the same time, the identity issue brings Russia back to Europe. Despite the dismal relations between Russia and the West, the Kremlin has remained eager to make use of the EAEU and the concept of the Eurasian Comprehensive Partnership as a means to reach out to Europe in integrative projects that revive the notion of a community that stretches from Lisbon to Vladivostok and now beyond into the Pacific region.

This chapter proceeds as follows. The evolution and performance of the CSTO, SCO, and EAEU are discussed in the first three sections followed by an assessment of the Russian effort (still in the process of development) to organize the Comprehensive Eurasian Partnership. I then discuss the role of multilateral organizations as a component of Russian regionalism before turning to an examination of identity politics and the role of great power status as a means of domestic legitimation. The conclusion summarizes the main themes of the chapter.

The CSTO: An Underutilized Structure?

The 1992 Tashkent Treaty of Collective Security laid the groundwork for the emergence of the CSTO. The CSTO was established in 2002 with the aim of coordinating security cooperation with the Commonwealth of Independent States (CIS) members (although membership in the organization has been limited to Russia, Belarus, Armenia, Kazakhstan, Kyrgyzstan, and Tajikistan, with Uzbekistan an occasional member). Moscow has sought to present the CSTO as a counterpart (and counterbalance) to NATO and has pushed its somewhat reluctant partners for the development of a rapid deployment force to intervene in instances of conflict. To date, however, the CSTO has never been involved in any real military action (although it holds annual training exercises). Russia did not seek CSTO involvement in its 2008 war with Georgia or in its 2014 military intervention in Ukraine. The Kremlin presumably felt that the participation of a regional organization was demeaning to its image as a great power. For their part, the other CSTO members have been highly ambivalent about Russia's 2008 war with Georgia as well as the 2014 annexation of Crimea (Kropatcheva 2016). Moreover, the CSTO declined to become involved in the 2010 political crisis in Kyrgyzstan in which inter-ethnic riots broke out between Kyrgyz and Uzbeks in the southern part of the state. Roza Otunbayeva, the acting chair of the Kyrgyz provisional government, requested a peacekeeping deployment from President Dmitry Medvedev. Not only was this appeal rejected, but Russia also declined to seek to mobilize the CSTO as an actor that might seek to resolve the crisis (Matveeva 2013).

The passivity of the CSTO indicates a lack of commitment to multilateral intervention on the part of all of its members. The tensions between CSTO members, as well as the pivotal role of Russia in the structure, were starkly highlighted in the fall of 2016 when its members failed to approve the transfer the chair of the organization from its long time Russian incumbent, Nikolai Bordyuzha, to an Armenian candidate. The disinclination of Russia to utilize the CSTO for military ends raises the question as to its primary function. To be sure, the CSTO operates to strengthen the bilateral linkages between Russia and the member states. It also signals Russian interests in Afghanistan and the influx of drugs flowing into Russia from Central Asia. But there is also a symbolic element to Russia's cultivation of the CSTO, insofar as it is meant to signal Russia as a great power whose presence can deter Western efforts at infiltration. Russian efforts to portray the CSTO as a counterpoint to NATO are not convincing. Nor does the Russian narrative correspond to the empirical reality. But Russian rhetoric does indicate the Kremlin's desire to make use of the CSTO as contributing to Russian prestige, as well as illustrating its commanding presence in the CIS region (Matveeva 2013, 492; Aris 2016).

THE EXPANSION OF THE SCO: TO WHAT ENDS?

The origins of the SCO lay in the 1996 Treaty on Deepening Military Trust in Border Regions signed by the so-called Shanghai Five (China, Russia, Tajikistan, Kyrgyzstan, and Kazakhstan). During Putin's first year in office in 2000, the Shanghai Five was reconstituted as the SCO (also including Uzbekistan as a member). The Kremlin had paid very limited attention to the Shanghai Five in the Yeltsin era, leaving China as the driving force behind the organization. The Putin presidency sought to redress this imbalance, while focusing on the structure as a means to preserve Russia's presence in Central Asia. Formally, the SCO is charged with three primary tasks: cooperation in (1) politics and security, (2) trade and economic activity, and (3) the development of cultural and humanitarian ties. There is a Regional Anti-terrorist Structure (RATS) located in Tashkent. The SCO also conducts occasional joint military exercises that typically focus on dealing with the evolution of a colour revolution scenario. With the exception of RATS, the SCO largely lacks an institutionalized structure. Decisions are made by consensus largely within the format of meetings of presidents and prime ministers of the member states.

In the 2000s, the SCO became the locale for a clash of interests between Russia and China. China was eager further to develop the economic functions of the SCO, seeking to establish a SCO development bank as well as the evolution of the structure into a free-trade zone. Both initiatives were opposed by Russia. For their part, the Central Asian leaders had no objection to a SCO development bank, but they also feared that the initiation of a free-trade area with Beijing would intensify Beijing's economic presence in the region as well as resulting in a flood of Chinese goods pouring across their borders. Beijing's frustration with the SCO as a means of economic cooperation was apparently a factor in its decision to launch its Silk Road project (also known as the Belt and Road Initiative or BRI) (Gabuev 2015; Lukin 2015, 4). It was presumably not a coincidence that Chinese president Xi Jinping announced the land based segment of the initiative during a 2013 visit to Kazakhstan. Beijing's decision to focus on the BRI in Central Asia, and in fact, throughout the broader post-Soviet space, is a tacit acknowledgement of its lack of interest in the future direction of the SCO. It appears that the Chinese leadership, having failed to achieve its goal by working within the organization, has selected to bypass it. This has left Russia as the biggest promoter of the SCO, which it has attempted to shape to its preferences.

The 2016 meeting of the SCO in Tashkent approved India and Pakistan as incoming members of the organization, with Iran also expected to join in the future. Russia has been the staunchest advocate of the expansion of the SCO, a measure that China has opposed, although not officially. The addition of India and Pakistan as members raises the question as to the future evolution of the organization. A key problem with the SCO has been its largely formalistic existence. The SCO is an inert structure, which "plans to act more than it acts" (Malashenko 2015). It is by no means clear that the addition of India and Pakistan as members will revitalize the organization. Rather, the addition of these two states—which have a highly strained, if not outright conflictual relationship—will likely diminish the focus of the organization on the member states of Central Asia, threatening to make the organization even more ceremonial, or, in the words of Alexander Gabuev (2017), "a useless club." This is not the opinion of the Kremlin, which apparently anticipates that the body can evolve into another platform that provides Russia with the opportunity to act as a great power on the world stage. Putin himself alluded to the latter scenario in describing the addition of India and Pakistan as a means of turning the SCO into "a very powerful international association that commands respect and is relevant both in the region and worldwide" (Kremlin.ru 2016a).

The EAEU: An Economic or Political Entity?

The EAEU, formally established on January 1, 2015, is an institution with a long pedigree, the latest stage in a two decade long integration process in the post-Soviet space. In addition to founding members Russia, Belarus, and Kazakhstan, Armenia and Kyrgyzstan joined the union later in 2015.

Moldova has an observer status, an option that has also been extended to Tajikistan. The EAEU has an institutionalized bureaucracy centred in Moscow headed by the Eurasian Economic Council. It seeks to integrate the economies of the member states rooted in the premise (albeit with many exclusions) of free trade and the free movement of goods, services, capital, and labour. The Kremlin has largely recruited members through a bilateral process of deals and benefits.

A major attraction of the EAEU is the provision of Russian subsidies, which includes the remittances received by states—notably Armenia and Kyrgyzstan—as a result of the free flow of labour to Russia (Roberts and Moshes 2016; Vieira and Guedes 2016). Although Kazakhstan and Belarus were willing participants, Armenia and Kyrgyzstan were less enthusiastic about joining the EAEU. Armenia previously had hopes of signing an Association Agreement with the EU, but presumably felt that it could not ignore Russia's position as a security protector. Speaking about the Ukrainian government's rejection of EAEU membership, Kyrgyz president Almazbek Atambayev noted in December 2013 that Kyrgyzstan, unlike Ukraine, "unfortunately did not have much of an alternative" (Popescu 2014, 20).

The maintenance of state sovereignty is a key preoccupation of all of the non-Russian member states, which speaks to an underlying fear of Russian intrusion into their internal affairs. The leaderships of Belarus and Kazakhstan have voiced these sentiments most fervently. Although in some ways its most dedicated proponent, Kazakh President Nursultan Nazarbaev, has insisted that the EAEU function solely as an economic not a political structure. Citing the predominance of state sovereignty, Nazarbaev has continuously reiterated that Kazakhstan will not hesitate to withdraw from the EAEU if it feels that its interests are threatened.[1] Although less emphatic than Nazarbaev, Belarusian president Alexander Lukashenko has similarly described Belarusian participation in the EAEU as a matter of cost-benefit calculations: "Belarus' position on the future EAEU will depend on what it can derive; if it is nothing, then what is the point to this alliance?" (Cheng 2015).

The Russian strategy to attract members to the EAEU through the granting of economic benefits suggests that participation is the EAEU is potentially disadvantageous to Russia itself as an economic proposition. Dmitry Trenin (2011) argued prior to the EAEU's establishment that Russia could never succeed in any integration projects in the region in the absence of permanent subsidies. Western analysts are divided as to whether the EAEU can succeed as an economic union (Tarr 2016; Hartwell 2016;

Aslund 2016). The Kremlin's narrative on the EAEU incorporates a specifically political component. As Suvi Kausikas (2015, 111) has noted: "Russia's own EEU project was never just about economics. In fact, it was perhaps not about economics at all." Putin's 2011 article in *Izvestia* in which he set forth his conception of a Eurasian Union focused largely on its economic benefits but was by no means devoid of a geopolitical element (Putin 2011). Putin denied that the Eurasian Union sought to resurrect the Soviet Union. He, however, noted that a Eurasian Union could serve as a pole in the international system as well as a bridge between Europe and the Asia-Pacific Region. He was also explicit that the Eurasian Union could contribute to the "community of economies … stretching from Lisbon to Vladivostok," signifying the development of a partnership between the Eurasian Union and the EU.

Since Putin's return to the presidency in 2012, the Russian narrative on the EAEU has evolved to place an increasing stress on its civilizational component, a perspective that also casts Russia as a great power in the international system. Here, the concept of the "Russian World" is seen to extend into the post-Soviet space. In a speech given to the 2014 Seliger Youth Forum, Putin associated the EAEU with the "Eurasian Idea" and the "Greater Russian World" (Akapov 2014). This idea is popular amongst a number of Russian political commentators. Alexander Lukin, for example, argues that a "clash of values" exists between the West and the Eurasian region. In his view, economic considerations are important, but secondary to the Eurasian integration project (Lukin 2014, 54). What he considers really distinctive and a unifying principle is the common values shared by the peoples of the region—commitment to family, traditional morality, a belief in religion, and so on—that contrast markedly with the relativistic permissive values of the West.

The failure of Russia to convince Ukraine to join the EAEU has undeniably struck a heavy blow to its prospects. In the wake of this event, the Kremlin ratcheted up its civilizational discourse. As Andrei Tsygankov (2015, 291) has noted, "The more the EU presented Ukrainian membership in the organization as a 'civilizational choice,' the more Putin and his associates viewed the Eurasian Union as a values based community." The Russian annexation of Crimea was also subsequently presented to the Russian population as testimony to Russia's great power status. Discourse on the EAEU has also been affected by the perceived need to present Russia as a great power, in this case, as an independent pole in the international system that serves as the lynchpin of Eurasia.

Alexander Libman's (2017) research on the EAEU additionally indicates the divergence between rhetoric and empirical reality. Whereas Russian discourse posits the ability of the EAEU to act to reshape the global economy, in fact the capabilities of the union are far more circumscribed. Evidence indicates that the Kremlin, having created the EAEU and its institutions, is not committed to making it work, but rather makes use of the institution as a demonstration of its global influence (Dragneva and Wolczuk 2017).

The Greater Eurasian Partnership: Moving Beyond the Post-Soviet Space

In the last few years, the Kremlin began to publicize the concept of a "Greater Eurasia" or a "Comprehensive Eurasian Partnership" as a loosely structured multilateral regional organization that extends beyond the boundaries of the post-Soviet space. In his December 2015 address to the Federal Assembly, Putin floated the idea of forming an economic partnership between the EAEU, the SCO, the Association of South East Asian Nations (ASEAN), and other states (Kremlin.ru 2015). Putin's June 2016 speech at the St. Petersburg International Economic Forum significantly enlarged upon this theme, calling for a "more extensive Eurasian partnership" that would involve establishing a network of bilateral and multilateral trade agreements between interested states and multilateral organizations (Kremlin.ru 2016b). The Russian relationship with China is envisioned to occupy a central role in this arrangement. In May 2015, Russia and China signed an agreement calling for the joint development of the EAEU with China's BRI (Zhong E. Lianbang 2015). In June 2016, shortly after the St. Petersburg International Economic Forum, the Russian-Chinese Joint Statement that was released after Putin's official visit to China advocated building a "Comprehensive Eurasian Partnership" that would include the possible involvement of the SCO and ASEAN in addition to the EAEU and China (Zhong E. Lianbang 2016). Subsequently, however, the SCO has also been identified as the organization most capable of guiding the development of the Comprehensive Eurasian Partnership (Karaganov 2016; Yefremenko 2016).

The Valdai Discussion Club has been closely associated with the concept of the Comprehensive Eurasian Partnership. In the past few years, the Club has issued a series of reports dealing with the Russian turn to the East. *Toward the Great Ocean-3*, published in 2015, discussed the development of a Central Eurasian movement (Valdai Club 2015). The Valdai Discussion Club introduced the concept of "Greater Eurasia" which subsequently became part of official discourse as the "Greater Eurasian Partnership" (Lukin and Yakunin 2018). Sergei Karaganov, in particular, has written extensively on Russia's relationship with Eurasia and has gone further than most commentators in proposing principles for the construction of a Greater Eurasia. In his view, these would include unconditional respect for political pluralism, an unconditional respect for sovereignty and territorial integrity, a refusal to create new military unions, or expand existing ones, and a commitment to the development of cooperation and security in a network that would locate Russia as a key security provider (Karaganov 2018).

The Eurasian Comprehensive Partnership is, to say the least, a vague and inchoate concept. It lacks an institutionalized structure and no meetings have been held to plot out its development. It exists, rather, solely in the realm of rhetoric. The Kremlin has proposed an economic format for this body as a loosely integrated structure of regional multilateral organizations. Nonetheless, this is inevitably also a political project. At its core, the Eurasian Comprehensive Partnership locates Russia at the centre of the Eurasian land mass posed to play a central role in the orchestration of political and security affairs on the Eurasian continent. In this format, it implies that Russia can simultaneously serve as a counterbalance to both Europe and to China. This is a vision that is reminiscent of Sir Halford Mackinder's articulation of the Heartland thesis and his dictum that the state that controls the Heartland commands Eurasia and beyond (Mackinder 1904).

Although couched in the language of cooperation and mutual benefit, the Comprehensive Eurasian Partnership seeks to position Russia as a dominant presence in the Eurasian region. Marcin Kaczmarski and Witold Rodkiewicz (2016) consider that the Greater Eurasian project is intended to "conceal and legitimize the growing asymmetry in Russian-Chinese relations." They argue that Russia has adopted a policy of bandwagoning rather than counterbalancing. This perspective is accurate, drawing upon the logic of political realism, but it does not completely capture Russia's intentions.

Rather, the Comprehensive Eurasian Partnership can also be seen as a counter response to China's Silk Road initiative that sets up Russia and not China as the dominant hegemon in the region (Lukin 2018). The extent to which Russia is proposing a division of labour in the region such that it plays a security role while China attends to economic affairs is not clear. It is notable, however, that Putin's speech at the May 2017 BRI

International Forum in Beijing followed upon Chinese practice in evoking a civilizational theme. Whereas the Chinese refer to participants in the BRI as members of a "Culture of Common Destiny," Putin described the move towards Greater Eurasia as a "civilization-wide" project (Kremlin.ru 2017; also see Callahan 2016). Chinese commentary on the Comprehensive Eurasian Partnership exhibits a distinct sensitivity to its hegemonic tendencies (Wong 2018). Moreover, while the 2016 Russian-Chinese Joint Statement referred to the Comprehensive Eurasian Partnership (*ou ya quanmian huoban guanxi*), current Russian-Chinese documents refer to the more circumscribed Eurasian Economic Partnership Agreement (*ou ya jingji guanxi xieding*), a change that was presumably initiated by the Chinese leadership.

The Kremlin's promotion of the Comprehensive Eurasian Partnership has generally been interpreted as evidence of Russia's pivot to the East. Dmitry Trenin (2015), for example, has noted that reaching out to the non-West is the only option open to Russia. The Comprehensive Eurasian Partnership, however, can be seen as a complementary extension of the EAEU insofar as both locate Russia as the central conduit to Europe. Putin has been very explicit about this facet of the project. In his speech to the St. Petersburg International Economic Forum, he explicitly noted that "the 'greater Eurasia' project is, of course open for Europe....Let me repeat that we are interested in Europeans joining the project for a major Eurasian partnership" (Kremlin.ru 2016b). This is a theme that he has subsequently reiterated indicating that the integration and trade agreements that the Kremlin has in mind include cooperation with the EU (Kremlin.ru 2017).

Multilateral Structures and Russian Regionalism

The Kremlin has a dualistic view of its participation in multilateral regional structures. On the one hand, they are viewed as an end in themselves and a means of asserting Russian influence in the post-Soviet space. On the other hand, Russian leadership of multilateral organizations is seen as an indication of Russia's status as a great power in the international system. These multilateral structures represent vectors or poles of Russian power in a multipolar world. The Kremlin's perspective on globalization is also complex. Russia is opposed to what it perceives as Western unilateralism in the international system, which also signifies the predominance of Western norms and values that are portrayed as universal. At the same time, Russia is a neo-revisionist rather than a revisionist power. It does not pose an alternative framework for the international order. In distinction to unilateralism, the Kremlin asserts multipolarity as a system characteristic, as well as claiming the supremacy of Westphalian values of state sovereignty and non-interference in the internal affairs of other states. This is a realist perspective, in which dominant states manage the political, economic and security affairs of the international system, an order, as Artyom Lukin (2018) has noted, that resembles the operation of the Concert of Powers in Nineteenth Century Europe.

The Russian view of regionalism envisions it as a reactive consequent of globalization. Natasha Kuhrt (2014, 146) observes that "Russia seeks to remain global by acting regionally." Involvement in regional institutions confers status on Russia at the global level. Simultaneously, however, the Kremlin envisions its cultivation of regional multilateral institutions as a means of defensive protection from encroachment from the West (and to a lesser extent, China) (Kaczmarski 2017). Participation in regional affairs serves to decrease dependency on the West (Lane 2016; Krickovic 2014). The Kremlin's cultivation of multilateral institutions is viewed as a means of reducing the threat of the development of a colour revolution scenario in the post-Soviet space, including of course in Russia itself. This is a fear, moreover, that is largely shared by the other elites in the region and serves as an incentive for them to join in multilateral associations with Russia (Allison 2008).

Russian Regionalism and Identity Issues

To a considerable extent, Russia's efforts to assume a regional dominance can be explained with reference to political realism. Russia seeks to assert its regional influence as the basis to act as a pole in an international system that is presumably evolving towards multipolarity. Its leadership over multilateral organizations in the area serves as an underlying bulwark for its claim to great power status. The realist lens, however, provides only a partial explanation, which also indicates the relevance of social constructivism and the role of ideas and the factor of national identity in interpreting Russian behaviour. Russian national identity is unformed and a work in progress. It has lacked an ideological component to replace the theoretical canon of Marxism-Leninism, although the current recourse to civilizational discourse provides a partial compensation. The projection of Russia as a great power, however, serves as more than a geopolitical construct; it rather constitutes a core element of Russian national identity. Russian dominance in regional organizations is perceived to indicate Russia's great power status, although this is a development that tends to promote the priority of form over substance.

Although realist analysis assumes that projections of great power status are grounded in power capabilities, Russian assessments of great power status can take on a virtual format. At times, Russia's seeming indifference to the institutionalization of regional multilateral organizations reflects a lack of capabilities. But it can also indicate the ideational functions of these structures. Thus, the Kremlin asserts the CSTO as a counterpoint to NATO although it has never actually been used in a security operation. The Kremlin's conviction (reminiscent of the Soviet era) that bigger is better with the enlargement of the SCO ignores the extent to which Pakistani and Indian enmity can further erode its substantive performance. Similarly, the Kremlin's practice of luring members into the EAEU through the payment of subsidies suggests that it views economic calculations as subsidiary to political goals.

Both the EAEU and the Russian elaboration of the Comprehensive Eurasian Partnership situate Russia as a lynchpin between Europe and Eurasia. In this context, social constructivism is also useful in indicating the importance of integration with Europe as a matter of Russian national identity. Ideational themes play a key role in Russian-Europe relations (Samokhvalov 2018). Europe remains a defining other for Russia either as a source of emulation or as a counter reference (Neumann 1996). The EAEU and the Comprehensive Eurasian Partnership indicate the continued importance to Russia, despite the dismal state of Russian-European relations and its turn to the east, of integration with Europe. In this sense, the EAEU should not be seen as an end in itself but a means to realize the integration of Russia into Europe. This can also be seen as a continuation of Mikhail Gorbachev's "common European home" (Gorbachev 1987). Putin himself has been adamant that he views European participation as a vital link in the construction of an integration community that would stretch from Lisbon to Vladivostok. According to Richard Sakwa (2016, 11), the EAEU "only seriously makes sense when viewed as part of Russia's long-term commitment to the greater European idea."

The academic literature on great power status largely contemplates it as an attribute that is not claimed by a state, but conferred by other actors in the international system (Paul et al. 2014). On the one hand, Russia seeks acknowledgement of its great power status from the dominant actors in the international system. On the other hand, it asserts great power status as self-conferred as an integral facet of the regime. In this respect, Russia's claims to great power status are directed less to external actors than to the Russian citizenry. The legitimacy of the Russian regime is typically considered to rest on several pillars that include the provision of political stability and economic security (Hutcheson and Petersson 2016). But it is also the case that the identification of Russia as a great power is a fundamental basis of regime support (Wilson 2018). In a 2017 opinion poll by the Levada Center (2017), 72 per cent of the respondents considered that Russia was a superpower. Of those polled 82 per cent stated that it was necessary for Russia to preserve its role as a great power. The orientation of the Russian populace to consider Russia as a great power reflects both historical legacy and the unremitting efforts of the regime. The domestic commitment of the Kremlin to projecting Russia as a great power to the citizenry, in fact, often takes precedence over the achievement of other foreign policy goals (Feklyunina 2012).

Conclusion

Russia's primary orientation towards its participation in regional integration structures is political. This is not to say that these organizations do not perform other simultaneous socio-cultural, economic, and security functions, but it is to assert the abiding presence of the Kremlin's political motivations and goals. The Russian leadership seeks to make use of multilateral organizations as a means to justify its claims to regional hegemony, which in turn is seen to confirm Russia's great power status. The Russian elaboration of the multipolar world, which locates great powers as representatives of sectoral poles of influence both indicates and confirms Russia's entitlement to great power status as a regional hegemon. The concept of a multipolar world composed of several great powers which collectively arrange the affairs relevant to the operation of the international system is not only a realist concept but a rather old-fashioned, realist concept reminiscent of the interaction of states in Nineteenth Century Europe. It is a view, however, that is comfortable to the Kremlin, which points to its strengths in the military and security realm, and downplays Russian economic weakness as well as the extent to which globalization has transformed the behaviour of state and non-state actors in the international system.

The realist paradigm, however, only provides a partial explanation for Russia's obsessive quest to be recognized as a great power. Great power status, as previously noted, is also a fundamental component of Russian national identity. The importance of this identity has been if anything magnified in the wake of the collapse of the Soviet Union and the loss of its superpower status. Great power identity, moreover, is not simply an integral component of Russian identity: it is at the same time a fundamental pillar of regime legitimacy. The domestic presentation of Russia as a great power to the Russian citizenry (and to the political elites themselves) is more important than recognition of great power status by the international community. Thus the Kremlin's concern with presenting the image of a great power takes precedence over the actual institutionalization of structures. This behaviour makes certain aspects of Russian behaviour, such as the provision of economically inefficient subsidies to members of the EAEU or the Russian desire to expand the SCO, more comprehensible. The Kremlin's efforts to use the EAEU and the concept of the Eurasian Comprehensive Partnership as a means of reaching out to Europe, albeit on Russian terms, indicates the strength of the European idea in Russia's political consciousness

The Russian leadership's discourse concerning Russia as a great power can be viewed as a validation to some extent of the constructivist view that reality is a social construct and that states are able to create and project their own reality to a targeted audience. It is also the case that the concept of great power status is a social construct rooted in the reception of a projected image. The empiricist, however, assumes that there will be objective limitations to this strategy sooner or later. Russia is destined by virtue of geography to play a prominent role in the Eurasian region. But it faces a challenge in aligning its ambitious rhetoric about the performance of the multilateral organizations in the area with material reality.

Note

1. It was Nazarbaev as well who insisted on the inclusion of the term "economic" into the title of the EAEU, rather than the more ambiguous Eurasian Union (see Samruk Kazyna n.d.; Kazakhstan 2050 n.d.).

References

Akapov, Petr. 2014. Kazakhstan s nami. *Topwar.ru*, September 2. https://topwar.ru/57328-kazahstan-s-nami.html

Allison, Roy. 2008. Virtual Regionalism, Regional Structures and Regime Security in Central Asia. *Central Asian Survey* 27 (2): 185–202. https://doi.org/10.1080/02634930802355121.

Aris, Stephen. 2016. Still in Search of Its Place: The CSTO as a Collective Political-Military Framework. *Russian Analytical Digest* 196 (23) (December). http://www.css.ethz.ch/en/services/digital-library/articles/article.html/f04f3ce4-f251-4afe-9ec0-5d03053dd070/pdf

Aslund, Anders. 2016. Putin Gets It Wrong Again: Eurasian Economic Union Hurts Russia. *New Atlanticist*, February 1. http://www.atlanticcouncil.org/blogs/new-atlanticist/putin-gets-it-wrong-again-eurasian-economic-union-hurts-russia

Callahan, William A. 2016. China's 'Asia Dream': The Belt Road Initiative and the New Regional Order. *Asian Journal of Comparative Politics* 1 (3): 226–243. https://doi.org/10.1177/2057891116647806.

Cheng, Min. 2015. Ou ya jingji lianmeng siwen. *Qiushi*, January 12. http://www.qstheory.cn/international/2015-01/12/c_1113963249.htm

Dragneva, Rilka, and Kataryna Wolczuk. 2017. The Eurasian Economic Union: Deals, Rules, and the Exercise of Power. *Chatham House Research Paper*, May 2. https://www.chathamhouse.org/sites/default/files/publications/research/2017-05-02-eurasian-economic-union-dragneva-wolczuk.pdf

Feklyunina, Victoria. 2012. Russia's International Image and Its Energy Policy: An Unreliable Supplier? *Europe-Asia Studies* 64 (3): 448–469. https://doi.org/10.1080/09668136.2012.661923.

Gabuev, Alexander. 2015. Another BRIC(S) in the Great Wall. *Carnegie Moscow Center*, July 7. https://carnegie.ru/commentary/60628

———. 2017. Bigger, Not Better: Russia Makes the SCO a Useless Club. *Carnegie Moscow Center*, June 23. https://carnegie.ru/commentary/71350

Gorbachev, Mikhail. 1987. *Perestroika: New Thinking for Our Country and the World*. New York: Harper and Row.

Hartwell, Christopher. 2016. Improving Competitiveness in the Member States of the Eurasian Economic Union: A Blueprint for the Next Decade. *Post-Communist Economies* 28 (1): 49–71. https://doi.org/10.1080/14631377.2015.1124554.

Hutcheson, Derek, and Bo Petersson. 2016. Shortcut to Legitimacy: Popularity in Putin's Russia. *Europe-Asia Studies* 68 (7): 1107–1126. https://doi.org/10.1080/09668136.2016.1216949.

Kaczmarski, Marcin. 2017. Non-Western Visions of Regionalism: China's New Silk Road and Russia's Eurasian Economic Union. *International Affairs* 93 (6): 1357–1376. https://doi.org/10.1093/ia/iix182.

Kaczmarski, Marcin, and Witold Rodkiewicz. 2016. Russia's Greater Eurasia and China's New Silk Road: Adaptation Instead of Competition. *OSW/Commentary*, July 21. https://www.osw.waw.pl/en/publikacje/osw-commentary/2016-07-21/russias-greater-eurasia-and-chinas-new-silk-road-adaptation

Karaganov, Sergei. 2016. A Turn to Asia: The History of the Political Idea. *Russia in Global Affairs*, January 13. http://eng.globalaffairs.ru/pubcol/A-turn-to-Asia-the-history-of-the-political-idea-17926

———. 2018. The New Cold War and the Emerging Greater Eurasia. *Journal of Eurasian Studies* 9 (2): 85–93. https://doi.org/10.1016/j.euras.2018.07.002.

Kausikas, Suvi. 2015. The Eurasian Economic Union, Russia's Integration Policy and the EU Challenge. *Journal on Baltic Security* 1 (1): 108–116. https://doi.org/10.1515/jobs-2016-0002.

Kazakhstan 2050. n.d. N. Nazarbaev: Dlya Kazakhstana yevraziyskiy ekonomicheskiy soyuz – eto neobkhodimost'. http://strategy2050.kz/ru/news/5935

Kremlin.ru. 2015. Presidential Address to the Federal Assembly. December 3. http://en.kremlin.ru/events/president/news

———. 2016a. Interview to the Xinhua News Agency of China. June 23. http://en.kremlin.ru/events/president/news/52204

———. 2016b. Plenary Session of St. Petersburg International Economic Forum. June 17. http://en.kremlin.ru/events/president/news/52178

———. 2017. Belt and Road International Forum. May 14. http://en.kremlin.ru/events/president/news/copy/54491

Krickovic, Andrej. 2014. Imperial Nostalgia or Prudent Geopolitics? Russia's Efforts to Reintegrate the Post-Soviet Space in Geopolitical Perspective. *Post-Soviet Affairs* 30 (6): 503–528. https://doi.org/10.1080.1060586x.2014.900975.

Kropatcheva, Elena. 2016. Russia and the Collective Security Treaty Organization: Multilateral Policy or Unilateral Ambitions. *Europe-Asia Studies* 68 (9): 1526–1552. https://doi.org/10.1080/09668136.2016.1238878.

Kuhrt, Natasha. 2014. Russia and Asia-Pacific: From 'Competing' to 'Complementary' Regionalism? *Politics* 34 (2): 138–148. https://doi.org/10.1111/1467-9256.12053.

Lane, David. 2016. Post-Socialist Regions in the World System. *European Politics and Society* 17 (Sup. 1): 46–66. https://doi.org/10.1080/23745118.2016.1171274.

Levada Center. 2017. Gordost' i styd. March 1. https://www.levada.ru/2017/03/01/gordost-i-styd

Libman, Alexander. 2017. Russian Power Politics and the Eurasian Economic Union: The Real and the Imagined. *Rising Powers Quarterly* 2 (1): 81–103. http://risingpowersproject.com/quarterly/russian-power-politics-eurasian-economic-union-real-imagined

Lukin, Alexander. 2014. Eurasian Integration and the Clash of Values. *Survival* 56 (3): 46–60. https://doi.org/10.1080/00396338.2014.920144.

———. 2015. Shanghai Cooperation Organization: Looking for a New Role. *Russia in Global Affairs*, July 10. http://eng.globalaffairs.ru/valday/Shanghai-Cooperation-Organization-Looking-for-a-New-Role-17576

Lukin, Artyom. 2018. Putin's Silk Road Gamble. *Washington Post*, February 8. https://www.washingtonpost.com/news/theworldpost/wp/2018/02/08/putin-china/?noredirect=on&utm_term=.36269c354920

Lukin, Alexander, and Vladimir Yakunin. 2018. Eurasian Integration and the Development of Asiatic Russia. *Journal of Eurasian Studies* 9 (2): 100–113. https://doi.org/10.1016/j.euras.2018.07.003.

Mackinder, Halford. 1904. The Geographical Pivot of History. *The Geographical Journal* 23 (4): 421–437. https://doi.org/10.2307/1775498.

Makarychev, Andrey, and Vlatcheslav Morozov. 2011. Multilateralism, Multipolarity, and Beyond: A Menu of Russia's Policy Strategies. *Global Governance* 71 (3): 353–373. https://doi.org/10.5555/1075-2846-17.3.353.

Malashenko, Alexei. 2015. Tupiki 'nezapadnykh' integratsii. *Novaya Gazeta*, August 7. https://carnegie.ru/2015/08/09/ru.pub.60970

Matveeva, Anna. 2013. Russia's Changing Security Role in Central Asia. *European Security* 22 (4): 478–499. https://doi.org/10.1080/09662839.2013.775121.

Ministry of Foreign Affairs. 2016. Concept of the Foreign Policy of the Russian Federation. December 1. http://www.mid.ru/en/foreign_policy/official_documents/-/asset_publisher/CptICkB6BZ29/content/id/2542248

Neumann, Iver. 1996. Self and Other in International Relations. *European Journal of International Relations* 2 (2): 139–174. https://doi.org/10.1177/1354066196002002001.

Paul, T.V., Deborah Welch Larson, and William C. Wohlforth, eds. 2014. *Status in World Politics*. New York: Cambridge University Press.

Popescu, Nicu. 2014. Eurasian Union: The Real, the Imaginary, and the Likely. *Chaillot Paper* 132 (September). https://www.iss.europa.eu/sites/default/files/EUISSFiles/CP_132.pdf

Putin, Vladimir. 2011. A New Integration Project for Eurasia: The Future in the Making. *Izvestia*, October 3. http://en.kremlin.ru/events/president/news/6152, http://www.russianmission.eu/en/news/article-prime-minister-vladimir-putin-new-integration-project-eurasia-future-making-izvestia-3

Roberts, Sean, and Arkady Moshe. 2016. The Eurasian Economic Union: A Case of Reproductive Integration? *Post-Soviet Affairs* 32 (6): 542–565. https://doi.org/10.1080/1060586X.2015.115198.

Sakwa, Richard. 2016. How the Eurasian Elites Envisage the Role of the EEU in Global Perspective. *European Politics and Society* 17 (Sup. 1): 4–22. https://doi.org/10.1080/23745118.2016.1171038.

Samokhvalov, Vsevolod. 2018. Russia and Its Shared Neighborhoods: A Comparative Analysis of Russia-EU and Russia-China Relations in the EU's Eastern Neighborhood and Central Asia. *Contemporary Politics* 24 (1): 30–45. https://doi.org/10.1080/13569775.2017.1408171.

Samruk Kazyna. n.d. Nursultan Nazarbaev, president Kazakhstana: Yevraziiskii soyuz ot idei k istorii budushchego. http://sk.kz/topblog/view/44

Tarr, David. 2016. The Eurasian Economic Union of Russia, Belarus, Kazakhstan, Armenia and the Kyrgyz Republic: Can It Succeed Where Its Predecessor Failed? *Eastern European Economics* 54 (1): 1–22. https://doi.org/10.1080/00128775.2015.1105672.

Trenin, Dmitry. 2011. *Post-Imperium*. Washington, DC: Carnegie Endowment for International Peace.

———. 2015. Russia Far from Isolated in Non-West Community. *China Daily*, July 8. http://www.chinadaily.com.cn/opinion/2015-07/08/content_21211016.htm

Tsygankov, Andrei. 2015. Vladimir Putin's Last Stand: The Sources of Russia's Ukraine Policy. *Post-Soviet Affairs* 31 (4): 279–303. https://doi.org/10.1080/1060586X.2015.1005903.

Valdai Club. 2015. Toward the Great Ocean-3: Creating Central Eurasia. June 4. http://valdaiclub.com/files/17658

Vieira, Alena, and Vstoskaya Guedes. 2016. Eurasian Integration: Elite Perspectives Before and After the Ukraine Crisis. *Post-Soviet Affairs* 32 (6): 566–580. https://doi.org/10.1080/1060586X.2015.1118200.

Wilson, Andrew. 2005. *Virtual Politics: Failing Democracy in the Post-Soviet World*. New Haven: Yale University Press.

Wilson, Jeanne L. 2018. Russia's Relationship with China: The Role of Domestic and Ideational Factors. *International Politics*. https://doi.org/10.1057/s41311-018-0167-8.

Wong, Ka-Ho. 2018. A Comparative Study of the Greater Eurasian Partnership: The Chinese and Russian Perspectives. *Analytical Media/Eurasian Studies*, June 1. http://greater-europe.org/archives/5160

Yefremenko, Dmitry. 2016. The Birth of a Greater Eurasia. *Russia in Global Affairs*, February 13. http://eng.globalaffairs.ru/number/The-Birth-of-a-Greater-Eurasia-18591

Zhong E. Lianbang. 2015. Zhonghua renmin gongheguo yu eluosi lianbang guanyu sichou zhi lu jingji dai jianshe he jianshe duijie hezuo de lianhe shengming (quanwen). *Qstheory*, May 9. http://www.qstheory.cn/zhuanqu/zywz/2015-05/09/c_1115228503.htm

———. 2016. Zhonghua renmin gongheguo he elusi lianbang lianhe shengming. *Xinhuanet*, June 26. http://news.xinhuanet.com/politics/2016-06/26/c_1119111908.htm

(Mis)interpreting the Eurasian Economic Union? Images of the EAEU in Russia and the West

Alexander Libman

INTRODUCTION

The Eurasian Economic Union (EAEU) of 2015, originally established as the Customs Union of Russia, Belarus and Kazakhstan in 2010, has been so far the most successful regional economic organization in post-Soviet Eurasia. Unlike its predecessors plagued by large implementation gaps, unrealistic goals and predominance of rhetoric over action, the EAEU actually managed to become a functioning regional organization. Most

---

This chapter draws on Alexander Libman, "Russian Power Politics and the Eurasian Economic Union: The Real and the Imagined," *Rising Powers Quarterly* 1, no. 1 (2017): 81–103. http://risingpowersproject.com/quarterly/russian-power-politics-eurasian-economic-union-real-imagined. The research is supported by the MOE Project of Key Research Institute of Humanities and Social Sciences in Universities of China (Center for Russian Studies of East China Normal University), Project Number: 16JJDGJW004.

A. Libman (✉)
Ludwig Maximilians University of Munich, Munich, Germany

E. Parlar Dal, E. Erşen (eds.), *Russia in the Changing International System*, https://doi.org/10.1007/978-3-030-21832-4_5

certainly, one should be cautious about overestimating the success of the EAEU, first, because the implementation of agreements is not absolute (particularly if major political interests of individual countries come into play); second, because there are questions about the EAEU's ability to fully achieve the goals set in the 2015 treaty; and third, because of the persistence of numerous internal market barriers (see Eurasian Economic Commission 2017). However, the EAEU's achievements should not be underestimated. It became an active customs union (although after Kazakhstan's accession to the World Trade Organization covering only about 60 per cent of the entire trade nomenclature) and managed to achieve free movement of capital and labour across the borders of its members (Vinokurov 2018).

In order to understand the role the EAEU plays in international affairs, it is important to look not only at its functioning but also at how the organization is viewed by the political elites of the member states and external partners as well as the epistemic communities. It is not rare for important international organizations to be associated with various perception gaps, when different groups of actors attribute different roles and potential to the regional organization or have different expectations about how that regional integration should develop in the future (e.g. Christiansen et al. 1999; Elgström 2007). The most successful organizations (like the EU) actively shape their perception to enhance their legitimacy or increase their influence. From the point of view of the observers, the EAEU did not emerge out of thin air. It followed a long sequence of regional organizations established by the Eurasian countries since 1991. This "shadow of the past" was primarily the "shadow of past failures," given the very poor performance of almost all EAEU predecessors. Furthermore, the EAEU was created at a particular point of the development of the Russian political regime and of the political relations between Russia, the EU and the US. As this chapter attempts to argue, this resulted in a substantial *perception gap* between the actual practices of the EAEU and the image of the EAEU in the eyes of the decision-makers, experts and scholars. Understanding this perception gap can be important for studying the general patterns of the Eurasian politics. Libman and Obydenkova (2018), for example, show that Russian policy towards other states of Eurasia is strongly influenced by how the EAEU is perceived by the Russian elites and public.

The goal of this chapter is to review the perceptions of the EAEU in Eurasia and beyond. My main focus is going to be on the expert scholarly debate, which is easier to analyse given the abundance of empirical material (texts produced by researchers studying the particular case). However, many of the features I identify in this paper inform the political discourse or are informed by it. Among the countries of the EAEU, I focus on Russia and how the organization is perceived there. I then confront this perception with the view of the EAEU in what one could describe as "the West" (although I am aware about how imprecise this reference is) as the international academic discourse is mostly taking place in the EU and US. This comparison is warranted, given the still substantial barriers in the communication existing between the research communities in Russia and abroad, which relatively few researchers are systematically able to cross.[1] Interestingly, I find that both Russian and international observers share an important common feature in their view of the EAEU: the focus on the geopolitical role of the organization and in particular its alleged ability to enhance Russia's influence in the global arena. From this point of view, however, the research on the EAEU faces an important problem: the institutional design of the regional organization does not seem to be particularly suitable to promote the Russian hegemony as the subsequent discussion of this chapter will show.

EAEU in the Eyes of the Russian Epistemic Communities

Unlike the Western discourse on Eurasian regionalism, which only recently became prominent enough to warrant a systematic analysis, the Russian discourse on regional integration in post-Soviet Eurasia has always been substantial. As a result, a certain way of perceiving the regional integration in Eurasia emerged. Libman (2012) in his survey of the scholarly literature refers to it as a "standard post-Soviet integration paper," typically based on four claims: that regional integration is inevitably beneficial for the countries of Eurasia; that the only way to integrate Eurasia is to emulate the EU; that the only factor precluding this emulation is the lack of political will of the leaders; and that the West is hostile towards any attempt of reintegrating Eurasia.

The establishment of the EAEU as an entity much more relevant for the economic policy triggered an even larger attention to the topic. A search in the *Elibrary.ru* database conducted on September 1, 2018, revealed 1784 journal articles containing the word "Eurasian Economic Union" in their title.[2] Still, the debate on the EAEU similarly seems to follow a number of common perceptions and ideas. In a nutshell, it appears to be based on three main assumptions.

First, regionalism is perceived not as a tool of *constraining the sovereignty* of individual countries (as it is done, for instance, in the EU studies or in many fields of comparative regionalism literature), but rather as a factor *empowering* them in world politics. Regional organizations are seen as bargaining coalitions, where countries come together to collectively support their position against other "power poles" or as tools of promoting economic competitiveness, which should again increase the countries' power. Butorina (2005) offers a comprehensive picture of the world consisting of several competing and complementary regional projects aiming to influence the institutions and the structure of the global economy.

Second, as a result, the main task of a country willing to promote its influence in the global economy and its vision of how it should develop is to join such a regional coalition or to develop one's own coalition: regional organizations (like the EU and NAFTA) and projects (like the Belt and Road Initiative) are interpreted through this lens: "joining forces makes it easier to fight, to develop, to create a power centre in the world of global contradictions and conflicts" (Leshukov 2016). Similarly, the EAEU should become a new power pole in the global world as post-Soviet integration allows its members to "maximize the benefits from globalization and to minimize its inevitable drawbacks" (Glinkina 2015, 12).

From this follows the third assumption. By creating the EAEU, Russia is able to increase its influence in the global economy and more actively participate in its design. By joining a different coalition, Russia would be forced to accept this coalition's vision of the global economy. Within the EAEU, it can protect and develop the Russian position on this matter. Some even go as far as to claim that the EAEU is necessary for the survival of the Eurasian nations in the globalized world (Fonarev 2012).

The reasons for why Eurasian integration is indeed strengthening Russia as a geopolitical player are rarely discussed explicitly. The assumption seems to be that Eurasian regionalism provides Russia with greater resources through cooperation with the neighbouring countries and that it safeguards Russia's specific "Eurasian" status, which is necessary to ensure "the security, the territorial integrity of Russia, to strengthen its international reputation and sovereignty" (Titarenko 2009). Eurasian integration is also seen as a way of refocusing the role of the region's economies in the global division of labour from resource exports to technology (Lagutina 2015).

The specific varieties of this general framework, as implemented in individual studies, differ a lot. In particular, Russian observers differ in their perception of "hostility" of other projects and power poles towards the

EAEU. For many of them, while some level of competition between projects is inevitable (because they represent different views on how the global economy should work), there is still substantial space for cooperation and interaction. In fact, precisely this interaction could constitute the main competitive advantage of the EAEU. Others see the dividing lines between the EAEU and other projects as deep and unresolvable. For instance, the EAEU's main goal should be to counter the Western influence in Eurasia. As a result, a continuum of different views on the EAEU emerges, with authors emphasizing the extent of its inherent competition against the West to different extent.

The following papers exemplify different stances of Russian scholars within this continuum. Butorina and Zakharov (2015, 53) represent a less confrontational view of the EAEU. While they clearly subscribe to all three assumptions presented earlier and argue that "an obvious, but officially not declared mission of the EAEU is to form a pole of geopolitical gravitation and a new centre of power, alternative to the European and the American ones," they do not focus on the contradiction between the EAEU and the alternative regional organizations and rather highlight the internal preconditions for the EAEU to live up to its potential. Braterskiy (2015, 59), who again suggests that "the main goal of the Russian foreign policy is to create a regional economic community with substantial economic sovereignty and strong political influence, i.e. a new centre of influence in the world economy," is more open about the possible tensions with the West. While the Russian policy is not seen as anti-American in its nature, it should inevitably lead to limiting the US influence in Eurasia. Vasilyeva (2015, 100) goes further in this direction. After echoing the discussed ideas by claiming that "the idea of Eurasian integration particularly fits the Russian geopolitical interests, as it creates real preconditions for Russia's positioning as a central country of Eurasia," she clearly suggests that the EAEU is designed to limit the fragmentation of post-Soviet Eurasia in the interests of external actors (China, the US and EU). Finally, Svetlichnyi (2012) takes an extreme stance, suggesting that it is the main tool of preventing the US attempts to strip Russia of the status of great power and surround it with hostile nations. Krotov and Muntian (2015) provide a combination of two views (this approach is also echoed by many other observers and, as it will be shown further, matters a lot in the political discourse). The EAEU is seen as potentially benefitting from cooperation with other regional organizations and willing to engage in it, but unable to do so because of the position of the Western powers (especially the US) and their rejection of the EAEU as a partner. This actually reflects the real scepticism many in the EU and the US express towards cooperating with the EU.

Interestingly, while highlighting the strengthening of the Russian bargaining power through the EAEU and explicitly acknowledging post-Soviet countries as a special "zone of influence" of Russia (Zhuravlev 2015), Russian discourse does not see it as a contradiction to the interests of other smaller countries of Eurasia. The EAEU is seen as an association of equals (as opposed to the explicitly asymmetric structure of the European Neighbourhood Policy, see Krotov and Muntian 2015) or as the only avenue of "independent development following one's own agenda" for countries between competing power poles of China and the EU (Knyazev 2016, 154). Most likely, this view continues the already described tradition of the "standard post-Soviet integration paper" with its assumption about the beneficial nature of Eurasian integration for all participants. Summing up, Kheyfets (2015, 35) ironically refers to the view of the EAEU I have described in this paper as "dreaming geopolitics"—pointing out to how different it is from the reality of Eurasian regionalism I discuss in the following section.

EAEU in the Eyes of the Western Observers

Research on the EAEU in the international academia is substantially smaller, although recently it resulted in the publication of a number of highly prominent books and articles. As of September 2018, the Web of Science database includes 67 journal articles with the title containing the words "Eurasian Economic Union," out of which 27 have been published in the Russian and Kazakhstani journals. There are only eight articles in the Science Direct database bearing the word "Eurasian Economic Union" in their title. The views of the Western observers are substantially more diverse than those of the Russian scholars, partly because unlike Russia no large field of studies exists, where the formation of a mainstream point of view could be possible. Still, one can highlight a number of arguments on the EAEU shared by many writing about this organization in the EU or US—though again one has to point out the existence of numerous diverging views.

Kirkham (2016) provides a review of the extant literature on the EAEU and concludes that the predominant discourse on this topic is to analyse the organization "through the prism of Russian foreign policy strategy, with notions of empire and hegemony." The views of the EAEU as a predominantly Russia-led and to a large—or even to a full—extent politically motivated project are very widespread in the discussion (Saivetz 2012; Delcour and Wolczuk 2013; Kühn 2017; Diesen 2017; Sergi 2018). This is a direct continuation of how post-Soviet regionalism was seen already prior to the initiation of the EAEU (Sushko 2004). The motives for the Russian actions could be diverse. Russia could attempt to reaffirm its dominance in post-Soviet Eurasia (Rivera and Garashchuk 2016); to protect what it perceives as its "sphere of influence" from the external actors, particularly the EU (Cadier 2014); to deal with the global uncertainty (Krickovic 2014) and with globalization (Lane 2015); or even to project a specific economic model (Johnson and Köstem 2016). As such, the EAEU is assumed to have no independent actorness. It is rather designed and shaped by Russia as it seems fit.

Unlike the Russian discourse on the EAEU, the international observers, however, challenge two other premises of the organization: the voluntary nature of membership of the individual countries and the inevitable success of the organization as a tool for protracting Russian power. A widespread point of view is that for many countries of Eurasia, membership in the EAEU comes at a cost and can be an outcome of Russian pressure (or more precisely a combination of Russian sanctions and rewards) rather than fulfilling their own objectives. More importantly, the EAEU is seen as a rather weak organization unable to fulfil the promises of the grandeur Russian elites link to it. It is associated with both structural and institutional features of the EAEU, making it unable to achieve a real progress in the domain of regional integration or at least resulting in a significant underperformance as opposed to the expectations (e.g. Roberts and Moshes 2016; Mohammeddinov 2017). Popescu (2014), in an insightful paper, suggests that the geopolitical ambitions dominating the Russian drive to create the EAEU are precisely the reason why the organization turns out to be less successful, as it makes the necessary steps for implementing (a more limited, but viable) economic integration project insufficiently attractive for Russia. In short, what appears to be a natural and necessary tool for securing Russia's high status in global politics for the Russian observers is seen as a much less effective and efficient organization with frequently coerced membership by their Western counterparts.

THE REAL AND THE IMAGINED EAEU

Thus, both Russian and international observers seem to share a common viewpoint on the EAEU, considering it as a tool designed to promote or strengthen Russian power in the international arena. Russian observers argue that the EAEU could be successful in achieving this objective, and that by doing it, it does not encroach upon the interests of other states of Eurasia. Western observers appear to express much more scepticism about the EAEU's ability to reach this goal, and also point out that the EAEU membership is frequently a result of direct or hidden coercion exercised by Russia against other states. The question, however, remains whether the EAEU *in its current institutional design* is indeed a suitable entity for achieving the goal of strengthening Russian geopolitical interests. Here, the evidence is much less conclusive as the mainstream opinion appears to be.

One has to acknowledge that the empirical evidence on this topic remains rather limited (Gast 2017), as there has been little research actually looking at the functioning of the EAEU bureaucracy and policymaking practices. Importantly, I do not claim that Russia did not *imply* the use of the EAEU as an entity for its geopolitical agenda, while participating in the original design of the organization. On the contrary, there are reasons to believe that this perception may explain the extent of commitment Russia showed to the organization (Libman 2018). The question is, however, whether the EAEU *as it materialized* based on negotiations with other members and the actual practices of its bureaucracy fits these geopolitical expectations and, in particular, actually empowers Russia as a global actor. The available evidence casts doubt upon it.

Generally speaking, there exists a design of regional organizations— which Hancock (2009) refers to as "plutocratic regionalism"—explicitly based on the delegation of authorities to the leading country rather than to smaller states. The Southern African Customs Union was an example of this approach before the end of apartheid, based on South Africa unilaterally setting customs duties and redistribution some of the customs revenue to other countries. The EAEU, however, does not follow this approach. Instead, it is structured as an apparent replica of the EU, with the Eurasian Economic Commission (EAEC) as a decision-making body claiming some supranational authorities. The Customs Union Commission (the first governing body of the EAEU) decision-making was based on weighted voting scheme, which provided more power to Russia than to other members. In the EAEC, the governing body of originally the Customs Union and later the EAEU, which replaced the Customs Union Commission in 2011, this approach was abandoned, with a single majority voting approach (where Russian votes count just as much as votes of the other members) or consensus decision-making. The EAEC Board (the main executive body of the EAEU) currently consists of ten representatives, two from each country, each running one's own ministry or agency. While they are able to make decisions through simple majority, de-facto decision-making is always consensus-based. In the case of disagreements, the EAEC bureaucrats seem to have a very strong preference to make no decision at all and instead shift it to the political leadership—that is, to the higher-level institutions (EAEC Council consisting of the deputy prime ministers of the member countries, and the Supreme Eurasian Council including the presidents of the five states), which are intergovernmental in nature and make all decisions by consensus.

As a result, the EAEC is frequently incapable of making any drastic decision in the case of contradictions. In some cases (Libman and Vinokurov 2018; Vinokurov 2018), the EAEC made decisions not in favour of Russia, rather promoting the interests of the smaller countries, or even overruled domestic Russian decisions. At least in one case, the EAEU blocked a Russian initiative in a policy area, which the Russian leadership considered to be extremely important. In 2014, presidents of Belarus and Kazakhstan rejected the Russian proposal to exit the free-trade agreement with Ukraine which Russia envisioned as a possible reaction on Ukraine's decision to join the Association Agreement with the EU. Russia still cancelled the free-trade regime in 2016 but did it unilaterally and had to introduce additional measures to prevent Ukrainian goods entering the Russian market through Belarus. In this case, the existence of the EAEU did not help Russia in mobilizing other Eurasian countries in favour of its foreign policy and in fact rather made it more difficult for Russia to implement the decision it intended.

The EAEU is associated with an extensive redistribution mechanism in favour of smaller countries (Knobel 2015; Andronova 2016), for example, through the reallocation of revenue from customs duties and pricing of energy. Belarus was particularly successful in receiving concessions from Russia in terms of export duties on raw oil supplied to Belarusian refineries. This redistribution mechanism is not unique for the EAEU. In many regional organizations with a strong asymmetry of power, the leading state accepts the role of a regional paymaster (Mattli 1999). However, if the main goal of the regional organization is indeed defined as increasing global power and influence, it should go hand in hand with greater allegiance of the smaller countries towards the foreign policy agenda of the leader. In Eurasia, this does not appear to be the case. In fact, if one looks at the critical foreign policy decisions made by Russia, one can hardly see a very strong degree of loyalty of Eurasian states towards them. Thus, not a single EAEU member recognized the annexation of Crimea in 2014 or the independence of Abkhazia and South Ossetia in 2008. Some EAEU countries seem to be rather using the contradictions between Russia and the EU and US to strengthen their own position in international politics rather than unequivocally ally with Russia. In many cases, the main achievement of Russia is the mere membership of a country in the EAEU and compliance with the EAEU norms, but whether this membership produces further dependence or enhances policy alignment with Russia is questionable.

One can go as far as to argue that in the current form, EAEU rather functions as an additional veto player making rapid changes in the economic policy more difficult than in case Russia were doing it alone (Libman and Ushkalova 2013). This situation is unlikely to change in the future. First, smaller states (especially Kazakhstan) clearly try to avoid excessive Russian influence through the EAEU. This factor, in fact, was crucial for the entire evolution of post-Soviet regionalism (Hancock and Libman 2016). As a result, they are unlikely to agree on any decision-making mechanism or power delegation scheme, which will give too much influence to Russia. Russia, in turn, is constrained in its ability to pressure the smaller members. It is questionable whether it could coerce them through economic measures. Again, Kazakhstan is the most prominent case, but even Belarus shows successful resistance to Russian coercion in multiple cases. Furthermore, an attempt to systematically exercise coercion against one member would alienate other countries and hence result in Russia losing international allies—which is an outcome Russia, especially after the Ukrainian crisis, can hardly afford. Second, as mentioned, a general feature of the EAEU countries' bureaucracies, which they demonstrate at all levels, is the lack of initiative and attempt to avoid any independent decision-making in a somewhat debatable situation—both because of how bureaucrats are trained and because of how they are socialized. There is no reason to expect that Russian or Kazakhstani bureaucrats will start behaving in a different way if they are delegated to the EAEU.

In addition, while the Russian rhetoric frequently emphasizes a much broader ambition of the EAEU, the actual language of the EAEU documents and charters shows clear constraints on the scope and objective of the organization. Although some studies attempt to link the EAEU to a particular ideology (especially "Eurasianism," which is in itself a very broad concept) (Pryce 2013; Lukin 2014), this is mostly done focusing on the Russian rhetoric or on the interpretation of Russian actions. The EAEU, as such, carefully avoids any ideological statements or commitments even to the extent to which they were usual in the preceding organizations like the Commonwealth of Independent States (CIS).[3] There is no officially declared political integration agenda in the EAEU, mostly because of the clear resistance of Kazakhstan, insisting on the EAEU remaining a purely economic organization. Even symbolic political steps (like an EAEU inter-parliamentary assembly) were ultimately rejected by Kazakhstan. Similarly, differences between economic systems and economic policy objectives of the EAEU countries (the state-led Belarusian economy, the Russian economy with its growing inclination towards protectionism and Kazakhstan with a much more liberal approach to economic decision-making) are so large that a common industrial policy is beyond the reach of the EAEU countries. Major progress in the EAEU was achieved in much more basic aspects of integration, like the free movement of people and capital, common customs tariff and abolition of internal customs borders.

This, of course, does not mean that the EAEU is unable to produce any significant benefits for the Russian geopolitical agenda. From this point of view, the EAEU can be seen as a commitment device, which precludes smaller states from signing association agreements with the EU. Because the EAEU is a customs union, any authority to conduct negotiations on the trade regime (an obviously crucial part of the Deep and Comprehensive Free Trade Areas or DCFTAs established within the association agreements) is transferred to the EAEC. Russia perceives the signing of association agreements as a risk to its influence on the neighbouring countries of Eurasia (whether this perception is true is, of course, another and a very debatable matter). This effect of the EAEU, however, is really important for merely one of the member countries—Armenia. For other countries, association agreements with the EU are irrelevant either because of their geography (Central Asian states) or their political regimes (Belarus). The importance of this issue is also linked to the particular tool the EU chose to develop relations with the Eastern European partners—the DCFTAs. Whether this is the only tool the EU has at its disposal, and whether it is even the best possible tool to achieve the main goal of the EU—improvement of governance and economic growth in the Eastern European states—is debatable. The signing of the Comprehensive and Enhanced Partnership Agreement with Armenia in 2017 indicates the existence of an alternative, which potentially could function even with the EAEU members.

Importantly, my argument is not that the EAEU is fundamentally unsuccessful. As mentioned, it was precisely the success of the EAEU, which makes this organization worth studying. However, the EAEU appears to be unsuccessful as an entity aiming at enhancing the Russian global power. This is not (only) an outcome of the deficits of the EAEU (the economic weakness of the member states, limits of the regionalism, which have to be undoubtedly mentioned and considered in the analysis), but to a large extent (also) a feature of the *fundamental institutional design* of the EAEU. Essentially, observers in Russia focus on a highly idealized image of the EAEU based on a very specific view of the role of regional organizations in international relations. Observers outside Eurasia, while analysing the EAEU, seem to pay much more attention to what Russia wants to achieve with it rather than to the specific integration outcome—a functioning institution to be compared with other regional projects from the comparative regionalism point of view.

Conclusion

The analysis of how the EAEU is perceived in the scholarly community in Russia and the West reveals an important puzzle. While most observers see the EAEU as a Russia-led project aiming at strengthening the country's economic and political power, and while Russia itself seems to share this view,[4] the institutional design of the EAEU does not necessarily fit this goal. This perception gap can be approached from two perspectives. One is to ask why Russia ultimately accepted such a design, assuming that its goals were indeed connected to using the EAEU as a tool for dominance. A much more interesting question in the context of this chapter is another one. Why do observers and students of the EAEU continue focusing on the geopolitical motives of the EAEU rather than on the actual functioning of the organization?

As for the Russian position, one could potentially explain it by two factors. On the one hand, Russia, similar to many other countries in the world, "downloads the global script" of the EU, that is, uses the European model as a blueprint for developing its own variety of regionalism (Börzel and van Hüllen 2015). The model of "EU-like" regionalism is indeed frequently perceived as the only legitimate model of regionalism (plutocratic integration, on the other hand, can be seen as illegitimate empire-building—an accusation the EAEU gets anyway) and, more importantly, potentially the only one known to the experts engaged in designing regional organizations. Over time, this seems to have changed. Starting from 2017, Russia has also proposed the project of "Greater Eurasian Partnership," which seems to be more informed by the Belt and Road

Initiative and "transcontinental" mega-regional agreements like the Trans-Pacific Partnership (Timofeev et al. 2017; Li 2018). However, as of now, this project remains purely rhetorical, unlike the EAEU. Second, the deviation of the EAEU from the Russian expectations could reflect the bargaining outcomes with smaller countries, which, even when supporting the EAEU (like Kazakhstan), use a wide array of measures to limit the Russian influence.

The second question indeed poses a serious challenge. As a comparison, one can hardly imagine an EU studies project, which ignores the work of the EU institutions (like the Council, the Commission and the Parliament) and instead explains the EU through a version of the European idea—say the United States of Europe concept.[5] The latter is without doubt an important ideational factor contributing to the development of the EU, yet the students of the EU typically focus on the actual functioning of the EU bureaucracy and decision-making. While for Russian experts one could, to some extent, link the situation with the willingness to adjust one's statement to the political discourse[6]—a goal not irrelevant in an authoritarian state, the level of interventions of the government in the academic discourse is (as of now) sufficiently low to actually make this explanation the predominant one. And it clearly does not fit the position of the Western observers.

Hypothetically, the gap between the perception of the EAEU and the practices of the organization can be explained by three factors. First, it can simply reflect lack of evidence. To my knowledge, there have been very few (if any at all) systematic empirical studies of the operation of the EAEU bureaucracies (a very recent exception is Staeger and Bobocea 2018). Most studies are based on either expert interviews or secondary data. As a result, one is forced to use more easily available sources like the information on the (much better researched) foreign policy goals.[7] Second, one should not underestimate the importance of informal politics in the case of the EAEU. The predominance of autocracies among the members of the organization is likely to increase their inclination to use informal instruments. In many cases, this informal politics will occur outside the institutions of the EAEU, at the level of bilateral relations of the member countries, which, however, will be informed and motivated by the existence of the EAEU. From this point of view, focusing on the EAEU as an organization is in fact potentially much less important than looking at its geopolitical image. For example, while the EAEU could fail to serve as a conduit for Russian geopolitical objectives, Russia could quite consciously allow this (as a concession to smaller states), expecting their loyalty in geopolitical issues unrelated to the EAEU in exchange (Libman and Obydenkova 2018).[8] Finally, the discussion of the EAEU could be heavily influenced by the approaches, which existed before the establishment of the organization: studies on Eurasian regionalism and even on the relations between the republics of the USSR. In the past, the weakness of regional organizations in Eurasia hardly warranted detailed investigation of their functioning. If anything, they could have been interesting as rhetorical instruments used by their members for propaganda purposes or as elements of the foreign policy of the Eurasian countries—especially Russia. The typical discussion of the EAEU could simply follow this logic.

As mentioned, understanding how the EAEU is perceived by epistemic communities is not a purely academic exercise. Epistemic communities influence foreign policy decisions and perceptions. And hence the actions of the Western countries and Russia could to some extent be explained by the image of the EAEU existing in the minds of decision-makers (exposed to the discourses summarized in this chapter) rather than by the actual functioning of the EAEU. For example, substantial reluctance towards a dialogue with the EAEU on the side of many EU actors could be linked to the perception of the EAEU as a Russian hegemonic project. Russia's willingness to pressure countries to join the Customs Union in the 2010–2014 period could also be linked to the predominance of the way of thinking described in this chapter. Again, certainly, it would be naïve to reduce the foreign policy decisions to the stereotypes and perception gaps. However, they also play a role (e.g. Vertzberger 1990), and thus should not be neglected.

NOTES

1. The existence of these barriers can be linked to both lack of resources and language knowledge. There is, however, a substantial tradition in Russia consciously insisting on separating Russian scholarly debate from the international one, either referring to the epistemological specifics of the Russian scholarly tradition (Yurevich 2015) or to the political tension in the relations with the West (Fenenko 2016).
2. Elibrary.ru indexes most of the Russian-language academic journals. See elibrary.ru.
3. On how problematic it is to try to fit the "real" EAEU into the Eurasianist rhetoric, see Laruelle (2015).

4. Or, at least, did it until recently. Libman (2018) argues that there is evidence of declining interest of the Russian leadership in Eurasian regionalism since 2015.
5. https://en.wikipedia.org/wiki/United_States_of_Europe
6. Obviously, one cannot make unambiguous claims about the direction of causality between the official discourse and the discourse of the epistemic communities.
7. Identifying the actual governance practices of the EAEU could, however, be a very difficult task. For instance, one should, as mentioned, hardly find any evidence of actorness of the EAEU bureaucracy vis-à-vis the nation states— the authoritarian nature of the post-Soviet countries and the bureaucratic traditions in these countries play an important role in this context. However, the actorness of the EAEU bureaucracies could manifest itself in relations with the individual national agencies, with the EAEU competing with them for attention and recognition from national leaders. This type of interaction would be very difficult to grasp empirically.
8. As mentioned, however, there is very little evidence that Russia is successful in this strategy.

References

Andronova, Inna. 2016. Yevraziyskiy ekonimicheskiy soyuz: potentsial i ogranicheniya dlya global'nogo i regional'nogo liderstva. *Vestnik Mezhdunarodnykh Organizatsiy* 11 (2): 7–23.

Börzel, T., and V. van Hüllen, eds. 2015. *Governance Transfer by Regional Organizations*. Basingstoke: Palgrave Macmillan.

Braterskiy, Maksim. 2015. Izolyatsionizm protiv geopolitiki: dvoystvernnaya rol' yevraziyskogo soyuza v sisteme global'nogo upravleniya. *Vestnik Mezhdunarodnykh Organizatsiy* 11 (2): 58–70.

Butorina, Olga. 2005. Ponyatie regional'noy integratsii: novye podkhody. *Kosmopolis* 3: 136–145.

Butorina, Olga, and Aleksandr Zakharov. 2015. O nauchnoy osnove yevraziyskogo soyuza. *Yevraziyskaya Ekonomicheskaya Integratsiya* 2: 52–68.

Cadier, David. 2014. Eastern Partnership vs Eurasian Union? The EU–Russia Competition in the Shared Neighbourhood and the Ukraine Crisis. *Global Policy* 5 (1): 76–85. https://doi.org/10.1111/1758-5899.12152.

Christiansen, Thomas, Knut Jorgensen, and Antje Wiener. 1999. The Social Construction of Europe. *Journal of European Public Policy* 6 (4): 528–544. https://doi.org/10.1080/135017699343450.

Delcour, Laure, and Kataryna Wolczuk. 2013. Eurasian Economic Integration: Implications for the EU Eastern Policy. In *Eurasian Economic Integration: Law, Policy and Politics*, ed. Rilka Dragneva and Kataryna Wolczuk, 177–203. Cheltenham: Edward Elgar.

Diesen, Glenn. 2017. *Russia's Geoeconomic Strategy for a Greater Eurasia*. Abingdon: Routledge.

Elgström, Ole. 2007. Outsiders' Perceptions of the European Union in International Trade Negotiations. *Journal of Common Market Studies* 45 (4): 949–967. https://doi.org/10.1111/j.1468-5965.2007.00755.x.

Eurasian Economic Commission. 2017. *Barriers, Derogations and Restrictions in the Eurasian Economic Union*. Moscow: Eurasian Economic Commission.

Fenenko, Aleksey. 2016. Pochemu v Amerike ne lyubyat publikovat' rossiyskikh avtorov? *Mezhdunarodnye Protsessy* 14 (1): 172–180. https://doi.org/10.17994/IT.2016.14.1.44.12.

Fonarev, Mikhail. 2012. Tendentsii i perspektivy rasshireniya politicheskogo vliyaniy i granits yevraziyskogo soobshestva. *Yevraziyskiy Soyuz* 1: 69–76.

Gast, Ann-Sophie. 2017. Regionalism in Eurasia: Explaining Authority Transfers to Regional Organizations. *Free University of Berlin Working Paper*. http://www.polsoz.fu-berlin.de/en/v/transformeurope/publications/working_paper/wp/wp82/WP_82_Gast_WEB_neu.pdf

Glinkina, Svetlana. 2015. Geopoliticheskoe sopernichestvo na postsovetskom prostranstve kak faktor zderzhivaniya sotrudnichestva v ramkakh SNG. In *Ekonomicheskoe Vzaimodeistvie Stran-Chlenov SNG v Kontekste Yevraziyskogo Integratsionnogo Proekta*, ed. Leonid Vardomskiy and Artem Pylin, 11–32. Moscow: IE RAN.

Hancock, Kathleen. 2009. *Regional Integration: Choosing Plutocracy*. Basingstoke: Palgrave Macmillan.

Hancock, Kathleen, and Alexander Libman. 2016. Eurasia. In *Oxford Handbook of Comparative Regionalism*, ed. Tanja Börzel and Thomas Risse, 202–224. Oxford: Oxford University Press.

Johnson, Juliet, and Seçkin Köstem. 2016. Frustrated Leadership: Russia's Economic Alternative to the West. *Global Policy* 7 (2): 207–216. https://doi.org/10.1111/1758-5899.12301.

Kheyfets, Boris. 2015. Tri videniya stran-uchstnits Yevraziyskogo Ekonimicheskogo Soyuza. In *Ekonomicheskoe Vzaimodeistvie Stran-Chlenov SNG v Kontekste Yevraziyskogo Integratsionngo Proekta*, ed. Leonid Vardomskiy and Artem Pylin, 33–44. Moscow: IE RAN.

Kirkham, Ksenia. 2016. The Formation of the Eurasian Economic Union: How Successful Is the Russian Regional Hegemony? *Journal of Eurasian Studies* 7 (2): 111–128. https://doi.org/10.1016/j.euras.2015.06.002.

Knobel, Aleksandr. 2015. Yevraziyskiy Ekonomicheskiy Soyuz: Perspektivy razvitiya i vozmozhnyye prepyatstviya. *Voprosy Ekonomiki* 3: 87–108.

Knyazev, Yuriy. 2016. Rossiya v izmenivsheysya geopoliticheskoy situatsii: uchastiye v integratsionnykh proyektakh. *Svobodnaya Mysl* 3: 149–162.

Krickovic, Andrej. 2014. Imperial Nostalgia or Prudent Geopolitics? Russia's Efforts to Reintegrate the Post-Soviet Space in Geopolitical Perspective. *Post-Soviet Affairs* 30 (6): 503–528. https://doi.org/10.1080/1060586X.2014.900975.

Krotov, Mikhail, and Valeriy Muntian. 2015. Yevraziyskiy ekonomicheskiy soyuz: istoriya, osobennosti, perspektivy. *Upravlencheskoe Konsultirovanie* 11: 33–47.

Kühn, Werner. 2017. The Eurasian Economic Union: Risks and Opportunities of an Emerging Bipolar Europe. *Zeitschrift für Europarechtliche Studien* 20 (2): 185–234.

Lagutina, Marina. 2015. Global'nyi region kak element mirovoy politicheskoy sistemy XXI veka. *Sravnitel'naya Politika* 2: 16–21.

Lane, David. 2015. Eurasian Integration as a Response to Neoliberal Globalization. In *The Eurasian Project and Europe*, ed. David Lane and Vsevolod Samokhvalov, 3–22. London: Macmillan.

Laruelle, Marlene. 2015. Eurasia, Eurasianism, Eurasian Union: Terminological Gaps and Overlaps. *PONARS Eurasia Policy Memo*, no. 366. http://www. ponarseurasia.org/memo/eurasia-eurasianism-eurasian-union-terminological-gaps-and-overlaps

Leshukov, Vladimir. 2016. Yevraziyskiy Ekonomicheskiy Soyuz: tendentsii razvitiya i riski. *Masterskaya Yevraziyskikh Idei*. http://eurasianworkshop.com/?p=1114

Li, Yongquan. 2018. The Greater Eurasian Partnership and the Belt and Road Initiative: Can the Two Be Linked? *Journal of Eurasian Studies* 9 (2): 94–99. https://doi.org/10.1016/j.euras.2018.07.004.

Libman, Alexander. 2012. Studies of Regional Integration in the CIS and in Central Asia: A Literature Survey. *EDB Center for Integration Studies Report*, no. 2. https://eabr.org/en/analytics/integration-research/cii-reports/studies-of-regional-integration-in-the-cis-and-central-asia-a-literature-survey

———. 2018. Regionale Wirtschaftliche Organisation in Eurasien: Die Eurasische Wirtschaftsunion. *Russland-Analysen* 353: 3–6.

Libman, Alexander, and Anastassia Obydenkova. 2018. Regional International Organization as a Strategy of Autocracy: The Eurasian Economic Union and Russian Foreign Policy. *International Affairs* 94 (5): 1037–1058.

Libman, Alexander, and Daria Ushkalova. 2013. Foreign Trade Effects of the Customs Union Between Belarus, Kazakhstan, and Russia. *George Washington University Central Asia Program Central Asia Economic Paper*, no. 8. http://centralasiaprogram.org/wp-content/uploads/2015/04/Economic_Papers_8_May_2013.pdf

Libman, Alexander, and Evgeny Vinokurov. 2018. Autocracies and Regional Integration: The Eurasian Case. *Post-Communist Economies* 30 (3): 334–364. https://doi.org/10.1080/14631377.2018.1442057.

Lukin, Alexander. 2014. Eurasian Integration and the Clash of Values. *Survival* 56 (4): 43–60. https://doi.org/10.1080/00396338.2014.920144.

Mattli, Walter. 1999. *The Logic of Regional Integration*. Cambridge: Cambridge University Press.

Mohammeddinov, Mikhail. 2017. What's the Point of the Eurasian Economic Union? *Russian Politics* 2 (3): 334–363. https://doi.org/10.1163/2451-8921-00203004.

Popescu, Nicu. 2014. Eurasian Union: The Real, the Imaginary and the Likely. *Chaillot Paper*, no. 132. https://www.files.ethz.ch/isn/183574/CP_132.pdf

Pryce, Paul. 2013. Putin's Third Term: A Triumph of Eurasianism. *Romanian Journal of European Affairs* 13 (1): 25–43.

Rivera, Pablo, and Anna Garashchuk. 2016. The Eurasian Economic Union: Prospective Regional Integration in the Post-Soviet Space or Just Geopolitical Project? *Eastern Journal of European Studies* 7 (2): 91–110.

Roberts, Sean, and Arkady Moshes. 2016. The Eurasian Economic Union: A Case of Reproductive Integration? *Post-Soviet Affairs* 32 (6): 542–565. https://doi.org/10.1080/1060586X.2015.1115198.

Saivetz, Carol. 2012. The Ties That Bind? Russia's Evolving Relations with Its Neighbors. *Communist and Post-Communist Studies* 45 (3–4): 401–412. https://doi.org/10.1016/j.postcomstud.2012.07.010.

Sergi, Bruno. 2018. Putin's and Russian-Led Eurasian Economic Union: A Hybrid Half-Economics and Half-Political 'Janus Bifrons'. *Journal of Eurasian Studies* 9 (1): 52–60. https://doi.org/10.1016/j.euras.2017.12.005.

Staeger, Ueli, and Christian Bobocea. 2018. Bureaucratic Authority and Mimesis: The Eurasian Economic Union's Multiple Integration Logics. *International Spectator* 53 (3): 38–54. https://doi.org/10.1080/03932729.2018.1490506.

Sushko, Oleksandr. 2004. The Dark Side of Integration: Ambitions of Domination in Russia's Backyard. *Washington Quarterly* 27 (2): 119–131. https://doi.org/10.1162/016366004773097740.

Svetlichnyi, Sergey. 2012. Yevraziyskiy Soyuz: protivodeistvie strategii anakondy. *Geopolitika i Bezopasnost* 1: 103–106.

Timofeev, Ivan, Yaroslav Lissovolik, and Liudmila Filippova. 2017. Russia's Vision of the Belt and Road Initiative: From the Rivalry of the Great Powers to Forging a New Cooperation Model in Eurasia. *China and World Economy* 25 (5): 62–77. https://doi.org/10.1111/cwe.12214.

Titarenko, Mikhail. 2009. Yevraziystvo kak paradigma sosushchestvovaniya i rastsveta mnogoobraziya kul'tur i tsivilizatsiy. *Ekonomicheskie Strategii* 5–6: 18–23. http://www.inesnet.ru/article/evrazijstvo-kak-paradigma-sosushhestvovaniya-i-rascveta-mnogoobraziya-kultur-i-civilizacij

Vasilyeva, Natalya. 2015. EAES: Rossiyskiye geopoliticheskie interesy. *Upravlencheskoe Konsultirovanie* 11: 98–104.

Vertzberger, Yaacov. 1990. *The World in Their Mind: Information Processing, Cognition and Perception in Foreign Policy Decisionmaking*. Stanford: Stanford University Press.

Vinokurov, Evgeny. 2018. *Introduction to the Eurasian Economic Union*. Basingstoke: Palgrave Macmillan.

Yurevich, Andrey. 2015. Imeet li nauka natsional'nye osobennosti? *Psikhologicheskiy Zhurnal* 36 (1): 123–132.

Zhuravlev, Vitaliy. 2015. Geopoliticheskie aspekty yevraziyskoy integratsii. *Vestnik Nauik i Obrazovaniya* 10: 139–144.

CHAPTER 6

Russia and China in Global Governance

Marcin Kaczmarski

INTRODUCTION

The increasing material capabilities and external activities of rising powers have led to a broad debate on the future of global governance, especially given its embodiment in Western political values and Western primacy in international politics (Kirton and Larionova 2018; Larson 2018). Non-Western powers and non-liberal powers have exerted increased influence on practices of global governance. The authoritarian conflict management, which relies on the use of force and military victory in civil conflict, for instance in the case of Chechnya or Sri Lanka, has emerged as the most serious alternative to liberal peace-building (Lewis et al. 2018). It is supplemented by the emerging version of Chinese "peace model" in Africa (Alden et al. 2017). International law in this regard is either circumvented or re-interpreted. Russia attempted to justify the annexation of Crimea as fulfilling international law criteria (Allison 2017), whereas China rejected the verdict of the International Arbitral Court pertaining to the South China Sea (Zhao 2018).

The scholarly debate on how rising powers shape global governance tends to be focused on China (Beeson and Zeng 2018; Fook 2017; Kennedy 2017), with less attention to Russia (for exceptions, see Belokurova

M. Kaczmarski (✉)
University of Glasgow, Glasgow, UK

E. Parlar Dal, E. Erşen (eds.), *Russia in the Changing International System*, https://doi.org/10.1007/978-3-030-21832-4_6

2017; Kanet 2018). The most contentious issue concerns China's long-term intentions. Some scholars recognize that China has been adapting to the international order, attempting to influence it from the inside. Chan et al. (2018) concluded in their latest contribution that "a greater stake and more extensive engagement with the international community has inclined Beijing to become a more responsible stakeholder". These voices are balanced by those scholars who see China as undermining the existing structure of global governance with its practices (Hameiri and Jones 2018; Hearson and Prichard 2018). There appears to be a greater consensus on Russia's approach, with the emphasis on Moscow's dissatisfaction with the existing order (for a broader discussion, see Götz and Merlen 2018, and other articles in their special issue).

Despite the surge of scholarly interest towards Sino-Russian relations, cooperation between the two states in the realm of global governance remains understudied (for exceptions, see Grant 2012; Kaczmarski 2018; Snetkov and Lanteigne 2014; Yu 2019). Scholars point at the informal division of labour between the two states in global governance. Russia remains active in the realm of international security governance, whereas China has increased the level of its participation in areas of economic, financial and environmental governance. Pundits ascribe these differences to the different potential of the two states as well as their related varied scope of interests in a well-functioning global governance system. However, this division of labour between Russian and China has evolved for the last couple of years. Beijing has increased its engagement with international security governance, while Moscow has lost some of its (already limited) interest in such areas as environmental or economic governance. This chapter aims at exploring this shift and its implications. Rather than analysing Sino-Russian relations in distinct areas of global governance, it proposes a different approach and identifies three patterns of interactions between the two countries: direct cooperation, parallel activities and contradictory/divergent activities.

DIRECT COOPERATION

Direct cooperation between Russia and China has the greatest potential to influence the existing patterns of global governance. Acting together, Moscow and Beijing may either reinforce dominant practices or successfully challenge them. Close collaboration also makes it easier for the two states to gain followers of their practices. What is characteristic for most cases of cooperation is that one of the two states usually takes a lead on a specific issue, while the other decides to follow.

Full-Fledged Collaboration: International Security Governance

Russian-Chinese cooperation in the sphere of international security governance stands out with regard to crisis and conflict management. Both states coordinate their positions on a number of issues related to regional and global crises and challenges, which are also regularly confirmed in their annual joint declarations (for details, see Kaczmarski 2018). The UN Security Council provides the institutional setting within which Moscow and Beijing translate their common positions into substantial actions and influence the course of events. One could indicate four important cases of Sino-Russian cooperation in this regard: Arab revolutions and the Syrian civil war, Iranian nuclear programme, North Korean nuclear crisis and the Rohingya refugees' emergency.

Russia has taken the lead with regard to crisis management in the Middle East after the Arab revolutions. Both in the case of the revolution in Libya in March 2011 and in the case of the Syrian civil war since 2011 onwards, Moscow convinced Beijing to follow the Russian position and regularly received Beijing's official support. The crucial step in the Libyan crisis was the decision of Russia and China to abstain during the voting in the UN Security Council, which paved the way for the Western-led intervention in the military conflict between Muammar Gadhafi and the Libyan opposition. Moscow's acquiescence seemed to be of vital importance, especially given Beijing's low-profile approach at that time.

In the case of the Syrian civil war, China joined Russia in vetoing the resolutions proposed by the Western states in 6 out of 11 cases between 2011 and 2018.[1] In the first phase of the domestic conflict, both states shielded the Syrian ruling regime from political pressure and criticism of the international community. Following the use of chemical weapons by the Assad regime, Moscow and Beijing prevented the imposition of any sanctions on Syria. Whereas it was Moscow that proposed the US to jointly eliminate chemical weapons from Syria in 2013, China joined the operation in a subsidiary role. Another way in which Russia and China demonstrated their shared position with regard to the Syrian conflict was to abstain during some votes on the provision of cross-border aid to Syria (CNBC 2018).

Russia and China also coordinated their positions in the UN Security Council throughout the process of managing the Iranian nuclear dossier. Both states supported several sets of sanctions between 2006 and 2010, thus exerting additional pressure on Tehran. At the same time, they jointly condemned the Western states for applying unilateral sanctions during the negotiation process. In the late 2000s, it was the evolution of the Russian position that was subsequently accepted by China. Beijing took a more assertive stance only in 2010. However, they played less publicly visible roles in the negotiations that ultimately led to the Joint Comprehensive Plan of Action (JCPOA) agreed in 2015. Following the US withdrawal from the agreement under Donald Trump in May 2018, Russia and China repeatedly confirmed their willingness to maintain the agreement and criticized the re-imposition of American sanctions on Iran.

The crisis surrounding North Korea's nuclear programme, on the other hand, illustrated China's leading role, especially in its most recent phase since 2017. Russia dropped its opposition to harsher sanctions proposed by the Western states after China agreed to increased political and economic pressure on Pyongyang (Rodkiewicz 2018).

Moscow and Beijing have also adopted similar policies towards one of the most serious humanitarian crises of the late 2010s—the persecution of the Rohingya minority in Myanmar. The two states maintained their usual line and attempted to limit the scope of conditions under which the UN Security Council could authorize the interference in domestic affairs by the international community. Thus, they both shielded Myanmar's government from any criticism in the UN Security Council (Fair 2018) and insisted that the issue concerned only Myanmar and Bangladesh, and as such should not be "internationalized", effectively blocking any statements that could exert pressure on the authorities of Myanmar (Schwirtz 2018; Japan Times 2018; RFERL 2017). They also opposed any measures to be taken by the UN General Assembly (The Guardian 2017).

The area of arms control and disarmament represents the case of partial coordination between Russia and China. Both states share an unwillingness to engage with certain areas of international security governance. The ban of anti-personnel mines, rejected by Moscow and Beijing, provides one such example. In particular, Russia and China remain unwilling to support compliance verification in most of the global governance schemes. The attempts to limit illegal "conflict diamonds" trade faced this kind of opposition on the part of both states (Westerwinter 2016).

In other areas, such as space security, both Russia and China have promoted a shared agenda. They proposed a joint treaty at the Conference on Disarmament banning the militarization of outer space for the first time in 2008 and they later proposed a revised version in 2014 (Tronchetti and Hao 2015). In terms of the non-proliferation regime, which remains one of the cornerstones of international security governance, Russia and China also tend to coordinate their efforts. Apart from collaboration during proliferation-related crises discussed earlier, they engage with other pillars of the non-proliferation regime. Whereas Moscow and Beijing support non-proliferation in general, they tend to be cautious towards Western initiatives that would increase the powers of the international community, such as the Proliferation Security Initiative. Russia and China also consistently opposed the authorization of inspections of suspected ships on high seas (Eilstrup-Sangiovanni 2016, 157–58).

The Shanghai Cooperation Organization (SCO) represents an intermediate level of Russian-Chinese cooperation between regional and global security governance. For most of its existence since 2001, the SCO was limited to Central Asia despite Moscow's ambitions to transform it into a global security organization. Beijing preferred to maintain the organization's focus on regional cooperation and use it as a platform against the so-called three evils of separatism, extremism and terrorism. The question as to whether the SCO should be enlarged was a major bone of contention between Russia and China (Ambrosio 2017; Lanteigne 2018). The deadlock was ultimately solved in 2017, when the SCO finally enlarged to include India and Pakistan. This has significantly contributed to the organization's global profile, even though it still remains unclear whether the new and old members can manage to reinvigorate the SCO agenda. Tensions between China and India as well as the conflict between India and Pakistan pose the most significant obstacle to broader collaboration and a more prominent role for the SCO in international security governance.

Elements of Collaboration: Economic, Environmental and Cyberspace Governance

Cooperation between Russia and China in such areas of global governance as economy, environment and cyberspace remains limited. This has to be ascribed to different potential and different roles both states play in these domains.

In the realm of economic, financial and trade governance, in most cases, it is Beijing that leads the cooperation. There are two main platforms that Russia and China use for their cooperation: G-20 and BRICS. As Russia has played a rather minor role within the G-20, this forum has remained rather unused. The most important—but still symbolic rather than substantial—step undertaken by China and Russia was to establish new financial frameworks within BRICS in 2014. The New Development Bank and the Contingent Reserve Arrangement are to perform functions parallel and similar to those of the World Bank and the IMF. The fact that Shanghai was made the seat of the New Development Bank confirmed China's leadership within the BRICS group (Cooper 2017; Liu 2016; Qobo and Soko 2015). The impression that Beijing played a bigger role in the sphere of financial governance was also reinforced by China's establishment of the Asian Infrastructure Investment Bank (AIIB). It seems that Russia had no other choice but to join the Chinese initiative.

Cooperation between Russia and China in the area of environmental governance remains even more limited. Moscow and Beijing approach environmental governance from different angles. The level of Russia's emissions is much lower than that of the Soviet Union, mostly due to its long-term industrial decline. China's levels of emissions, in turn, multiplied for the last several decades. As a result, cooperation between the two states in this realm is an exception rather than a rule. Moscow and Beijing find common ground in issues related to climate change, in particular in opposing what they regard as excessive measures. For instance, in one of the few cases of closer cooperation, Russia and China acted in a coordinated manner in their joint opposition to the EU plan to make airlines buy emission schemes in 2011.

Russia and China also share the same view regarding the need to introduce new norms and rules to the cyberspace. According to this view, state sovereignty should embrace the cyberspace and a state should be entitled to impose its national rules in the cyber domain. Therefore, both states promote the idea of "internet sovereignty". The most far-reaching step Moscow and Beijing took in this sphere was to propose the "International Code of Conduct for Information Security" in 2011. However, whereas this proposal helped to make clear Russia and China's positions on cyber governance, it was not backed up by many other countries (Ebert and Maurer 2013; Farnsworth 2011).

Parallel Activities

Parallel activities form the dominant pattern of Russian-Chinese relations in global governance. These activities might be interpreted as an informal and often unintentional "division of labour" in global governance. Taken together, they have the potential to change the existing arrangements in favour of Moscow and Beijing.

Different Tools: Security Governance

The most outstanding feature of Russia and China's parallel approaches to international security governance is the use of different tools to address particular crises and influence the situation on the ground in the long-term perspective. These are often unilateral means that nonetheless have implications for the practices of global governance. The Russian leadership prefers the use of force and military-related means such as arms sales and delivery, whereas the Chinese leadership employs economic and development assistance instruments. Moscow seems more ready to act in extraordinary circumstances such as civil wars and revolutions and support incumbents as the case of the Syrian civil war demonstrated. Beijing, in turn, is only ready to prop up non-democratic regimes in mundane situations. China is rather willing to provide financial assistance and investments—with both state-owned enterprises and private companies—and looks for new markets and ways to "outsource" their overcapacity.

Peacekeeping operations illustrate the different approaches of Russia and China to their roles in international security governance. The level of participation of Chinese troops in peacekeeping operations has been steadily increasing in the last decade. In 2013, for instance, Beijing sent an infantry detachment of about 500 troops to serve in the UN peacekeeping mission in Mali. This was the first overseas deployment of Chinese combat troops in a peacekeeping role. In 2014, Beijing also sent a battalion of 850 soldiers to South Sudan (Godement et al. 2018). The number of Chinese troops deployed reached the level of 3000 on average between 2015 and 2017 (Cho 2018).

Russia, in turn, has practically withdrawn from any participation in UN peacekeeping operations, even though this policy was never admitted publicly. One may speculate that the Russian leadership regarded peacekeeping operations as neither increasing Russia's international prestige, nor bringing tangible economic benefits. The last Russian mission under the aegis of the UN took place in 2006 in Lebanon, even though in this case the Russian unit operated separately from the major UN mission.[2] It is only recently that Moscow decided to engage in conflict management "on the ground". In December 2017, for instance, Russia convinced the UN Security Council to make an exception that enabled the Russian training mission and weapons to be sent to the Central African Republic (News 24 2018). However, at this stage, it is impossible to predict how durable Russia's engagement is going to be.

Both Russia and China have also been participating in anti-piracy missions in the Horn of Africa since 2008. They did not join the existing multinational operations, but dispatched their ships independently (Percy 2016). It is difficult, however, to assess the scope of substantial cooperation between the navies of the two countries. According to Beijing's estimates, during the decade of the operation, the Chinese navy escorted 3400 ships, that is, 51 per cent of all the escorted ships (Ministry of National Defense 2019). Unlike China, Russia did not publicize its participation in anti-piracy operations.

Nuclear arms control represents another area of international security governance in which Russia and China chose to pursue separate paths. Due to its superpower nuclear arsenal, Russia has been the number-one interlocutor for the US. China, in turn, preferred to stay outside of most of nuclear arms control and arms reduction agreements, as it regarded its nuclear arsenal to be too small. However, the gradual withdrawal of the US from arms control agreements—including the Anti-ballistic Missiles (ABM) Treaty in 2002—followed by growing Russian-Western tensions, made Moscow less interested in maintaining the existing arms control architecture. Eventually, Russia withdrew from conventional arms control regimes such as the Treaty on Conventional Forces in Europe (CFE), even though it still strived to maintain nuclear arms control in place. The New START treaty, signed in 2010, led to further reductions in Russian and American arsenals, while also enhancing Russia's prestige in the West.

The deterioration of Russian-Western relations over the annexation of Crimea, however, made the prospects for arms control bleaker. In the mid-2010s, Washington accused Russia of breaking the Intermediate-Range Nuclear Forces Treaty (INF). Moreover, the US saw this treaty as an unnecessary limitation in the face of the growing missile threat from China. The withdrawal of both the US and Russia from the INF Treaty in 2019 removed one of the last remaining elements of the arms control regime. Yet, it should be noted that China has been unwilling to commit itself to any nuclear arms control agreements. The most recent confirmation of this point was made by the Chinese representative during the Munich Security Conference in February 2019 (Channel News Asia 2019). It is also possible that the major remaining Russian-American arms control treaty—the New START—will expire if one of the two parties decides not to prolong it. Ultimately, this may result in both Russia and China not taking part in any major nuclear arms control agreements in the future.

Leader and a Minor Participant: Economic Governance

In the realm of global economic governance, parallel activities are the dominant modus operandi as China is usually at the forefront of economic and financial governance, while Russia has been taking a back seat for the last two decades. China has been a member of the World Trade Organization (WTO) since 2001, whereas Russia joined this organization only in 2012. Furthermore, with the expansion of the G-20 mechanism, China became a member of the global financial regulators such as the Financial Stability Board and the Basel Committee on Banking Supervision.

China's engagement in global economic and financial governance is much more sophisticated than Russia's approach as Beijing pursues a dual-track policy. It attempts to reinforce its position in the existing institutions and at the same time continues to establish its own parallel institutions. China has worked hard to increase its share both in the IMF (from 3.67 per cent in the mid-2000s to 6.09 per cent in 2018) and in the World Bank. The IMF later also decided to include the yuan as its reserve currency. Simultaneously, China has established the AIIB in 2015, despite the open opposition from the US and convinced a number of US allies from Europe and Asia to join the AIIB (Ren 2016).

Russia, in turn, has remained on the margins of global economic and financial governance. Whereas China has sufficient economic resources to upgrade its position within the international financial architecture, Russia has to struggle to retain its position in global financial and economic institutions. Despite joining the WTO, Russia has not opened up to trade and it actually became one of the states erecting the largest number of trade restrictions (Solanko 2016, 6–7). Contrary to China, Russia has not managed to join the core group of WTO negotiators either—that is, the states which effectively exercise veto power in the negotiation process (Jordan 2017, 465).

In addition, Russia and China do not cooperate in the realm of development assistance and their patterns of engagement in this area differ significantly. Russia attempted to set up a separate national development assistance institution in 2007, when it adopted its first development cooperation strategy, which was updated in 2014 (De Cordier 2016; Ministry of Foreign Affairs 2014). Following several years of bureaucratic turmoil and the global economic crisis, the Kremlin decided to hand over development issues to the Federal Agency for the Commonwealth of Independent States, Compatriots Living Abroad and International Humanitarian Cooperation, commonly known as Rossotrudnichestvo. Handing over the development cooperation portfolio to an agency responsible for cooperation in the post-Soviet space attests to the limited regional scope of Russia's ambitions. Russia's official development assistance (ODA) hovered around $500 million between 2010 and 2012 and exceeded $1 billion in 2015 and 2016 (these figures include debt cancellation). Bilateral ODA is 75 per cent of overall ODA, while Russia's development assistance remains concentrated in the post-Soviet space, Kyrgyzstan, Armenia and Azerbaijan being the major recipients (Zaytsev and Knobel 2017, 14 & 18). Syria joined this group of recipients following Russia's intervention in the civil war in that country in 2015.

China's development assistance is global in scope and provides developing states with more substantial financial resources, although it sometimes entices particular recipients into a debt trap. Beijing prefers to finance the construction of infrastructure with a focus on the African states. According to the OECD figures, China's ODA in 2015 was $3.1 billion, of which more than 90 per cent was distributed via bilateral channels. Chinese infrastructure investments have narrowed economic inequalities within developing countries (Bluhm et al. 2018). Other assessments provide higher estimates, but the details of particular agreements are quite rarely released publicly. This generous policy does not preclude some negative effects in that states supported by China are still prone to being caught in the debt trap, as it used to be the case with previous Western and Soviet assistance. Nevertheless, China's growing experience in development assistance and its plans to broaden it have urged Beijing to establish a national development assistance agency in 2018 (Kitano 2018).

Changing Roles: Environmental Governance

In the 2000s, Russia appeared to be a strong supporter of the fight against climate change and a relevant actor—being responsible for 5 per cent of the global emissions. Back in 2004, the EU supported Russia's bid for WTO membership in exchange for Moscow's participation in tackling climate change (Parker and Karlsson 2010). This turned out to be Russia's last contribution to the climate change regime. Global warming did not seem to be much of a concern for Russia, which could even benefit from some of its effects such as the opening of the Northern Sea Route.

In 2009, it was China which—together with the US—blocked the emergence of a new climate agreement during the summit in Copenhagen, leaving Russia and the EU on the side-lines. Beijing took the initiative, leading the BASIC countries (Brazil, India, South Africa) in opposition to a new agreement that would have replaced the Kyoto protocol after 2012. China refused to bind itself in any way to reductions of greenhouse-gas emissions and thus it was accused of torpedoing the outcome of the summit.

In recent years, however, the roles of China and Russia seem to have been reversed. Beijing is now ready to reduce carbon emissions and a series of pledges paved the way for the conclusion of the 2015 Paris Agreement (Godement 2015). It also promised financial assistance for developing countries so that they could meet their own targets (Hilton and Kerr 2017). Indeed, after the US withdrawal from the Paris Agreement under President Trump, China has come to portray itself as a leader in climate change mitigation. Xi Jinping went so far as to call for the creation of "ecological civilization" (Xinhuanet 2019).

Yet, it should be noted that in the case of China, its interest in global environmental governance is both domestic-driven and half-hearted. On the one hand, the ruling party realizes that its legitimacy is increasingly relying not merely on economic growth but also on the less tangible "life quality" of which relatively clean environment is a crucial element. Hence, Beijing-ordered crackdown on the polluting factories. On the other hand, China remains ready to "outsource" its environmental problems by investing in polluting factories or coal-fuelled power plants far beyond its borders (Reuters 2019). With regard to the latter, China emerged as "the largest global provider of public financing for foreign coal-fired power plants" (Umbach 2019, 7).

While Russia also joined the Paris Agreement, scholars observed an important shift in the discourse on climate change in Russia towards a much more sceptical attitude (Tynkkynen and Tynkkynen 2018). This shift coincides with the unambitious target declared by Russia for the Paris Agreement. Moscow promised to limit greenhouse gas emissions to 70–75 per cent of the 1990 level by 2030, which will not be difficult given that in 2012 Russia's emissions were already below 68 per cent of the 1990 level. As Korppoo and Kokorin (2017) put it, "adopting a deeper target would be more credible than the current commitment, even if it were not fully achieved".

CONTRADICTORY/DIVERGENT ACTIVITIES

The number of spheres in which China and Russia act in opposite ways in global governance still remains limited. Russia's conflict with the West over Ukraine and the suspension of Russia's membership in the G-8 in particular eliminated one of the contradictions between Russia and China. In the

2000s, Russia aspired at G-8 membership and the Russian chairmanship at this platform in 2006 was the highest point. Even though Russia's agenda, which was focused on energy governance, was not fully implemented, Moscow's membership in the G-8 placed it in the group of developed states. China, meanwhile, considered itself to be a developing country. These differences translated in Moscow and Beijing's diverging approaches regarding such issues as responsibility for the fight against climate change. Developing states including China have promoted the policy of divided responsibility, recognizing developed states as those which should bear the brunt of tackling the challenge of climate change. Although the emergence of G-20 as a key forum in the aftermath of the 2008–2009 global economic crisis as well as China's skyrocketing rise partially bridged the gap between Moscow and Beijing, it was only after the G-7 returned to its original membership structure that Russia and China found themselves on the same page regarding this issue.

At the same time, however, it should be emphasized that China's stake in maintaining the stability and openness of the global economy has significantly increased in the past decade. Russia's failed attempts to embark on the path of modernization, coupled with Moscow's autarkic tendencies that followed Western sanctions as well as Russian counter-sanctions, meant that Russia's interest in an open global economy decreased.

The different levels of benefits that Russia and China gained from post–Cold War economic globalization have shaped their attitudes towards anti-globalization and populist processes, which became the hallmarks of the 2010s. China has much more to lose if the protectionist stance, which has become dominant in the US since Trump's election, forced other global players to retaliate. From this perspective, it is justified to argue that China remains interested in maintaining political-economic stability and economic openness in the outside world. At the same time, both the US and EU seem to be losing their patience with China's model of state capitalism. Their refusal to grant China a market-economy status within the WTO in 2016 was the first sign. Nevertheless, Beijing has been attempting to achieve two goals simultaneously: to portray itself as a defender of economic globalization and to maintain state support for economic growth and technological progress.

Russia finds itself at the opposite end of the spectrum. Although its ruling elites have benefited enormously from the financial openness of the Western world, the Russian economy has not. Given its limited economic potential, Russia cannot expect to thrive on economic globalization—it is rather susceptible to losing any competitive edge. This lack of skin in the game has urged the Russian leadership to engage in international brinkmanship, ranging from the annexation of Crimea to cultivating ties with and financial support for both right-wing and left-wing radical movements in the West and interference with democratic election processes. Moscow appears to believe that it has more to gain by stirring up instability and uncertainty at the international level than by playing by the rules.

The energy sector also points out the potential of divergence between Russia and China's activities in the realm of global governance. Russia's interests as a major exporter and China's interests as a major importer clash on a number of issue including the price of natural resources and the long-term stability of demand secured by long-term contracts versus market-based dynamics of prices. Certain aspects of both states' economies, such as the domination of the energy sector by state-owned enterprises, mitigate some of these differences. Nonetheless, Russia prefers solutions favouring energy providers, whereas China favours those supporting energy customers. Russia's cooperation with OPEC with the aim to keep oil prices at a certain price for instance works against China's interests.

CONCLUSION

Russia and China share some similarities in their approaches to global governance. Both states disagree with some basic features of the Western vision of international order—particularly those that place limitations on state sovereignty and the impunity of national governments with regard to domestic politics. Russian and Chinese ruling elites recognize global governance as a Western concept that aims at broadening Western interests (Grant 2012). Yet, the similar "starting point" notwithstanding, the positions of Moscow and Beijing in global politics and economy vary substantially, thus heavily influencing their approaches and policies.

This chapter illustrated the spectrum of Russia and China's engagement with global governance, from close coordination of their policies through parallel activities that constitute an informal "division of labour" to contradictory policies leading to divergence between the two powers. Moscow and Beijing cooperate closely in those areas of global governance, in which they can block unwelcomed developments. Under such circumstances, their political-diplomatic instruments—permanent membership in the UN Security Council in particular—turn out to be the most efficient way for achieving results.

In the areas of global governance that require more pro-active policies, Russia and China tend to conduct parallel and often uncoordinated activities, tailored to their respective advantages. In the case of Russia, these include military and political support. For China, it is most often economic and financial assistance. This kind of specialization has contributed to the emergence of a "division of labour" between Moscow and Beijing, posing a dual challenge to the West.

However, the long-term outlook for Sino-Russian cooperation seems uncertain. As illustrated in the third section, short-term "division of labour" may evolve into a more fundamental divergence, especially with regard to economic globalization and maintaining the openness of the global economy. Beijing's attempts to strengthen its voice in international politics while at the same time maintaining stability of the global order contradict Moscow's use of political and economic instability for the purpose of increasing its global weight.

Notes

1. The veto list is available at https://research.un.org/en/docs/sc/quick.
2. For the last time, Russia took a meaningful part in the multilateral peace-keeping operation in the Balkans, withdrawing in 2003.

References

Alden, Chris, et al., eds. 2017. *China and Africa: Building Peace and Security Cooperation on the Continent*. Cham: Springer.

Allison, Roy. 2017. Russia and the Post-2014 International Legal Order: Revisionism and Realpolitik. *International Affairs* 93 (3): 519–543. https://doi.org/10.1093/ia/iix061.

Ambrosio, Thomas. 2017. The Architecture of Alignment: The Russia–China Relationship and International Agreements. *Europe-Asia Studies* 69 (1): 110–156. https://doi.org/10.1080/09668136.2016.1273318.

Beeson, Mark, and Jinghan Zeng. 2018. The BRICS and Global Governance: China's Contradictory Role. *Third World Quarterly* 39 (10): 1962–1978. https://doi.org/10.1080/01436597.2018.1438186.

Belokurova, Elena. 2017. A Russian Perspective on Global Governance. In *Global Governance from Regional Perspectives: A Critical View*, ed. Anna Triandafyllidou, 141–160. Oxford: Oxford University Press.

Bluhm, Richard, et al. 2018. Connective Financing: Chinese Infrastructure Projects and the Diffusion of Economic Activity in Developing Countries.

AidData Working Paper, no. 64. http://docs.aiddata.org/ad4/pdfs/WPS64_ Connective_Financing_Chinese_Infrastructure_Projects_and_the_Diffusion_ of_Economic_Activity_in_Developing_Countries.pdf

Chan, Steve, et al. 2018. Discerning States' Revisionist and Status-quo Orientations: Comparing China and the US. *European Journal of International Relations.* https://doi.org/10.1177/1354066118804622.

Channel News Asia. 2019. China Rebuffs Germany's Call for US Missile Deal with Russia. February 17. https://www.channelnewsasia.com/news/asia/china-rebuffs-germany-s-call-for-us-missile-deal-with-russia-11250882

Cho, Sunghee. 2018. China's Participation in UN Peacekeeping Operations since the 2000s. *Journal of Contemporary China.* https://doi.org/10.1080/10670 564.2018.1542216.

CNBC. 2018. Russia, China Abstain in UN Vote on Syria Cross-Border Aid. December 13. https://www.cnbc.com/2018/12/14/russia-china-abstain-in-un-vote-on-syria-cross-border-aid.html

Cooper, Andrew F. 2017. The BRICS' New Development Bank: Shifting from Material Leverage to Innovative Capacity. *Global Policy* 8 (3): 275–284. https://doi.org/10.1111/1758-5899.12458.

De Cordier, Bruno. 2016. Russia's International Aid Donorship: From Diplomatic Status Symbol to 'Frontline Aid'? *Global Affairs* 2 (1): 21–34. https://doi.org /10.1080/23340460.2016.1127453.

Ebert, Hannes, and Tim Maurer. 2013. Contested Cyberspace and Rising Powers. *Third World Quarterly* 34 (6): 1054–1074. https://doi.org/10.1080/01436 597.2013.802502.

Eilstrup-Sangiovanni, Mette. 2016. Power and Purpose in Transgovernmental Networks: Insights from the Global Nonproliferation Regime. In *The New Power Politics: Networks and Transnational Security Governance*, ed. Deborah Avant and Oliver Westerwinter, 131–168. Oxford: Oxford University Press.

Fair, Christine C. 2018. Rohingya: Victims of a Great Game East. *The Washington Quarterly* 41 (3): 63–85. https://doi.org/10.1080/0163660X.2018.1519356.

Farnsworth, Timothy. 2011. China and Russia Submit Cyber Proposal. *Arms Control Today* 41 (9): 35–36. https://www.armscontrol.org/act/2011_11/ China_and_Russia_Submit_Cyber_Proposal.

Fook, Lye L. 2017. China and Global Governance: A More Active Role on a Selective Basis. *China: An International Journal* 15 (1): 214–233.

Godement, Francois. 2015. China: Taking Stock Before the Paris Conference. *European Council on Foreign Relations* (September). https://www.ecfr.eu/ page/-/CA_1509_Climate.pdf.

Godement, Francois, et al. 2018. The United Nations of China: A Vision of the World Order. *European Council on Foreign Relations* (April). http://www.ecfr. eu/page/-/the_united_nations_of_china_a_vision_of_the_world_order.pdf.

Götz, Elias, and Camille-Renaud Merlen. 2018. Russia and the Question of World Order. *European Politics and Society.* https://doi.org/10.1080/23745118.2 018.1545181.

Grant, Charles. 2012. *Russia, China and Global Governance*. London: Centre for European Reform. https://carnegieendowment.org/files/Grant_CER_Eng.pdf.

Hameiri, Shahar, and Lee Jones. 2018. China Challenges Global Governance? Chinese International Development Finance and the AIIB. *International Affairs* 94 (3): 573–593. https://doi.org/10.1093/ia/iiy026.

Hearson, Martin, and Wilson Prichard. 2018. China's Challenge to International Tax Rules and the Implications for Global Economic Governance. *International Affairs* 94 (6): 1287–1307. https://doi.org/10.1093/ia/iiy189.

Hilton, Isabel, and Oliver Kerr. 2017. The Paris Agreement: China's 'New Normal' Role in International Climate Negotiations. *Climate Policy* 17 (1): 48–58. https://doi.org/10.1080/14693062.2016.1228521.

Japan Times. 2018. U.N. Security Council Considers Move to Push Myanmar on Rohingya Crisis, but Russia and China Boycott Talks. December 18. https://www.japantimes.co.jp/news/2018/12/18/asia-pacific/u-n-security-council-considers-move-push-myanmar-rohingya-crisis-russia-china-boycott-talks#.XG1-ZugzbIV.

Jordan, Pamela A. 2017. Diminishing Returns: Russia's Participation in the World Trade Organization. *Post-Soviet Affairs* 33 (6): 452–471. https://doi.org/10.1080/1060586X.2017.1388473.

Kaczmarski, Marcin. 2018. Convergence or Divergence? Visions of World Order and the Russian-Chinese Relationship. *European Politics and Society*. https://doi.org/10.1080/23745118.2018.1545185.

Kanet, Roger E. 2018. Russia and Global Governance: The Challenge to the Existing Liberal Order. *International Politics* 55 (2): 177–188. https://doi.org/10.1057/s41311-017-0075-3.

Kennedy, Scott, ed. 2017. *Global Governance and China: The Dragon's Learning Curve*. Abingdon/New York: Routledge.

Kirton, John, and Marina Larionova, eds. 2018. *BRICS and Global Governance*. London: Routledge.

Kitano, Naohiro. 2018. China's Foreign Aid: Entering a New Stage. *Asia-Pacific Review* 25 (1): 90–111. https://doi.org/10.1080/13439006.2018.1484617.

Korppoo, Anna, and Alexey Kokorin. 2017. Russia's 2020 GHG Emissions Target: Emission Trends and Implementation. *Climate Policy* 17 (2): 113–130. https://doi.org/10.1080/14693062.2015.1075373.

Lanteigne, Marc. 2018. Russia, China and the Shanghai Cooperation Organization: Diverging Security Interests and the 'Crimea Effect'. In *Russia's Turn to the East*, ed. Helge Blakkisrud and Elana Wilson Rowe, 119–138. Cham: Palgrave Pivot.

Larson, Deborah Welch. 2018. New Perspectives on Rising Powers and Global Governance: Status and Clubs. *International Studies Review* 20 (2): 247–254. https://doi.org/10.1093/isr/viy039.

Lewis, David, John Heathershaw, and Nick Megoran. 2018. Illiberal Peace? Authoritarian Modes of Conflict Management. *Cooperation and Conflict* 53 (4): 486–506. https://doi.org/10.1177%2F0010836718765902.

Liu, Ming. 2016. BRICS Development: A Long Way to a Powerful Economic Club and New International Organization. *The Pacific Review* 29 (3): 443–453. https://doi.org/10.1080/09512748.2016.1154688.

Ministry of Foreign Affairs. 2014. Concept of the Russian Federation's State Policy in the Area of International Development Assistance. April 20. http://www.mid.ru/en/foreign_policy/official_documents/-/asset_publisher/CptICkB6BZ29/content/id/64542.

Ministry of National Defense. 2019. Chinese Naval Fleets Escort 3,400 Foreign Ships over Past 10 Years. January 1. http://eng.mod.gov.cn/news/2019-01/02/content_4833368.htm.

News 24. 2018. C. Africa Rebels Rearm After Military Gets Russia Weapons: UN Panel. August 1. https://www.news24.com/Africa/News/c-africa-rebels-rearm-after-military-gets-russia-weapons-un-panel-20180801.

Parker, Charles F., and Christer Karlsson. 2010. Climate Change and the European Union's Leadership Moment: An Inconvenient Truth? *Journal of Common Market Studies* 48 (4): 923–943. https://doi.org/10.1111/j.1468-5965.2010.02080.x.

Percy, Sarah. 2016. Counter-Piracy in the Indian Ocean: Networks and Multinational Military Cooperation. In *The New Power Politics: Networks and Transnational Security Governance*, ed. Deborah Avant and Oliver Westerwinter, 245–268. Oxford: Oxford University Press.

Qobo, Mzukisi, and Mills Soko. 2015. The Rise of Emerging Powers in the Global Development Finance Architecture: The Case of the BRICS and the New Development Bank. *South African Journal of International Affairs* 22 (3): 277–288. https://doi.org/10.1080/10220461.2015.1089785.

Ren, Xiao. 2016. China as an Institution-Builder: The Case of the AIIB. *The Pacific Review* 29 (3): 435–442. https://doi.org/10.1080/09512748.2016.1154678.

Reuters. 2019. Shuttered at Home, Cement Plants Bloom Along China's New Silk Road. January 31. https://www.reuters.com/article/us-china-silkroad-cement-insight/shuttered-at-home-cement-plants-bloom-along-chinas-new-silk-road-idUSKCN1PO35T.

RFERL. 2017. China, Russia Block UN Statement on Myanmar Violence, Diplomats Say. March 17. https://www.rferl.org/a/china-russia-united-nations-myanmar-rakhine-rohingya/28376375.html.

Rodkiewicz, Witold. 2018. *China's Junior Partner: Russia's Korean Policy.* Warsaw: Centre for Eastern Studies. https://www.osw.waw.pl/sites/default/files/PW_72_China%E2%80%99s%20junior%20partner_net.pdf.

Schwirtz, Michael. 2018. Anguish at U.N., but No Action Plan, for Rohingya Atrocities. *The New York Times*, August 28. https://www.nytimes.com/2018/08/28/world/asia/un-rohingya-myanmar-blanchett.html.

Snetkov, Aglaya, and Marc Lanteigne. 2014. 'The Loud Dissenter and Its Cautious Partner': Russia, China, Global Governance and Humanitarian Intervention. *International Relations of the Asia-Pacific* 15 (1): 113–146. https://doi.org/10.1093/irap/lcu018.

Solanko, Laura. 2016. Opening Up or Closing the Door for Foreign Trade: Russia and China Compared. *BOFIT Policy Brief*, no. 8. https://helda.helsinki.fi/bof/bitstream/handle/123456789/14372/bpb0816.pdf?sequence=1.

The Guardian. 2017. China and Russia Oppose UN Resolution on Rohingya. December 24. https://www.theguardian.com/world/2017/dec/24/china-russia-oppose-un-resolution-myanmar-rohingya-muslims.

Tronchetti, Fabio, and Liu Hao. 2015. The 2014 Updated Draft PPWT: Hitting the Spot or Missing the Mark? *Space Policy* 33 (1): 38–49. https://doi.org/10.1016/j.spacepol.2015.05.004.

Tynkkynen, Veli-Pekka, and Nina Tynkkynen. 2018. Climate Denial Revisited: (Re)contextualising Russian Public Discourse on Climate Change During Putin 2.0. *Europe-Asia Studies* 70 (7): 1103–1120. https://doi.org/10.1080/09668136.2018.1472218.

Umbach, Frank. 2019. China's Belt and Road Initiative and Its Energy-Security Dimensions. *RSIS Working Paper*, no. 320. https://www.rsis.edu.sg/wp-content/uploads/2019/01/WP320.pdf.

Westerwinter, Oliver. 2016. "Bargaining in Networks: Relationships and the Governance of Conflict Diamonds." In *The New Power Politics: Networks and Transnational Security Governance* Deborah Avant & Oliver Westerwinter, 196-223. Oxford: Oxford University Press.

Xinhuanet. 2019. Xi's Article on Building Ecological Civilization to Be Published. January 31. http://www.xinhuanet.com/english/2019-01/31/c_137790087.htm.

Yu, Bin. 2019. From Global Governance to Global Disorder? Implications for Russia and China. In *Sino-Russian Relations in the 21st Century*, ed. Jo Inge Bekkevold and Bobo Lo, 191–214. Cham: Springer.

Zaytsev, Y., and A. Knobel. 2017. Ekonomicheskaya pomoshch Rossii drugim stranam v 2016 godu. *Monitoring Ekonomicheskoi Situatsii v Rossii* 17 (55): 14–18.

Zhao, Suisheng. 2018. China and the South China Sea Arbitration: Geopolitics Versus International Law. *Journal of Contemporary China* 27 (109): 1–15. https://doi.org/10.1080/10670564.2017.1363012.

Geopolitical Economy of Russia's Foreign Policy Duality in the Eurasian Landmass

Emre İşeri and Volkan Özdemir

INTRODUCTION

Due to a "global power shift" (Hoge 2004) that has induced systemic change, the political-economic weight of the Asia-Pacific region (APR)—primarily led by China—has been increasing.[1] These global geopolitical economic changes have been reshaping the hierarchy of international politics, thereby providing significant opportunities and challenges for the

This chapter draws on Emre İşeri & Volkan Özdemir, "Geopolitical Economy of Russia's Foreign Policy Duality: Lockean in Its East and Hobbesian in Its West." *Rising Powers Quarterly* 2, no. 1 (2017): 53–79. http://risingpowersproject. com/quarterly/geopolitical-economy-russias-foreign-policy-duality-lockean-east-hobbesian-west. The authors would like to thank Research Assistant Ahmet Çağrı Bartan at Yaşar University for his research inputs and edits.[1]

E. İşeri (✉)
Department of International Relations, Yaşar University, Izmir, Turkey
e-mail: emre.iseri@yasar.edu.tr

V. Özdemir
EPPEN-Institute for Energy Markets and Policies, Ankara, Turkey
e-mail: ozdemir@eppen.org

E. Parlar Dal, E. Erşen (eds.), *Russia in the Changing International System*, https://doi.org/10.1007/978-3-030-21832-4_7

113

system's secondary powers (Williams et al. 2012).[2] At a time of new economic (dis)order (i.e. changing trade balances, increasing protectionism, price volatilities and an American-led unconventional energy revolution), this is particularly the case for Russia as an "aspiring great power" (Rangsimaporn 2009; Mankoff 2012).

As one of the largest energy exporting countries, but with a shrinking European market, Russia dreams of regaining its powerful status in the east, as an Eastern vector or pivot to Asia, aiming to exploit untapped potential resources—particularly in East Siberia and the Russian Far East (ESRFE)—and export them to the widening Asia-Pacific market. Moreover, China and Russia, which were labelled as "competitors" and "revisionist powers" in the National Security Strategy (NSS) of the US (White House 2017) under the Trump administration, have intensified their political relations (e.g. support for each other in the UN Security Council regarding Ukraine/Crimea, Syria, North Korea) and military relations (e.g. Joint Military Exercises). This process has prompted Chinese State Councillor and Foreign Minister Wang Yi to declare the state of bilateral relations with Russia as "the best level in history" in April 2018 (Xinhuanet 2018). To the west, in contrast, Russia acts assertively in its geographically imagined near abroad (i.e. Ukraine) and the Middle East—particularly in Syria.

In this light, the chapter aims to explain this foreign (economic) duality of Russia in the Eurasian landmass. It draws on the understudied concept of geopolitical economy and a neoclassical realist perspective that bridges the divide between domestic-international (spatial), ideational-material (cognitive) and temporal (present-future) dimensions. It assumes that political elites' "state-level assessments and imaginations about future material capabilities create the geopolitical contours for the formation of foreign policy" (Foulon 2015). Against this backdrop, the chapter argues that the interaction of the Russian elites' geopolitical economic perceptions of their resource-rent based country's role at a time of profound geopolitical economic changes in the systemic level causes discrepancy in Russia's foreign (economic) policy in the Eurasian landmass.

The first part of the chapter focuses on the two critical geopolitical economic changes in the international system level: the power shift to the East and new energy (dis)order, which offer both opportunities and challenges for Russia's great power prospects with a resource rent-based economy. The second part examines the Russian elites' perceptions about their country's role and foreign (energy) policy orientations with particular reference to its intensified energy links with China at a time of profound changes at the international level. The third part discusses "sense of geopolitical exposure" and "mismanagement of resource rent-based economy" as the two main challenges on the way of Russia's revival as a great power. The chapter concludes that the Russian elites' "sense of geopolitical exposure" alongside the problems of modernizing the country's economy through resource rents have rendered those critical geopolitical changes as structural challenges, rather than opportunities, for Russia's prospects of regaining its great power status.

GEOPOLITICAL ECONOMIC CHANGES IN THE TWENTY-FIRST CENTURY

The power shift to the East and the new energy (dis)order have emerged as two prominent underlying geopolitical economic changes for Russia's foreign (economic) policy in the twenty-first century. Before examining how those systemic changes have served as inputs to Russia's foreign (economic) policy output, it is useful to explain how those profound changes have been (re)shaping the hierarchy of international politics in general, and Eurasian and Russian politics in particular.

The Power Shift to the East

The debate over the US as a declining power and the rise of Asia has been around since the late 1960s. In this parallel, one should note Frank's concept of the "ReOrient" postulating the re-orientation of the global political economy towards Asia:

> Leadership of the world system ... has been temporarily 'centred' in one sector and region (or a few), only to shift again to one or more others. That happened in the nineteenth century, and that appears to be happening again at the beginning of the twenty-first century, as the 'centre' of the "world economy seems to be shifting back to the 'East'." (Frank 1998, 7)

Indeed, this phenomenon became evident in the 2000s, mainly due to the rise of China with its success in outperforming Asia for the past two centuries. Among those studies, Zakaria's *The Post-American World* (2008) asserts that the "third great power shift" is occurring which includes "the rise of the rest." The decline of the West or the US and multipolarity debates have been reinvigorated with the American-led global financial crisis in 2008 (Mahbubani 2009; Fouskas and Gökay 2012; Layne 2012; Dicken 2015; Fouskas and Gökay 2019). Mainly due to the success of its socialist market economy as an economic development model, China overcame the crisis with minimal negative impacts to become the world's second largest economy and the largest one in terms of purchasing power parity (Atlı 2013). The crisis underlined China's position as the engine of not only the Asian regional economy, but also the global economy (Xinbo 2010). From Beijing's perspective, China has been re-emerging to claim its rightful place in the international system, arguably harbingering "a return to geopolitical business as usual" (Beeson and Li 2015). In this vein, continental power China has been marching westwards along the Silk Road Economic Belt (SREB) and the Twenty-First-Century Maritime Silk Road, together known officially as the Belt and Road Initiative (BRI). Arguably, this ambitious initiative echoes the English political geographer Halford J. Mackinder's postulation in 1919 that a consolidated power integrating the transportation lanes of Europe, Asia and Africa into a single "World-Island" would command the world (Tsui et al. 2017, 37).

While China believes that it is a rising power on its way to becoming the world's largest economy, it has one enormous problem: energy needs (Bender and Rosen 2015). According to all energy projections, Asia's ongoing economic expansion—particularly in China and India—will drive continued growth in global energy demand over the next few decades. Accompanied by its strategic mistrust of the US control of maritime (energy) trade and energy rivalries with the Asian allies of the US (e.g. India, Japan and South Korea), China has been exposed as a continental power to growing geopolitical risk at a time of shifting energy trade balances (Newell and Iller 2013).

Energy-related geopolitical risks are not China's only concern, however, as it also confronts a price risk. That is, energy price volatility, which has been created by a climate of uncertainty and distrust among the energy actors, has become the most significant issue facing the global energy industry over the last decade (Henning et al. 2003). Accordingly, the title of a World Energy Council report was "Energy Price Volatility: The New Normal" (World Energy Council 2015). The new energy (dis)order has made resource rent-based economies like Russia much more unpredictable.

The New Energy (Dis)order

Recent technological advances have made previously untapped reserves of oil and gas reachable and this revolution is expected to transform the world's regional supply dynamics (Maugeri 2012). Indeed, it is projected that the US will become the largest oil producer by mid-2020s and a net energy exporter by 2030s. The International Energy Agency (2018) also estimates that US gas production will further outnumber Russia's production rates, whereas the biggest incremental gas demand will come from China. Already, the US has shifted its focus from importing increasing amounts of liquefied natural gas (LNG) to becoming a net LNG exporter, with potentially significant effects on spot market prices, the global LNG market and international price structures for natural gas contracts. Although this impact has been less pronounced than the impact caused by shale gas, North America's unconventional oil reserve potential (oil sands/tight oil) will likely have similar ramifications for global oil markets (Newell and Iller 2013).

This surge in oil production and fluctuations in financial markets are considered to be among the primary reasons for the sharp 40% oil price fall between June and December 2014 (Economist 2014; Özdemir 2014). Besides fluctuating prices, these abundant unconventional source discoveries in North America, combined with global demand patterns emanating from the APR, will likely transform the global energy trade balances (Newell and Iller 2013). As energy guru Daniel Yergin (2014) puts it, "the emergence of shale gas and tight oil in the U.S. demonstrates once again how innovation can change the balance of global economic and political power."

Before assessing the geopolitical economic implications of this new energy (dis)order, four main features of the revolution should be noted. First, production growth continues to be driven by North America. Second, there will be a slowdown after 2020. Third, other countries will enter the game—notably Russia and China—although their contribution will be limited (Rühl 2014). Given this context, it is safe to propose that by having the strategic card of becoming a net energy exporter, the US is the biggest winner. Fourth, this is in parallel with the EU's "Energy Security Strategy Paper" (European Commission 2014), which was published in response to the Ukraine crisis, aiming to ensure reliable supply. The strategy paper proposed various actions (e.g. supplier diversification, efficiency, completing the internal energy market, increasing renewable energy production) to decrease its dependence on Russian resources (around 30–35% for natural gas). For sure, American excess LNG production would likely contribute to the EU's ambition to diversify away from Russia. Since the shipments of the first American LNG carrier to Portugal in April 2016, the EU's LNG imports from the US have indeed increased from zero to 2.8 billion cubic metres (bcm), which accounts for more than 10% of total US LNG exports (Europa.eu 2018).

Russia's Geopolitical Economic Outlook

Unlike other major powers (US, EU and China), Russia's great power status has largely diminished from its superpower status in the second half of the twentieth century (Kuchins and Zevelev 2012). It is therefore not a surprise to note that in one of his speeches responding to the Western criticisms about Russia's democratic credentials, even President Vladimir Putin himself acknowledged such a decline by stating that "the collapse of the Soviet Union was the greatest geopolitical catastrophe of the century" (Independent 2005).

This geopolitical economic outlook correlates with Russia's ambition to regain a great power status that is directly linked with its geographical position and its physical characteristics as a security state which should be powerful enough to avert any threats (e.g. military or separatist groups) endangering the integrity of its extensive territories in the Eurasian landmass. Following the footsteps of former Prime Minister Yevgeny Primakov, who was the architect of Russia's multi-vector foreign policy with his frequent emphasis on "multipolarity," Putin has a vision of transforming Russia into an indispensable great power through "economic modernization" (for our purposes, the energy sector) and an independent foreign policy (Mankoff 2007).

In its foreign policy, Moscow has pursued a more independent approach in dealing with the rest of the world. Along with Putin's leadership style and a broad elite consensus on the role that the state should play, an increase in Russia's relative international power—mainly due to incrementally increasing energy revenues and declining American hegemony—has shaped the country's new foreign policy approach (Mankoff 2012).

According to Putin's vision, "Great-power status is … a necessary condition for Russia's more advanced engagement with the world" (Tsygankov 2005). Given its greatest fear that the emerging new geopolitical setting would enable the world's major economic powers to topple Russia as an aspiring great power, Moscow has been in a state of transition in its geo-political position and role in the international system (Morozova 2009; Gvosdev and Marsh 2013).

As it aims to regain its great power status, there has been a shift in understanding among Russians that economic rather than military factors, particularly energy wealth, are the primary components of Russia's power in the new era (Gvosdev and Marsh 2013). Russia is therefore ready to do whatever it is necessary, including changing its foreign (economic) policy orientation or geo-strategy, as shown by the foreign policy objectives in its 2008 Foreign Policy Concept:

> to preserve and strengthen its sovereignty and territorial integrity, to achieve strong positions of authority in the world community that best meet the interests of the Russian Federation as one of influential centres in the mod-ern world, and ... to create favourable external conditions for the modern-ization of Russia. (Kremlin.ru 2008)

Energizing Eastern Siberia and Russian Far East

Most recently, thanks to the advantages of its strategic location between Asia and Europe, Russia is set to change its orientation as power shifts to the APR, which could provide resources for the development of distant Russian regions that communist planners left out in the cold, namely ESRFE (Hill and Gaddy 2003). As the 2013 Foreign Policy Concept states, "Russia is interested in participating actively in APR integration processes, using the possibilities offered by the APR to implement pro-grams meant to boost Siberian and Far Eastern economy" (Ministry of Foreign Affairs 2013).

Indeed, Russia's willingness to cooperate with rising Asian powers like China will determine its chances of maintaining its current position at worst or its revival as the third-largest great power at best in the twenty-first cen-tury's new geopolitical setting. Despite concerns of becoming too depen-dent and open to geopolitical exposure to China and its deteriorating relations with the West even before the Ukraine crisis, Russia perceives great political-economic potential in its growing partnership with China, which is a natural partner in many critical foreign policy issues that strengthen Russia (Legvold 2006). However, Sino-Russian economic interdependence is lim-ited, with arms trade accounting for most of the trade volume as Russia is the second largest arms exporter to China. In the coming years, their intensified energy cooperation will likely urge China and Russia to adopt common positions towards non-energy-related issues and facilitate long-term deeper interaction (Yilmaz and Daksueva 2017).

Considering that "when a vector joins with a sector, we can see the emergence of foreign policy" (Gvosdev and Marsh 2013), its dominant energy sector along with the military sector prompted Russia to prioritize its Eastern vector, although such a position actually conflicts with the Russian elites' concerns about empowering China. As Tsygankov (2009) notes, this pro-China position is often favoured by the energy producers and military enterprises seeking feasible contracts in the growing Asian markets.

As a major producer and exporter of oil and natural gas, Russia's economy heavily relies on its energy exports. According to data from the Ministry of Finance (n.d.), for the period of January-April 2018, the share of oil- and gas-related revenue in Russia's federal budget was 46.9%. In 2016, Russia's oil production was 11,227 million barrels per day (bbl/d), while its annual natural gas production was 579.4 bcm. A significant portion of those resources are exported, which makes Russia the world's largest oil and gas exporter overall (BP 2017).

Connected by a variety of oil and natural gas pipelines, Europe has historically been Russia's main energy partner. Although Russian energy companies in the 1990s endeavoured to diversify away from European markets, they did not get the required support from the Russian state. Today, however, Russia prioritizes market diversification (i.e. the Asia-Pacific) and stresses developing resources towards the east (i.e. Eastern Siberia and Russia's Far East) (Balzer 2005; Poussenkova 2009). As it loses its share in the European market, Russia expects to increase its share in the Asia-Pacific energy market by 2030 from 8% to 25% in oil and from 0% to 20% in natural gas (Ministry of Energy 2010).

Despite declining rates of production over more than 40 years of operation, West Siberia—notably the Priobskoye and Samotlor fields—continues to provide the bulk of Russia's oil output. In the longer term, however, Sakhalin in the Far East, which currently contributes only 3%, along with untapped oil reserves in Eastern Siberia and the Russian Arctic, is expected to increase its share in total production figures (EIA 2014). Based on these optimistic production figures and overshadowing all other projects in post-Soviet Russia, the ESPO-2 became operational to link Skovorodino to Kozmino oil terminal, with an annual capacity of 35 million tons in January 2018 (RT 2018). This two-legged pipeline project will not only enable Russia to diversify its energy markets in Asia but also bolster prospects for the development of ESRFE. Indeed, Putin asserted that the new pipeline section will "considerably increase the infrastructure capacity of the regions in Russia's Far East" and considered the commissioning a "significant event" (Rousseau 2013).

By 2019, Gazprom is prepared to complete the 2500 km "Power of Siberia" gas pipeline that will export 38 bcm of gas from Eastern Siberia (Irkutsk and Yakutia fields) to China annually for the following 30 years. Arguably, this pipeline has been Gazprom's response to the US-led shale gas revolution and future export prospects of those unconventional resources to world energy markets, notably Europe and Asia.

In this vein, as of December 2017, the Yamal LNG project began its exports to Asian and European markets. Russia's current LNG exports come from the Gazprom-led Sakhalin-2 LNG project (Novatek n.d.). Along with ongoing upstream investments in Sakhalin, deposits in the Arctic and East Siberia have attracted increasing attention from the world energy sector. Even though production costs are much higher than those in Western Siberia, they are the only way to compensate for the declining production figures. Particularly in the Arctic area, there has been fierce competition, partly due to the emerging Northern Sea Route, as the meltdown changing the world's trade routes as transporting Russian goods to Asian economies will become much quicker and less costly.

On the western front, there have been serious setbacks in EU-Russia energy relations, such as the investigations by the European Commission (EC) against Gazprom and the implementation of EU legislation on new infrastructure projects developed by Gazprom. The Russian side is in talks with the EC over the construction of Nord Stream-2 under the Baltic Sea. However, the recent decision by the Polish Competition Authority to block Gazprom's European partners from participating in the project made the situation more complicated. In this sense, the EU is engaging in energy containment policy against Russia, which Moscow needs to counter at this challenging moment. Here, the launch of the Turkish Stream project with Ankara via the Black Sea offered a "solution" because Russia gains new leverage vis-à-vis the EU by officially incorporating Turkish Stream into the picture, which will give it an instrument in its negotiations with the EU regarding its larger aims. As a result, investigation by the EC concluded without a serious turmoil for Russia in May 2018 (Reed and Schreuer 2018). With this development, instead of established bilateral energy relations, there is now a more complex and dynamic energy triangle between the EU, Russia and Turkey.

CHALLENGES FOR RUSSIA AS AN ASPIRING GREAT POWER

As the power shift to the East has been reshaping the world, Russia is endeavouring to readjust itself as an aspiring great power to these new geopolitical economic changes by reorienting its foreign (economic) policy towards the east, primarily through its energy sector. In this venture, however, there are two major challenges: its sense of geopolitical exposure and modernizing its resource rent-based economy.

Sense of Geopolitical Exposure

Due to its control of vast territories in the Eurasian landmass, in terms of the length of its borders and the number of its neighbours (particularly the US, Japan, Korea, China and EU), Russia is the world's most exposed country. Scarred by historical invasions, its geographically insecure land power status has prompted Russia (and its predecessors) to establish buffer zones (Gvosdev and Marsh 2013), conceptualized as its "near abroad" (Secrieru 2006; Trenin 2009; Camerona and Orenstein 2012) in various official documents.

On its western flank, Russia's sense of geographical insecurity has been justified by the East-West Energy Corridor (Baku-Tbilisi-Ceyhan oil pipeline, Trans-Anatolian natural gas pipeline, etc.), Western-sponsored colour revolutions, NATO's Kosovo intervention and missile defence systems. Meanwhile, NATO and EU's enlargement as well as their Eastern Partnership strategy as well as their policy of signing association agreements with the countries in Russia's near abroad have added insult to injury for Russia's geopolitical interests. Therefore, the Ukraine crisis (since 2014) and the Georgian crisis of 2008 have not erupted out of thin air. Rather, they have served as the last straws (Trenin 2014) for Russia's security considerations with far-reaching geopolitical repercussions for Eastern Europe and beyond. In contrast to popular arguments in the West that overstate Russia's imperial impulses and/or personal ideological commitments over the latest crisis, Putin has castigated Western refusal to treat Russia as an equal partner and consider its security interests:

> [Western states] are constantly trying to sweep us into a corner because we have an independent position, because we maintain it and because we call things like they are and do not engage in hypocrisy. But there is a limit to everything. And with Ukraine, our western partners have crossed the line, playing the bear and acting irresponsibly and unprofessionally. (Washington Post 2014)

Since the end of the Cold War, as Larson and Shevchenko (2014) note, Moscow has displayed anger at the US unwillingness to grant Russia the status to which it believes it is entitled, especially during the Russian-Georgian war, Ukrainian crisis and Russia's takeover of Crimea. Similarly, Bagdonas (2012) argues that Russia's support for the Assad regime in the Syrian crisis is not primarily motivated by material interests alone, but also by its foreign policy doctrine of multipolarity and the desire to maintain its influence and reputation in the region. As Putin noted, "At first, they talked about the need to isolate Russia after well-known events, for example, in Crimea. Then it became clear that this is impossible, and with the beginning of our operations in Syria the understanding of the impossibility of such destructive actions against our country became completely obvious" (RT 2016). Regardless of media reports labelling Russia and the Assad regime as "the winners" of the Syrian conflict, one should question the price and cost of this intervention for Russia. Apart from the heightened risk of being dragged into "alien wars" and military confrontation with the US and its allies (e.g. Israel) in order to support a cause that is not vital for Russian interests (Souleimanov and Dzutsati 2018, 42), Russian elites' "more guns, less butter" strategy would further jeopardize its long-term, socio-economic development (Bradshaw and Connolly 2016, 162).

Mismanagement of Resource Rent-Based Economy

Following the collapse of the Soviet Union, the ESRFE has suffered from de-industrialization and de-population as China increased its presence in that region (Rousseau 2012). In this regard, it is vital for Russia to achieve those eastern provinces' dual integration by retaining them as parts of the country and integrating them with the growing Asian market. At this point, the important question is whether its political economy based on a "three-legged stool" (resource rents, resource addiction and rent management system) (Gaddy and Ickes 2015) would enable Russia to materialize this ambitious dual integration objective.

Notwithstanding Moscow's optimism that the private sector can provide the required investment to develop unproductive regions facing harsh climatic conditions, Russia's economy is far from providing a proper business climate for feasible investments. It therefore cannot prevent high rates of capital outflows (Yanık 2013). This is also the case for the country's energy sector, in which increasing governmental control and restrictions imposed on both domestic private producers and foreign investors have curtailed investment (Khrushcheva 2012).

Against this backdrop, solving its "Eastern Question" by providing fertile ground for investment is one of the most challenging tasks for Russia. The Ukraine crisis and annexation of Crimea have resulted in Western sanctions imposed on the Russian economy (including the energy sector), which further curtailed prospects to finance or attract huge energy infrastructure investment (new pipelines, refineries, LNG plants, etc.) required to foster development in those provinces. To make things more complicated, plunging oil prices have hit the resource rent-dependent Russian economy much harder than the Western sanctions (Birnbaum 2014). This reminds us that Russia is vulnerable to fluctuating energy prices and this jeopardy places financial restrictions on its ability to modernize its economy (Connolly 2011).

Another risk associated with Russia's dependence on its energy sector is related to problems with exerting political and economic influence in its Eastern vector. Partly due to the non-conventional energy revolution, Russia will face increasingly harsh competition from other LNG exporters—especially Australia, US and Qatar—for gaining access to the Asia-Pacific energy market, which has already diversified its imports (Victor 2013). Following the nuclear deal with the P5+1 countries, Iran has also become a potential energy supplier to those markets with depressed prices at the expense of Russia's energy sector (Mills 2015). However, after Trump became the president of the US, the deal has been questioned. Finally, it was unilaterally cancelled and Washington decided to impose new sanctions against Iran targeting the energy sector. Even though this seems like Trump's "unexpected present" to Russia at first glance (Matthews 2018), Moscow will eventually become one of the many energy suppliers with limited political-economic influence. Indeed, Russian Science Academy report in 2013 warned that Russia would have difficulty finding customers willing to pay reasonable prices for its energy exports, posing a risk to its energy sector and overall economy (ERIRAS 2013). Given Russia's increasingly strained relations with the West, this risk has escalated as well, particularly in price negotiations favouring China (Panin 2014). Hence, "Russia's pivot to Asia is being reduced to a pivot to China" (Hedlund 2015).

CONCLUSION

This chapter's main objective was to examine the interaction of geopolitical economic changes (i.e. global power shift and new energy (dis)order) and the Russian elites' perception of their country's role affecting its foreign (economic) policy orientation in the Eurasian landmass. For this purpose, it adopted the understudied concept of "geopolitical economy" and relied on a neoclassical realist account to discern how leader-level perceptions of a country's role with a resource rent-based economy could serve as an intervening variable in shaping/making its foreign (energy) policy in the transforming global political-economic system.

In this regard, it argues that the Russian economy, which had been mainly characterized by its energy exports to Europe, became incorporated into the world economy through diversification of its export routes (i.e. Asia) as the Sino-Russian political cooperation intensified. In fact, this energy shift is convergent with the main aim of Russian foreign policy, which views the country as one of the centres in a multipolar world order. It concludes that the future global political economic developments and the Russian elites' perception of those developments as well as their success in managing the country's energy wealth to promote domestic development would determine the new positioning of Russia in the transforming global system of the twenty-first century.

Overall, we consider our study as a baseline in terms of integrating the understudied "geopolitical economy" with a neoclassical realist account. This approach enabled us to develop a comprehensive perspective to discern how state elites' perceptions of their country's role interact with the global level and how domestic economy as an intervening variable shapes foreign (economic) policy. We applied our perspective to the case of Russia and tried to make sense of its foreign (economic) policy orientation at a time of critical geopolitical economic changes. Further case studies (cf. Amineh and Guang 2017; Van der Pijl 2018; Krieckhaus 2018) on "geopolitical economy" are needed to shed light on how the logic of state elites (geopolitics) and capital/wealth (geoeconomics) interact in shaping foreign (economic) policy decisions in different domestic political-economic settings.

Notes

1. Gilpin (1981, 39–41) proposes three (ideal) types of international changes: system change (nature of actors), systemic change (governance of system) and interactional change (interstate processes).
2. As an understudied approach, geopolitical economy's primary consideration is the distribution of political and economic power in the international system. The concept is associated with two political geographers Agnew and Corbridge (1995) examining the geographical dimensions of economic and political processes in the era of globalization. In the same vein, Desai

(2013, 2016) adopts geopolitical economic approach to shed light on the evolution of the capitalist world order's evolution and its twenty-first-century form of multipolarity. Desai's interpretation of the concept assumes states' central role in developing and regulating economies. States' mutual interactions—conflicting cooperative and collusive—and the international order they create are understood in terms of the character of their national economies, contradictions and the international possibilities and imperatives they generate.

References

Agnew, John, and Stuart Corbridge. 1995. *Mastering Space: Hegemony, Territory and International Political Economy.* London: Routledge.

Amineh, Mehdi P., and Yang Guang, eds. 2017. *Geopolitical Economy of Energy and Environment: China and the European Union.* Leiden: Brill.

Atlı, Altay. 2013. Değişen Çin ve Kriz Sonrası Dünya Düzenindeki Rolü. In *Küresel Kriz ve Yeni Ekonomik Düzen,* ed. Fikret Şenses, Ziya Öniş, and Caner Bakır, 285–310. Istanbul: Iletisim.

Bagdonas, Azuolas. 2012. Russia's Interests in the Syrian Conflict: Power, Prestige, and Profit. *European Journal of Economic and Political Studies* 5 (2): 55–77.

Balzer, Harley. 2005. The Putin Thesis and Russian Energy Policy. *Post-Soviet Affairs* 21 (3): 210–225. https://doi.org/10.2747/1060-586X.21.3.210.

Beeson, Mark, and Fujian Li. 2015. What Consensus? Geopolitics and Policy Paradigms in China and the United States. *International Affairs* 91 (1): 93–109. https://doi.org/10.1111/1468-2346.12188.

Bender, Jeremy, and Armin Rosen. 2015. This Pentagon Map Shows What's Really Driving China's Military and Diplomatic Strategy. *Business Insider,* May 13. http://www.businessinsider.com/this-map-shows-chinas-global-energy-ties-2015-5#ixzz3fIkHnfLl

Birnbaum, Michael. 2014. Falling Oil Prices Hit Russia Much Harder Than Western Sanctions. *Washington Post,* December 2. http://www.washingtonpost.com/world/europe/falling-oil-prices-hit-russia-much-harder-than-western-sanctions/2014/12/02/91a5a5c4-79b3-11e4-8241-8cc0a3670239_story.html

BP. 2017. Statistical Review of World Energy. https://www.bp.com/content/dam/bp/en/corporate/pdf/energy-economics/statistical-review-2017/bp-statistical-review-of-world-energy-2017-full-report.pdf

Bradshaw, Michael, and Richard Connolly. 2016. Barrels and Bullets: The Geostrategic Significance of Russia's Oil and Gas Exports. *Bulletin of the Atomic Scientists* 72 (3): 156–164. https://doi.org/10.1080/00963402.2016.1170372.

Camerona, David R., and Mitchell A. Orenstein. 2012. Post-Soviet Authoritarianism: The Influence of Russia in Its 'Near Abroad'. *Post-Soviet Affairs* 28 (1): 1–44. https://doi.org/10.2747/1060-586X.28.1.1.

Connolly, Richard. 2011. Financial Constraints on the Modernization of the Russian Economy. *Eurasian Geography and Economics* 52 (3): 428–459. https://doi.org/10.2747/1539-7216.52.3.428.

Desai, Radhika. 2013. *Geopolitical Economy: After US Hegemony, Globalization and Empire*. London: Pluto Press.

———, ed. 2016. *Analytical Gains of Geopolitical Economy*. Bingley: Emerald Group Publishing.

Dicken, Peter. 2015. *Global Shift: Mapping the Changing Contours of the World Economy*. London: Sage.

Economist. 2014. Why the Oil Price Is Falling. December 8. http://www.economist.com/blogs/economist-explains/2014/12/economist-explains-4

EIA. 2014. Russia Looks Beyond West Siberia for Future Oil and Natural Gas Growth. September 19. http://www.eia.gov/todayinenergy/detail.cfm?id=18051

ERIRAS. 2013. Global and Russian Energy Outlook Up to 2040. http://www.eriras.ru/files/Global_and_Russian_energy_outlook_up_to_2040.pdf

Europa.eu. 2018. EU-U.S. Joint Statement of 25 July: European Union Imports of U.S. Liquefied Natural Gas (LNG) Are on the Rise. August 9. http://europa.eu/rapid/press-release_IP-18-4920_en.htm

European Commission. 2014. European Energy Security Strategy. May 28. https://www.eesc.europa.eu/resources/docs/european-energy-security-strategy.pdf

Foulon, Michiel. 2015. Neoclassical Realism: Challengers and Bridging Identities. *International Studies Review* 17 (1): 635–661. https://doi.org/10.1111/misr.12255.

Fouskas, Vassilis K., and Bülent Gökay. 2012. *The Fall of the US Empire: Global Fault-Lines and the Shifting Imperial Order*. London: Pluto Press.

———. 2019. *The Disintegration of Euro-Atlanticism and New Authoritarianism: Global Power-Shift*. London: Palgrave Macmillan.

Frank, Andre Gunder. 1998. *ReOrient: Global Economy in the Asian Age*. Berkeley: University of California Press.

Gaddy, Clifford G., and Barry W. Ickes. 2015. Putin's Rent Management System and the Future of Addiction in Russia. In *The Challenges for Russia's Politicized Economic System*, ed. Susanne Oxenstierna, 11–32. London: Routledge.

Gilpin, Robert. 1981. *War and Change in World Politics*. New York: Cambridge University Press.

Gvosdev, Nikolas K., and Christopher Marsh. 2013. *Russian Foreign Policy: Interests, Vectors, and Sectors*. Los Angeles: CQ Press.

Hedlund, Stefan. 2015. China Benefits as West's Sanctions Drive Russia Eastwards. *World Review*, May 19. http://www.worldreview.info/content/china-benefits-wests-sanctions-drive-russia-eastwards#60

Henning, Bruce, Michael Sloan, and Maria De Leon. 2003. Natural Gas and Energy Price Volatility. *American Gas Foundation* (October). http://www.gas-foundation.org/researchstudies/volstudych5.pdf

Hill, Fiona, and Clifford Gaddy. 2003. *The Siberian Curse: How Communist Planners Left Russia Out in the Cold*. Washington: Brookings Institution Press.

Hoge, James F. 2004. A Global Power Shift in the Making. *Foreign Affairs* 83 (4): 2–7. https://doi.org/10.2307/20034041.

Independent. 2005. Putin: Collapse of the Soviet Union Was 'Catastrophe of the Century'. April 26. http://www.independent.co.uk/news/world/europe/putin-collapse-of-the-soviet-union-was-catastrophe-of-the-century-6147493.html

International Energy Agency. 2018. *Gas Market Report*. Paris: International Energy Agency.

Khrushcheva, Olga. 2012. The Controversy of Putin's Energy Policy: The Problem of Foreign Investment and Long-Term Development of Russia's Energy Sector. *CEJISS* 1: 164–188.

Kremlin.ru. 2008. The Foreign Policy Concept of the Russian Federation. http://archive.kremlin.ru/eng/text/docs/2008/07/204750.shtml

Krieckhaus, Jonathan. 2018. *Geopolitical Economy: The South Korean FTA Strategy*. Michigan: University of Michigan Press.

Kuchins, Andrew C., and Igor Zevelev. 2012. Russia's Contested National Identity and Foreign Policy. In *Worldviews of Aspiring Powers: Domestic Foreign Policy Debates in China, India, Iran, Japan, and Russia*, ed. Henry R. Nau and Deepa M. Ollapally, 181–210. Oxford: Oxford University Press.

Larson, Deborah W., and Alexei Shevchenko. 2014. Russia Says No: Power, Status, and Emotions in Foreign Policy. *Communist and Post-Communist Studies* 47 (3): 269–279. https://doi.org/10.1016/j.postcomstud.2014.09.003.

Layne, Christopher. 2012. This Time It's Real: The End of Unipolarity and the Pax Americana. *International Studies Quarterly* 56 (1): 203–213. https://doi.org/10.1111/j.1468-2478.2011.00704.x.

Legvold, Robert. 2006. US-Russian Relations: An American Perspective. *Russia in Global Affairs* 4: 157–169.

Mahbubani, Kishore. 2009. *The New Asian Hemisphere: The Irresistible Shift of Global Power to the East*. New York: Public Affairs.

Mankoff, Jeffrey. 2007. Russia and the West: Taking the Longer View. *The Washington Quarterly* 30 (2): 123–135. https://doi.org/10.1162/wash.2007.30.2.123.

———. 2012. *Russian Foreign Policy: The Return of Great Power Politics*. Maryland: Rowman & Littlefield.

Matthews, Owen. 2018. U.S. Gives Russia 'Unexpected Present' with Iran Sanctions and Oil Price Surge. *Newsweek*, May 30. https://www.newsweek.com/2018/06/08/irans-loss-will-be-putins-unexpected-present-us-sanctions-drive-oil-prices-948173.html

Maugeri, Leonardo. 2012. *Oil: The Next Revolution*. Cambridge: John F. Kennedy School of Government, Harvard University.

Mills, Robin. 2015. Winners and Losers from Iran's Eventual Return to Global Energy Markets. *The Nation*, July 19. http://www.thenational.ae/business/energy/winners-and-losers-from-irans-eventual-return-to-global-energy-markets

Ministry of Energy. 2010. Energy Strategy for Russia: For the Period Up to 2030. http://www.energystrategy.ru/projects/docs/ES-2030_(Eng).pdf

Ministry of Finance. n.d. Federal Budget. https://www.minfin.ru/ru/statistics/fedbud

Ministry of Foreign Affairs. 2013. Concept of the Foreign Policy of the Russian Federation. http://www.mid.ru/brp_4.nsf/0/76389FEC168189ED4425 7B2E0039B16D

Morozova, Natalia. 2009. Geopolitics, Eurasianism and Russian Foreign Policy Under Putin. *Geopolitics* 14 (4): 667–686. https://doi.org/10.1080/14650 040903141349.

Newell, Richard G., and Stuart Iller. 2013. The Global Energy Outlook. In *Energy & Security: Strategies for a World in Transition*, ed. Jan H. Kalicki and David L. Goldwyn, 25–68. Washington, DC: Woodrow Wilson Center Press.

Novatek. n.d.. http://www.novatek.ru/en/business/yamal/southtambey

Özdemir, Volkan. 2014. Oil Prices: Expectations vs. Price Setters. *Eppen.org*, December 10. http://www.eppen.org/en/index.php?sayfa=Yorumlar&link=&makale=157

Panin, Alexander. 2014. China Gets Upper Hand in Gas Deals Amid Russia-West Tensions. *The Moscow Times*, November 10. http://www.themoscowtimes.com/business/article/china-gets-upper-hand-in-gas-deals-amid-russia-west-tensions/510910.html

Poussenkova, Nina. 2009. Russia's Future Customers: Asia and Beyond. In *Russian Energy Power and Foreign Relations: Implications for Conflict and Cooperation*, ed. Jeronim Perovic, Robert W. Orttung, and Andreas Wenger, 132–154. New York: Routledge.

Rangsimaporn, Paradorn. 2009. *Russia as an Aspiring Great Power in East Asia*. Oxford: Palgrave Macmillan.

Reed, Stanley, and Milan Schreuer. 2018. EU Settles with Russia's Gazprom over Antitrust Charges. *New York Times*, May 24. https://www.nytimes.com/2018/05/24/business/energy-environment/eu-gas-gazprom.html

Rousseau, Richard. 2012. Will China Colonize and Incorporate Siberia? *Harvard International Review*, September 9. http://hir.harvard.edu/will-china-colonize-and-incorporate-siberia

———. 2013. The Kremlin's Strategic Plans for Siberia. *The Washington Review*, January. http://www.thewashingtonreview.org/pdf/articles/the-kremlins-strategic-plans-for-siberia.pdf

RT. 2016. Russia-China Military Ties 'at All-time High', No Threat to Other States. November 23. https://www.rt.com/news/367880-russia-china-cooperation-stability

————. 2018. New Russia-China Pipeline Doubles Beijing's Oil Import Capacity. January 2. https://www.rt.com/business/414846-russia-china-pipeline-double-capacity

Rühl, Christof. 2014. The Five Global Implications of Shale Oil and Gas. *Energypost*, January 10. http://www.energypost.eu/five-global-implications-shale-revolution

Secrieru, Stanislav. 2006. Russia's Foreign Policy Under Putin: 'CIS Project' Renewed. *UNISCI Discussion Papers* 10: 289–308. http://www.redalyc.org/html/767/76701018.

Souleimanov, Emil Aslan, and Valery Dzutsati. 2018. Russia's Syria War: A Strategic Trap? *Middle East Policy* 25 (2): 42–50. https://doi.org/10.1111/mepo.12341.

Trenin, Dmitri. 2009. Russia's Spheres of Interest, Not Influence. *The Washington Quarterly* 32 (4): 3–22. https://doi.org/10.1080/01636600903231089.

————. 2014. *The Ukraine Crisis and the Resumption of Great-Power Rivalry.* Moscow: Carnegie Moscow Center.

Tsui, Sit, et al. 2017. One Belt, One Road: China's Strategy for a New Global Financial Order. *Monthly Review* 68 (8): 36–45. https://doi.org/10.14452/MR-068-08-2017-01_4.

Tsygankov, Andrei P. 2005. Vladimir Putin's Vision of Russia as a Normal Great Power. *Post-Soviet Affairs* 21 (2): 132–158. https://doi.org/10.2747/1060-586X.21.2.132.

————. 2009. Eastern Promises. *Russia Now—The Washington Post*, December 18. http://www.washingtonpost.com/wp-adv/advertisers/russia/articles/opinion/20091218/eastern_promises.html

Van der Pijl, Kees. 2018. *Flight MH17, Ukraine and the New Cold War: Prism of Disaster.* Manchester: Manchester University Press.

Victor, David G. 2013. The Gas Promise. In *Energy & Security: Strategies for a World in Transition*, ed. Jan H. Kalicki and David L. Goldwyn, 88–106. Washington, DC: Woodrow Wilson Center Press.

Washington Post. 2014. Transcript: Putin Says Russia Will Protect the Rights of Russians Abroad. March 18. http://www.washingtonpost.com/world/transcript-putin-says-russia-will-protect-the-rights-of-russians-abroad/2014/03/18/432a1e60-ae99-11e3-a49e-76adc9210f19_story.html

White House. 2017. National Security Strategy (NSS) of the United States of America. https://www.whitehouse.gov/wp-content/uploads/2017/12/NSS-Final-12-18-2017-0905.pdf

Williams, Kristen, Steven Lobell, and Neal Jesse, eds. 2012. *Beyond Great Powers and Hegemons: Why Secondary States Support, Follow or Challenge.* Stanford: Stanford University Press.

World Energy Council. 2015. Energy Price Volatility: The New Normal. https://www.worldenergy.org/wp-content/uploads/2015/01/2015-World-Energy-Issues-Monitor.pdf

Xinbo, Wu. 2010. Understanding the Geopolitical Implications of the Global Financial Crisis. *The Washington Quarterly* 33 (41): 155–163. https://doi.org/10.1080/0163660X.2010.516648.

Xinhuanet. 2018. China, Russia Need to Strengthen Cooperation Amid Global Uncertainties: FM. June 4. http://www.xinhuanet.com/english/2018-04/06/c_137090788_2.htm

Yanık, Lerna K. 2013. Krizden Krize Rusya'da İktisadi Değişim ve Dönüşüm. In *Küresel Kriz ve Yeni Ekonomik Düzen*, ed. Fikret Şenses, Ziya Öniş, and Caner Bakır, 219–240. Istanbul: Iletisim.

Yergin, Daniel. 2014. The Global Impact of Shale Gas. *Project Syndicate*, January 8. http://www.project-syndicate.org/commentary/daniel-yergin-traces-the-effects-of-america-s-shale-energy-revolution-on-the-balance-of-global-economic-and-political-power

Yılmaz, Şerafettin, and Olga Daksueva. 2017. The Energy Nexus in China-Russia Strategic Partnership. *International Relations of the Asia-Pacific*. https://doi.org/10.1093/irap/lcx003.

CHAPTER 8

Russia's Strategies Towards BRICS: Theory and Practice

Alexander Sergunin

Introduction

Russia's contemporary foreign policy in general and in the BRICS context in particular is a vexed question both in the media and in the expert community. Since President Putin's speech at the 2007 Munich Security Conference, Russia's launch of a proactive Arctic strategy in 2007–2008 and the "five-day war" with Georgia in August 2008, the Western analysts have often described Russia's policies as aggressive, expansionist and even jingoistic or as a return to a "gunboat diplomacy" (Cohen and Hamilton 2011; Walt 2014). This criticism has been further strengthened with Russia's takeover of Crimea in 2014, subsequent support for the pro-Russian rebels in Ukraine's south-eastern Donbas region and military

This chapter was prepared within the framework of the research project sponsored by the St. Petersburg State University (Grant No. 17.37.226.2016).

A. Sergunin (✉)
Moscow State Institute of International Relations, Moscow, Russia

St. Petersburg State University, St. Petersburg, Russia

Nizhny Novgorod State University, Nizhny Novgorod, Russia

© The Author(s) 2020   133
E. Parlar Dal, E. Erşen (eds.), *Russia in the Changing International System*, https://doi.org/10.1007/978-3-030-21832-4_8

intervention in the Syrian civil war. According to some Western experts, due to its economic weakness and technological backwardness, Russia tends to rely on military-coercive instruments in protecting its national interests in the post-Soviet space and become assertive in its relations with the West (Walt 2014).

On the other side of the spectrum, there are observers—mostly from Russia—who are inclined to characterize Moscow's foreign policy in a complimentary way—as "non-aggressive", "peaceful", "purely defensive", oriented to "protection of its legitimate interests" and so on (Lukyanov 2010). In their view, Moscow does not pursue aggressive or revisionist policies. On the contrary, it seeks to solve international disputes by peaceful means, in accordance with international law and within the framework of international institutions including BRICS.

In the same vein, the BRICS grouping is viewed in the academic community in two different ways: (a) a revisionist force seeking to overthrow the existing international system, create an alternative world order, challenge the established Western powers and substitute the key financial institutions with new ones; (b) a group of major emerging economies searching for ways and plausible options to expand their currently limited capacity to set the agenda on a global scale, influence the decision-making process and promote changes in the international financial and economic architecture that will create a more favourable international environment for the development of the emerging and developing countries. The Russian and international literature offers quite a few works that draw on the various theoretical approaches in an attempt to balance the otherwise competing perspectives (Hansen and Sergunin 2014; Shakleina 2013).

The discussions on Russia's intentions towards and motivation for participation in BRICS are part of these ongoing debates. What are Russia's interests in BRICS? What strategic goals—geopolitical and economic—does Moscow want to achieve through participation in BRICS? Why does the Kremlin consider BRICS an important foreign and security policy priority? Which International Relations (IR) theories can better explain Russia's strategies towards and within BRICS? What kind of Russian international strategy is emerging in the BRICS context? Is this grouping helpful for Russia's reintegration into the existing world order—given Moscow's current semi-isolation in the international community as a result of the Ukrainian crisis? Or does the Kremlin plan to use BRICS—along with other multilateral institutions it created—to change the world order to its benefit? In order to provide a nuanced and accurate picture of Russia's participation in BRICS, these questions are addressed in this chapter.

Russia and BRICS: Theoretical Approaches

It is commonplace among the Western analysts to define contemporary Russia as a revisionist power. The dichotomy of "revisionist versus status-quo states" stems from the realist/neorealist *power transition theory* (PTT) developed by A.F.K. Organski (1958) and his followers (Tammen et al. 2000). This theory explains the causes of international conflicts and wars by the rise of emerging powers that become discontent with international rules established by the dominant powers. According to this theory, powerful and influential states such as the US that benefits from the established world order fall under the category of status-quo states, while states dissatisfied with their role in global affairs are often considered revisionist states. An important point when characterizing Russia is that the PTT is based on the assumption that the revisionist state aims at either achieving a radical change of the old rules or imposing new rules on the other international actors.

Mainly designed for the Cold War period, this theory can still probably work well in some cases even in the present-day situation. Yet, I argue that when applying it to the foreign policy behaviour of the BRICS countries, it does not hold much explanatory power. From the PTT perspective, the BRICS countries are seen as revisionist powers because some of them have ambitions to reform global institutions (e.g. India and Brazil pursue permanent membership in the UN Security Council, while BRICS as a whole pursues greater influence in the IMF and World Bank), extend their continental shelves and exclusive economic zones (like Russia's activities in the Arctic and Pacific oceans and China's activities in the East China Sea) and reclaim some territories previously lost in past geopolitical cataclysms (Russia's interest in Crimea or China's interest in Taiwan), that is, to change the existing rules. But in contrast with the PTT postulates, these quasi-revisionist states are in fact set to solve disputable questions in a "civilized" way—through negotiations, referenda and international institutions. All of the BRICS members repeatedly claim that they intend to solve all disputes by peaceful means through negotiations and on the basis of international law.

Furthermore, the creation of BRICS itself is a manifestation of Moscow's—as well as the other BRICS members'—intention to rely first and foremost on "soft power" rather than "hard power" in achieving foreign policy goals. The reforming of the global institutions is seen by these five countries as something to be achieved in a peaceful and non-coercive manner, through presenting their common position on the reform issue in the G20 and corresponding financial institutions and exerting pressure on the developed countries so as to make them admit the necessity of reform and provide emerging actors with greater space and power. The creation of new financial bodies under the auspices of BRICS, which is often regarded in the West as a revisionist move, is purely of complementary nature and not aimed at replacing the existing financial institutions. Firstly, BRICS financial bodies are a far cry from the IMF or World Bank, if one takes into account the financial resources available. Secondly, the BRICS Contingent Reserve Arrangement, for example, is complimentary to the IMF since it preserves a strong connection to the latter: the maximum access for the member country to financial resources is divided into de-linked and IMF-linked portions equal to 30 per cent and 70 per cent correspondingly (Leksyutina 2015, 169). All these demonstrate that the BRICS members cannot be regarded as purely revisionist powers.

Moreover, the problem with the revisionist/status-quo powers theory is that it largely ignores the existence of a third type of states—the reformists. The concept of a reformist state is relatively new in the IR literature. Scholars prefer to call them "pluralist" or "non-aligned" states. Similar to revisionist powers, such states are unsatisfied with the existing rules of the "game", but they do not want to change them radically. Rather, they focus on reforming and adapting them to new realities, while making them more suitable for the members of the global or regional community. Such states prefer to act on the basis of existing rules and norms rather than challenging them. All changes (reforms) should be made gradually, through negotiations and to the benefit of all the parties involved. It is safe to assume that all the BRICS countries perfectly fall into this category, including Russia. One can distinguish between more or less assertive reformist actors, but even the most assertive ones can hardly be characterized as revisionist states. As Toloraya (2015) explains, all the BRICS countries understand that it is impossible and unreasonable to destroy the established financial and economic architecture, regard Euro-Atlantic values and lifestyle as an example to follow in one way or another and rely on the West as the main source of technologies and investment as well as the main market for their exports.

As opposed to the realist/neorealist PTT, the neoliberal IR paradigm proposes the *soft power theory* to explain Russia's policies towards and within BRICS. The neoliberals argue that in the post–Cold War period, key international players prefer to exercise soft power rather than hard power. According to those subscribing to the soft power concept, the economic, socio-cultural, institutional and legal instruments are now much more effective than military power or direct political or economic pressure. For many states, hard power has become an exceptional tool and a last resort in their foreign relations rather than a day-to-day practice. Hard power is now mainly applicable to those international actors who violate international law or directly threaten national, regional or global security.

The concept of soft power has become increasingly attractive to the Russian leadership lately. For example, both Russia's foreign policy doctrine (Pravo.gov.ru 2016) and BRICS strategy (Kremlin.ru 2013b) indicate the need for developing soft power capabilities. Russia's increased interest in soft power has several explanations, including the hope that with the help of the soft power concept it would be possible to foster economic, political and socio-cultural integration in the post-Soviet space and attract partners from all parts of the world—including the BRICS countries. There has also been the need to improve Russia's international image which seriously suffered after a number of crises such as the 2008 "five-day war" with Georgia and the 2014 Ukrainian crisis.

Moscow worked hard to create a soft power potential including Russia's economic attractiveness for the BRICS partners (especially as a supplier of energy resources and as a transit country between Europe and East Asia), its diplomatic capabilities that are necessary for the competition of BRICS with the West and its strong cultural influence which is especially welcomed in the partner countries. The Kremlin created a soft power institutional framework which included *Rossotrudnichestvo*, the Russian governmental agency responsible for relations with the Commonwealth of Independent States (CIS) and compatriots living abroad; *Russkiy Mir* (Russian World) Foundation for the promotion of the Russian language, culture and education system abroad; Gorchakov Foundation for Public Diplomacy; Andrei Pervozvanny Fund; International Foundation for Working with Diasporas Abroad "Rossiyane"; International Council of Russian Compatriots; Moscow Foundation for International Cooperation; Library "Russian Language Literature Abroad"; and International Association of Twin Cities. Russian educational and cultural institutions are integral parts of this soft power arsenal as well.

While Russia's soft power strategies towards BRICS and some post-Soviet countries can be assessed as rather efficient, Moscow's public diplomacy with regard to many Western states and some former Soviet republics (e.g. the Baltic states, Georgia and Ukraine) is assessed critically by foreign policy-making and expert communities. The list of complaints against Russia includes the creation, maintenance and support of Kremlin-friendly networks of influence in the cultural, economic and political sectors, dissemination of biased information, local agenda-setting through the state-controlled Russian media and making the compatriots loyal to Kremlin.

Against this background, given the limitations and weaknesses of Russia's soft power, the collective soft power of BRICS can be seen as a plausible way to enhance Moscow's attractiveness in the world. In other words, Russia can bandwagon with the BRICS model that might be appealing to other developing and emerging countries. The same logic is applicable to other BRICS members as well. Individually, each of the five countries possesses limited soft power. Despite their rich cultural heritage and significant resources spent on public diplomacy (especially in the case of China and Russia), these countries have some characteristics that affect their capacity to influence other countries beyond traditional forms of power—for instance, high levels of poverty in India or violence in Brazil or the lack of political freedom in China. Yet, acting as a group in BRICS, the negative image of a particular country recede into the background, giving way to cumulative soft power capacity.

BRICS can be a source of attractiveness also because it succeeded in creating an operational framework where countries, which are very different politically, economically, socially and culturally, not only coexist, but leaving apart their differences (which are substantial, for example, in the case of China-India relations) act as a community capable of consolidated international action. The BRICS countries promote a model of international relations with such characteristics as the peaceful coexistence of various civilizations and religions, multilateralism, democratization of international affairs, adherence to principles of good faith, sovereign equality of states, non-interference in the internal affairs of states, international law and equal and indivisible security. On the other hand, the BRICS countries condemn such international practices as regime change by force, imposition of unilateral coercive measures, unilateral military intervention, economic sanctions in violation of international law and strengthening of a state's security at the expense of the security of others. Therefore, the BRICS members strive for a more just, equitable, democratic and multipolar international order based on the central role of the UN and respect for international law, where international problems and disputes are to be solved peacefully by collective efforts through political and diplomatic means (Xinhuanet 2017).

On the economic front, BRICS advocates a greater role for developing countries in the existing financial institutions and undertakes measures aimed at creating a more favourable international environment for the development of the emerging economies. Moreover, having been created on the basis of the five emerging economies' outstanding achievements, BRICS can be appealing to the developing countries as a successful development model. A number of developing countries including Turkey, Indonesia, Argentina, Egypt and Nigeria have already expressed their interest to become a BRICS member, while many other developing countries and non-Western organizations have been pleased to take part in the BRICS summits in an "outreach" format.

During its presidency of BRICS in the 2015–2016 period, Russia proposed a number of measures targeted at enhancing the collective soft power of BRICS and raising awareness of the activities of BRICS in the international community. These measures included coordinating practical approaches of the member countries to international development assistance; setting up a "Public Diplomacy Forum" in order to share best practices on covering BRICS' activity and elaborate common approaches; holding publicity campaigns devoted to the 70th anniversary of the victory in World War II; providing government support for the production of documentary films and television and radio programmes devoted to BRICS; launching the work of the BRICS Virtual Secretariat which has been designed to contain information on the activities, history, objectives and operating principles of BRICS (BRICS 2015). Moscow believes that the enhancement of the image of BRICS within a broader international community will have positive implications for Russia's soft power as well.

On top of all of that, soft power is not only about constructing a positive image of a country (or a group of countries) internationally or acting as an attractive development model with certain widely recognized values and principles. Of greater importance for a country is to play significant—and preferably leading—roles in the institutions that lay the basis for the existing international system. From this perspective, BRICS can also be very useful for generating Russia's soft power in terms of strengthening its agenda-setting and decision-making capacity. The creation of new financial institutions and promotion of the role of emerging economies in the existing institutions is obviously helpful in strengthening the agenda-setting capacity.

And, finally, Moscow also employs the group as an instrument to attract the other four BRICS members. That is a task worth the efforts since these four countries are key actors in their respective regions—together representing 40 per cent of world population, 17 per cent of world's land area and 20 per cent of world GDP (World Bank Database n.d.). One of Russia's five strategic objectives in BRICS as defined in the "Concept of Participation of the Russian Federation in BRICS" clearly specifies Moscow's interest in using this grouping to consolidate its soft power within the BRICS countries: "using participation in BRICS, to widen the Russian linguistic, cultural and informational presence in major countries of the world, to which BRICS members belong" (Kremlin.ru 2013b, 4).

Civic dialogue, academic forums, sister city programs, youth activities and other people-to-people platforms implemented lately within the framework of BRICS perfectly support Russia's plans to increase its attractiveness among the emerging powers. Reducing visa-related bureaucracy and facilitating travel with the BRICS countries further promotes Russia's people-to-people interactions with the member states (Stuenkel 2016, 358).

Altogether, cooperation within BRICS offers Russia an opportunity to define and project a new international role for itself which is different from its traditional image as a great hard power. The concept of soft power looks promising for the Kremlin because it can suggest selling not only raw materials, industrial products and high technologies to the BRICS "market" but also Russian higher education and culture. Supported by BRICS, Moscow hopes to ascertain its global authority by other means and in its new capacity not as a militarist and expansionist country, but as a soft power which is attractive for international partners economically, politically and culturally.

With regard to emerging powers, such as the BRICS countries, the *coexistence concept*—though without its Marxist connotation—has recently become popular again in the IR literature (Odgaard 2012). According to this school, countries with completely different socio-economic and political systems can peacefully coexist. The emerging powers agree to play by the existing rules, but they want to make them more just and adequate to the changing realities. They do not accept a dominant state(s) imposing rules on the rest of the world and favour a multipolar world model. The "coexistence" concept quite nicely fits the reformist states' political philosophy and can be applicable to the explanation of foreign policy behaviour of many emerging powers including Russia.

Moscow's renewed interest in the peaceful coexistence concept can be explained by several reasons. First and foremost, at some point, the Kremlin realized that previous models of Russia's relations with the West such as comprehensive security (late Gorbachev era), Russia as the "junior partner" of the West (early Yeltsin era), cooperative security (late Yeltsin and early Putin eras) and strategic or just partnership (second Putin era and Medvedev era) did not work. The return to an older, time-tested and seemingly reliable foreign policy concept was viewed as a logical step in the search for a proper doctrinal basis for Moscow's international strategy.

Furthermore, since mid-2000s Moscow has been increasingly dissatisfied with the West's reluctance to respect Russia's global and regional interests and treat Russia as an equal partner. Putin's Munich speech of 2007 marked the moment when the Kremlin started to redesign its foreign policy in a more assertive way. Over time, Russia's controversies with the West regarding international issues were augmented by their fundamental differences on the interpretation of core values such as democracy, rule of law, human and minority rights, freedom of speech and independent mass media. The West became increasingly critical of the Putin regime, accusing it of authoritarianism and human rights violations. Similar to the Cold War era, both the West and Russia tended to believe that they belonged to rather different socio-political systems. Under these circumstances, the Kremlin viewed the coexistence principle as a proper approach in dealing with the West.

It should be noted that not only Russia, but also other BRICS members prefer to use the peaceful coexistence concept. In this sense, they speak the same language and understand each other well. However, Russia's present-day interpretation of the coexistence concept is different from its Soviet original. The Soviet version was based on the Marxist-Leninist ideology, while the current version has no clear ideological roots. Furthermore, the strategic goals and roles of the coexistence concept in the Soviet and Russian foreign policies are different. In the Soviet era, the coexistence concept was a strategy for the transitional period when two antagonistic social systems had to reluctantly cohabit. However, the strategic aim of coexistence was still the elimination of world capitalism and achievement of the worldwide victory of socialism. The fight against imperialism would be continued, but by other means and in other spheres. Competition in the field of economy and technology as well as "ideological warfare" would take place instead of an open military confrontation between the two blocs.

Currently, Moscow has no such revolutionary/radical objectives. The present-day coexistence concept is more defensive than offensive. Moscow has no intention to destroy the dominant capitalist system. Rather, it wants to be integrated to this system on equal terms. The Kremlin does not aim to impose its values or model on other nations, as it only wants to be treated with respect and on a mutually beneficial basis.

The current interpretation of Russia's peaceful coexistence concept can be summarized in the following way. Similar to the old version of the concept, the Kremlin believes that countries with different socio-economic and political systems can coexist peacefully. However, in contrast with the Marxist-Leninist interpretation, the coexisting systems now belong to the same type of social and economic formation. At the same time, Moscow does not accept the dominance of one state or group of states and instead favours a multipolar world model (the concept which now prevails in the Russian foreign policy discourse) where Russia can find its legitimate and rightful place. The soft power instruments are preferable while military force should be the last resort or an exceptional tool which should be used when other means are exhausted.

In spite of numerous divergences with the West, Russia has a broad cooperative agenda with the US, EU and NATO that includes non-proliferation of weapons of mass destruction (WMD), arms control and disarmament, conflict prevention and resolution, fighting international terrorism and transnational crime, environment protection and climate change mitigation, civil protection, outer space and world ocean research, and humanitarian and cultural cooperation. On the other hand, the coexistence concept is mostly designed for Russia's relations with the West or developed countries. Moscow's relations with BRICS as well as post-Soviet states and developing countries are based on other theoretical/conceptual principles ranging from the moderate version of Eurasianism to various interpretations of the partnership model.

In explaining Russia's foreign policy behaviour which sometimes seems "irrational", "unpredictable" or even "emotional" to the outside observers, one can also refer to the *status theory* which is being developed in the context of the post-positivist IR paradigm. The collapse of the USSR, which is perceived by the current Russian leadership as the "greatest geopolitical disaster of the 20th century" and the concomitant loss of the superpower status have left Russia with an agonizingly uncertain status.

While Russia's nuclear arsenal still enables it to qualify as a top-tier country, its performance in almost all other areas places it among the states which were—until recently—inferior to it. This relatively sudden development has arguably resulted in a kind of status inconsistency or even "status panic", which post-Soviet Russia is still struggling to deal with. With the help of BRICS, Russia hopes to restore its great power status (including the political privileges and prestige accompanying it) as well as elevate its standing in relation to other world powers (Hansen and Sergunin 2014; Stuenkel 2016). Each of the five member countries is a leader in its respective region, which makes BRICS a meaningful grouping representing five regions and a bloc with global outreach.

To explain further the complexity of status-seeking behaviour, it should be noted that achievements in various fields do not necessarily bring the external recognition expected by a status-seeker (there can be a discrepancy between self-perception of status and externally-defined positions). This can, in turn, push a status-seeker towards engaging in symbolic actions and gestures to demonstrate capabilities (technological, economic, military, cultural, etc.) to win higher status recognition although such "symbolic policies" cannot match its economic, defence, socio-political and moral resources. For example, some analysts question whether Moscow's mega sports events such as the 2014 Sochi Winter Olympic Games or 2018 World Soccer Cup were really affordable and economically viable for Russia or did they simply aim to elevate Russia's status and international prestige? In the same vein, other experts are puzzled by the question as to whether Putin's decision to take over Crimea was a result of a careful calculation or a poorly thought out improvisation to "punish" Ukraine for ousting the pro-Russian Viktor Yanukovych regime and demonstrate that the West has crossed one more "red line" drawn by the Kremlin.

Why Is Russia Interested in BRICS?

Russia's interests and policy priorities in the case of BRICS are described in the document titled "Concept of Participation of the Russian Federation in BRICS" (Kremlin.ru 2013b) prepared by the Foreign Ministry on the eve of the BRICS Durban Summit in March 2013. As also indicated by this document, Moscow's interest in this international grouping is of both geoeconomic and geopolitical nature. Geoeconomically, the Kremlin has favoured the creation and development of BRICS due to the following reasons.

Like the other emerging economies, Russia has been discontent with the global economic and financial system which was established to benefit the "club" of highly developed countries. It is not a coincidence that BRICS has institutionally consolidated itself in the context of the global financial crisis of the 2008–2010 period. Its member states strongly believe that the West should be blamed for the "short-sighted" and "reckless" financial policies that led to the financial crisis and that the emerging economies should act together in this critical period. Their decision to establish a "New Development Bank" of $100 billion to finance infrastructure projects and a "Contingent Reserve Arrangement" of $100 billion to stabilize their currency markets aimed to create safeguards against new global crises and make them less dependent on the economic and financial rules imposed by the Western countries.

Moreover, the BRICS countries share common economic and financial problems as well as the need for large-scale modernization. For example, Brazil and India are permanently facing serious problems in stabilizing their currencies, since they are under pressure to maintain growth by encouraging domestic demand because of the generally high poverty levels. The Russian rouble has also depreciated considerably since the beginning of 2013—much earlier than the oil prices started to drop and the Western sanctions were introduced. As for China, before February 2014, the government was able to ensure exchange rate stability through strict regulatory measures, but later the policy of gradual depreciation of the yuan started. According to the World Economic Forum experts, China is now losing another main economic advantage: a cheap labour force. China now comes only 29th in the World Economic Forum's Global Competitiveness Index, with South Africa far behind in the 53rd place, while Brazil, India and Russia are in the 56th, 60th and 64th places, respectively (Kuzmin 2013). In the Kremlin's view, these structural economic problems can be solved through joint efforts. In addition to issues related with trade and finance, cooperation in areas such as industries, energy, agriculture, telecommunications, information technologies, research, healthcare, higher education and culture should be developed.

Moscow believes that the BRICS countries have an immense potential not only to solve the existing problems but also to ensure sustainable and prosperous socio-economic development (Kremlin.ru 2013a). However, to see BRICS solely through the lens of economic growth is to miss the point. As many analysts believe, BRICS may also become the main pole of the emerging multipolar world. For example, Fyodor Lukyanov, an authoritative columnist and president of the Valdai International Discussion Club, which is an influential Russian think-tank, emphasizes that "BRICS is primarily a political group that emerged in response to the obvious need for a more diverse and less Western-oriented global political structure" (Lukyanov 2011). Russian Foreign Minister Sergei Lavrov also repeatedly noted that BRICS has been first and foremost a geopolitical association for Russia (Lukyanov 2011).

There are several reasons for Russia's growing geopolitical interest in BRICS. First, it is becoming increasingly clear for the emerging powers that the structure of global institutions is inadequate for the twenty-first century's realities, while the plans to reform these institutions remain mostly on paper. It should be noted that while these five very different countries do not agree on everything, they are nonetheless united in their dissatisfaction with their status in the world, although their reasons are different and sometimes even incompatible (Stuenkel 2014). Existing political structures were built around the bipolar world of the Cold War and they have remained virtually unchanged since then. The BRICS member states rightly question the legitimacy of the existing system and request a global political structure that reflects the multipolar world order that is gradually taking shape. That is, for example, why all the BRICS countries favour a reform in the UN Security Council because the current system is viewed as a relic of the balance of power of 1945. However, these countries understand that it is not easy to implement such a reform and all structural and procedural changes should be made gradually and in a cautious way. On the other hand, they underline that the proposed UN reform should not undermine the role of this organization.

It is also clear for the five BRICS countries that current global problems demand entirely new approaches. They believe that the West has monopolized the global debate and by doing this impeded the search for fresh ideas and effective solutions that could only emerge from a more inclusive discussion. The BRICS countries have especially been concerned about the frequent use of military force by the US and its NATO allies in the post-Cold war era. The Russian strategic document on BRICS, for instance, underlines the need "to prevent the use of the UN, first of all the Security Council, to cover up the course towards removing undesirable regimes and imposing unilateral solutions to conflict situations, including those based on the use of force" (Kremlin.ru 2013b, 5).

Furthermore, all of the BRICS countries have found it difficult to increase their influence on the world stage within the framework of existing institutions and they have all been looking for ways to strengthen their geopolitical positions by forming a new global politico-economic structure. The fact that they represent different parts of the world gives even more weight to their aspirations.

BRICS is a particularly useful grouping for Russia, which has struggled since 1991 to find a suitable identity in the global political arena. Following the collapse of the Soviet Union, Russia was reduced to the level of a regional power. The BRICS grouping therefore offers Russia a chance to reassert its global aspirations and draw attention to its economic progress. Moreover, BRICS allows Russia to do this in a non-confrontational way, even though the US remains unconvinced that the group is not directed against anyone and still views BRICS as a threat to its own global influence.

Given Russia's proactive foreign policy, BRICS is especially valuable for Moscow for mobilizing political support—either directly or indirectly—for its international initiatives and actions. Having the political support of BRICS became more important for Moscow after its tensions with the West heightened due to the crises in Ukraine and later Syria. While facing strong criticism from the West, it is indispensable for Moscow to cultivate and form a support base in the world so as to avoid international isolation.

Russia also believes that BRICS can be helpful in promoting international security cooperation, more specifically in areas such as conflict resolution, non-proliferation of WMD, combating international terrorism, drug trafficking, piracy, money laundering and illegal migration. In short, Moscow favours the creation of joint institutions to coordinate the activities of BRICS in the field of international security (Kremlin.ru 2013b, 6–7).

Russia and BRICS: Priorities for Cooperation

Given Moscow's important geoeconomic and geopolitical interests in cooperation with BRICS, the following priority areas in Russia's strategy can be identified. First, BRICS is used by Russia for the reform of the international financial system. Motivated by a shared desire to create a more favourable international environment for the development of the emerging and developing countries, the BRICS member states have joined their efforts to facilitate the transformation of the global governance system. They seek to change the hierarchy in the system to obtain privileges that have so far been only enjoyed by the developed countries in the West. Such efforts above all aim to limit the control of the US and European countries in key international institutions by strengthening the representation and voting power of the emerging and developing countries at the IMF and World Bank and by providing access to senior level positions in the IMF, World Bank and World Trade Organization (WTO) for the representatives of the developing countries.

Despite the resistance of the Western countries, the World Bank agreed to the redistribution of 3 per cent of the voting rights in favour of the developing countries in 2010. As a result of this reform, BRICS strengthened its position within this global financial institution. Currently, with its 4.59 per cent voting share in the International Bank for Reconstruction and Development and 2.21 per cent voting share in the International Development Agency, China occupies the fourth position, while India and Russia occupy the seventh and eighth positions, respectively (Leksyutina 2017, 30; Leksyutina 2018, 92).

In January 2016, the IMF was reformed as well. The quotas of the BRICS countries were increased to 14.7 per cent which came closer to the 15 per cent stake of the US. Currently, China is the IMF's third-largest stakeholder (following the US and Japan), while India, Russia and Brazil occupy the eighth, ninth and tenth positions, respectively (Leksyutina 2017, 30).

In November 2015, the IMF Executive Board took another important decision. Since October 2016, the Chinese yuan has been included in the special drawing rights (SDR) basket along with other international currencies. The SDR basket now consists of the following five currencies: US dollar—41.73 per cent, Euro—30.93 per cent, Chinese yuan—10.92 per cent, Japanese yen—8.33 per cent and UK pound—8.09 per cent (Leksyutina 2017, 31).

Russia and the other BRICS countries, however, believe that the World Bank and IMF reforms are incomplete as their voting power in these financial institutions still does not correspond to their share in the world's GDP. Moreover, the global financial institutions have been traditionally governed by the representatives of the developed countries which is perceived by BRICS as a clear manifestation of the Western dominance in the world financial system.

Furthermore, the BRICS countries supplement the existing governance mechanisms with new ones like the New Development Bank and Contingent Reserve Arrangement. Yet, one should bear in mind that the establishment of new institutions is not aimed at changing the global rules or challenging the existing financial institutions. Rather, these institutions have been founded due to the older institutions' incapacity to adequately integrate the emerging economies. Thus, the newly established institutions are meant to complement the existing order and better project the power of the emerging economies.

The harmonization of the two mega Eurasian integration projects—the Russia-led Eurasian Economic Union (EAEU) and China-inspired "One Belt-One Road" (OBOR) which is later renamed as the Belt and Road Initiative (BRI)—is viewed by the Kremlin as another strategic goal of BRICS. Although Moscow was initially quite suspicious about the OBOR/BRI, Russia's tense relations with the West in the wake of the Ukrainian crisis forced it to revise its position in a more constructive way. On May 8, 2015, Russian President Putin and Chinese President Xi Jinping signed a joint statement on cooperation in the harmonization of the EAEU and OBOR/BRI. The Sino-Russian cooperative plans firstly aim to develop the Eurasian transport infrastructure with the active participation of other European, Central Asian, East Asian and South Asian countries (Leksyutina 2017). Among the most promising infrastructure plans, the following projects should be mentioned:

- "Transsib" (Trans-Siberian Railroad): the railway route connecting the European part of Russia with Siberia and the Far East, which makes it a truly Eurasian transport corridor connecting Eastern and Central Europe with the Korean peninsula, China and Mongolia.
- "North–South" transport corridor: a multimodal 7200 kilometre route to transport passengers and cargo from St. Petersburg to the port of Mumbai (through which goods will be carried from India, Iran and the Persian Gulf to Russia and further to Northern and Western Europe).
- The Northern Latitudinal Railway: a project to create a transport infrastructure in the Yamal-Nenets Autonomous District including a 707 kilometre East-West railway between Nadym and Labytnangi and an extension to Sabetta port on the Yamal peninsula with the goal of connecting these gas and oil-rich regions with the existing Russian rail system.
- "Belkomur" (White Sea-Komi Republic-Ural): a 1161 kilometre route connecting Northwestern Russia and Scandinavia with the Asian parts of Russia, Central Asia and Asia-Pacific countries.
- The Northern Sea Route (Polar Silk Road as defined by the Chinese): the most promising maritime route for international commercial navigation from East and Southeast Asia (i.e. China, India, Japan,

South Korea, Singapore) to Northern and Western Europe and vice versa.

Using BRICS as an instrument to overcome the economic crisis and compensate for the damage caused by the Western sanctions is another direction of Russia's BRICS strategy. Economic recession that began in Russia in 2014 due to the combination of a number of factors such as the volatility of the rouble, plunging oil prices and Western sanctions reconfirmed for Moscow the importance of being a member of the BRICS grouping. In contrast to Russia's poor economic performance in the 2014–2016 period, the other BRICS members performed quite well, which means that although Russia is not a successful economy anymore, it still continues to be associated with major emerging economies. In addition, cooperating within the framework of BRICS and using the advantages of the mutually complementary nature of the BRICS economies, Moscow seeks to diversify its foreign economic ties by developing its trade and investment relations with the other BRICS members as well as the regions under their economic influence.

It was during Russia's presidency in 2015 that the BRICS Economic Partnership Strategy through 2020 was adopted. Cooperation was developed in areas such as industries, energy, agriculture, telecommunications, information technologies and research. The Xiamen Summit in 2017 witnessed the conclusion of four new agreements in areas of economic and trade cooperation, innovation cooperation, customs cooperation and strategic cooperation between the BRICS Business Council and the New Development Bank.

Sino-Russian economic cooperation is especially productive. In addition to the steadily growing bilateral trade, numerous industrial projects are being developed including the construction of gas and oil pipelines, building of nuclear plants in China and LNG plants in Russia's Arctic region, developing the infrastructure of the seaports in Arkhangelsk and Murmansk and so on.

Moscow uses BRICS not only to counter the Western economic sanctions but also to avoid international isolation. In March 2014, for instance, the four BRICS members abstained from voting at the UN General Assembly on a draft resolution condemning Russia's annexation of Crimea. They also issued a joint statement against the proposal of the Australian foreign minister who requested the exclusion of Russia from the G20 Brisbane Summit in November 2014 and thus prevented the geopolitical isolation of Moscow by the West in the aftermath of the crisis in Ukraine

Russia also believes that BRICS can play an important role in the field of security cooperation which is exemplified by cooperation in arms trade and defence industry as well as joint military exercises, efforts for the prevention of proliferation of WMD, fighting international terrorism and countering transnational organized and cybercrime. The BRICS leaders also regularly meet to discuss "joint economic security measures" such as information exchange regarding speculative attacks on currency, stock and commodity markets, food security and cooperation in agricultural technology to help combat climate change. At the 2018 BRICS summit, for instance, South Africa proposed establishing a working group on peacekeeping in order to strengthen the role of BRICS in conflict resolution. Russia also favours strengthening the people-to-people exchanges and fostering closer cooperation in the areas of culture, sport and education. People-to-people exchanges among BRICS countries have already intensified through institutions such as the Young Diplomats Forum, Parliamentarian Forum, Trade Union Forum, Civil BRICS and the Media Forum. In 2018, South Africa also suggested to create a BRICS Gender and Women's Forum.

CONCLUSION

Overall Russia's policies towards and within BRICS represent a combination of ideational and material motives. On the one hand, the BRICS grouping is important for Moscow in terms of status seeking, as it believes that by joining forces with other major emerging economies, it will be easier to regain its great power status, shape the emerging world order and compel the West—particularly the US—to abide by the rules of that order. On the other hand, the Kremlin prioritizes its economic and strategic partnerships with the BRICS members, since they are important for Russia's well-being and sustainable development as well as for counterbalancing the West in the global geoeconomic and geopolitical setting.

Up to now, initiatives that have been developed by BRICS demonstrate that the grouping does not have a revisionist agenda. Instead, through their participation in BRICS, the five countries—and particularly Russia—aim to better incorporate themselves into the existing system and become "responsible" actors with international obligations as well as rights and powers. The international behaviour of Russia and BRICS can be properly understood, if one applies the peaceful coexistence concept and the reformist political philosophy behind it. The international activities of BRICS are strictly reformist in nature. Against this background, Russia's participation in BRICS indicates that Moscow wishes to redesign its foreign policy in a way to support and further develop international norms, rules and institutions and prefers non-coercive and soft power methods.

Moreover, it is safe to assume that Russia uses BRICS as an instrument to enhance its soft power vis-à-vis the other BRICS countries and, even more importantly, increase its soft power globally riding on the back of BRICS in world politics. The BRICS framework provides Moscow with additional prestige in the international community as well as greater legitimacy to its international activities. All these factors explain why the Kremlin attaches great importance to BRICS and why strengthening BRICS and its role in global affairs is viewed in Moscow as a basis for solidifying Russia's political and economic position in the international arena.

REFERENCES

BRICS. 2015. Concept of the Russian Federation's Presidency in BRICS in 2015–2016. http://en.brics2015.ru/russia_and_brics/20150301/19483.html

Cohen, Ariel, and R.E. Hamilton. 2011. *The Russian Military and the Georgia War: Lessons and Implications.* Carlisle Barracks: Strategic Studies Institute.

Hansen, Flemming S., and Alexander Sergunin. 2014. Russia, BRICS, and Peaceful Coexistence: Between Idealism and Instrumentalism. In *The BRICS and Coexistence: An Alternative Vision of World Order,* ed. Cedric de Coning, Thomas Mandrup, and Liselotte Odgaard, 75–99. Abingdon: Routledge.

Kremlin.ru. 2013a. Vladimir Putin's News Conference Following the G20 Summit. September 6. http://eng.kremlin.ru/news/5950

———. 2013b. Concept of Participation of the Russian Federation in BRICS. http://eng.news.kremlin.ru/media/events/eng/files/41d452b13d9c2624d228.pdf

Kuzmin, Viktor. 2013. New BRICS Reserve Pool to Fight Currency Shocks. *Russia Beyond the Headlines,* September 11. https://www.rbth.com/economics/2013/09/11/new_brics_reserve_pool_to_fight_currency_shocks_29263

Leksyutina, Yana. 2015. BRICS: Reforming Global Economic Governance System. *Public Administration and Civil Service* 1: 166–172.

———. 2017. Liderstvo v BRICS: prognozy i realii. *World Economy and International Relations* 61 (5): 25–33.

———. 2018. Functional Changes in China's Participation in the Multilateral Development Banks: From Borrower to Creditor Status. *International Organizations Research Journal* 13 (1): 80–98. https://doi.org/10.17323/1996-7845-2018-01-05.

Lukyanov, Fyodor. 2010. Russian Dilemmas in a Multipolar World. *Columbia SIPA Journal of International Affairs* 63 (2). http://jia.sipa.columbia.edu/russian-dilemmas-multipolar-world/

————. 2011. BRICS Goes from Fantasy to Reality. *Russia in Global Affairs*, April 17. http://www.globalaffairs.ru/redcol/BRICS-goes-from-fantasy-to-reality-15169

Odgaard, Liselotte. 2012. *China and Coexistence: Beijing's National Security Strategy for the 21st Century*. Washington, DC: Woodrow Wilson Center Press/Johns Hopkins University Press.

Organski, A.F.K. 1958. *World Politics*. New York: Alfred and Knopf.

Pravo.gov.ru. 2016. Kontseptsiya vneshnei politiki Rossiyskoi Federatsii. November 30. http://publication.pravo.gov.ru/Document/View/0001201612010045?index=0&rangeSize=1

Shakleina, Tatiana. 2013. Russia in the New Distribution of Power. In *Emerging Powers in a Comparative Perspective: The Political and Economic Rise of the BRIC Countries*, ed. Vidya Nadkarni and Norma Noonan, 163–188. New York: Bloomsbury.

Stuenkel, Oliver. 2014. Emerging Powers and Status: The Case of the First BRICS Summit. *Asian Perspective* 38 (1): 1–13.

————. 2016. Do the BRICS Possess Soft Power? *Journal of Political Power* 9 (3): 353–367. https://doi.org/10.1080/2158379X.2016.1232285.

Tammen, Ronald L., et al. 2000. *Power Transitions: Strategies for the 21st Century*. New York: Seven Bridges Press.

Toloraya, Georgy. 2015. Why Does Russia Need BRICS? *Russia in Global Affairs*, March 19. http://eng.globalaffairs.ru/number/Why-Does-Russia-Need-BRICS-17373

Walt, Stephen. 2014. The Bad Old Days Are Back. *Foreign Policy*, May 2. http://foreignpolicy.com/2014/05/02/the-bad-old-days-are-back/

World Bank Database. n.d. http://data.worldbank.org/indicator/NY.GDP.MKTP.CD

Xinhuanet. 2017. Full Text of BRICS Leaders Xiamen Declaration. September 4. http://www.xinhuanet.com/english/2017-09/04/c_136583396.htm.

CHAPTER 9

Ukraine Between Russia and the West: Russian Challenge to Euro-Atlantic Security

Sergii V. Glebov

INTRODUCTION

For the last five years, Russia's relations with the US, EU and NATO are being tested by the sharpest confrontation between the West and the East since the end of the Cold War. Under such circumstances, the decades-old idea of establishing a common European security and cooperation framework between Russia and the West received a heavy blow. Although Russia has been advocating a multipolar world order since the breakup of the USSR that would be subject to the supervision of the UN Charter, its own foreign policy actions in the last few years have been threatening the very idea of the same multipolar world order. In January 2017, the US Defence Secretary Ash Carter even accused Russian President Vladimir Putin with

This chapter draws on Sergii Glebov, "Russia as a Rising Isolated Power and the W(r)est: Wrestling Ukraine from the West and the New Euro-Atlantic Puzzle," *Rising Powers Quarterly* 2, no. 1 (2017): 145–167. http://risingpowersproject. com/quarterly/russia-rising-isolated-power-wrest-wrestling-ukraine-west-new-euro-atlantic-puzzle/

S. V. Glebov (✉)
Odessa Mechnikov National University, Odessa, Ukraine

© The Author(s) 2020
E. Parlar Dal, E. Erşen (eds.), *Russia in the Changing International System*, https://doi.org/10.1007/978-3-030-21832-4_9

153

the following words: "one of the ways he defines the success of his policy is not by results on the ground but the level of the discomfort he can create in the rest of the world and show to his people as the point of his policy" (Seib 2017).

Since 2014, Moscow's aggressive and controversial policies became more evident—invoking criticism from the majority of the UN Security Council members especially when they discuss the situation in Ukraine. Other members of the UN Security Council are no longer ready to tolerate a quasi-diplomatic behaviour from the Russian representatives. As Ambassador Lyall Grant from the UK's mission to the UN clearly stated at the Security Council meeting regarding Ukraine on August 28, 2014, "Violating international law and the UN Charter in such a brazen manner is not compatible with Russia's responsibilities as a permanent member of the Security Council" (Gov.uk 2014). At the same time, this also means that the UN community simply has no adequate diplomatic instruments to influence Russia at least diplomatically because of Moscow's tendency to take unilateral decisions.

In this context, Russia achieved to impose its own agenda in global politics by annexing Crimea, increasing its aggression in the eastern part of Ukraine through methods of hybrid warfare and demonstrating cynical behaviour in the UN Security Council. This agenda is best reflected by the so-called Ukraine crisis. Even though the author of this chapter is not in favour of using this vague concept which is generally perceived as something "internally Ukrainian," the origins of the concept actually date back to the Russian-Ukrainian negotiations about the Black Sea Fleet of the former USSR in the 1990s.

It is essential to remind that a treaty on friendship, cooperation and partnership between Russia and Ukraine was signed on May 28, 1997, based on the principle of mutual respect for territorial integrity and sovereignty. Yet, this happened only after Ukraine agreed to permit the Russian Black Sea Fleet to be based in Sevastopol until 2017 in accordance with the "Agreements on the Black Sea Fleet of the former USSR" signed just a few days before the Russian-Ukrainian treaty. It was clear that without maintaining its military presence on the territory of Ukraine and keeping its grip on Sevastopol and Crimea at least in the form of a formal land lease, Russia refrained from recognizing Ukraine's sovereignty and its existing borders and integrity as an independent actor and as a subject of international relations with whom Moscow initially was ready to establish ties of "friendship, cooperation and partnership" (Glebov 2007). Yet, even at that time, Crimea was a potential source of conflict between Russia and Ukraine. In less than 20 years, the Black Sea region similarly became the most significant potential source of conflict in the entire Euro-Atlantic security zone.

The goal of this chapter is to evaluate the regional and global impacts of the conflict in Ukraine in relation with the challenges posed by Russia to the security of the Euro-Atlantic community. Following a brief discussion on the changing conceptions of Russia's security identity since 2014, the chapter will focus on the dynamics of Russia's new confrontation with NATO, the global implications of the Russian actions in Ukraine and Crimea and the shifts in the security architecture of the Black Sea in light of Russia's strengthened military presence in the region.

CONCEPTUALIZING RUSSIAN SECURITY IDENTITY

Although it is ironic, almost one year before the Russian masked troops invaded and occupied the key locations in Crimea, executing the direct orders of the Kremlin, President Putin approved a foreign policy concept. In this document, Russia identified itself "as an integral and inseparable part of European civilization" and claimed that it had "common deep-rooted civilizational ties" with "the Euro-Atlantic states" (Ministry of Foreign Affairs 2013, IV: 54, 56). Therefore, it can be argued that before 2014, Russia at least had an official desire to identify itself with the West—the collectively wealthy and attractive group of "Euro-Atlantic states," which implies a conceptual unity between liberal, democratic and value-oriented communities in the eyes of the Russian leaders. Before 2014, this group was basically represented by the member states of the G7 as well as the EU and NATO.

At the same time, however, it should be indicated that for the current political regime in Russia, which pretends to be one of the designers of the new world order, to be *with the West* does not mean to be *part of the West*. Thus, the foreign policy concept approved by Putin in 2016 acknowledges that "the world is currently going through fundamental changes related to the emergence of a multipolar international system" (Ministry of Foreign Affairs 2016, II: 4). It also states that while "the cultural and civilizational diversity of the world and the existence of multiple development models are clearer than ever," Russia has chosen its own path towards the "formation of new centres of economic and political power" (Ministry of Foreign Affairs 2016, II: 4). The foreign policy concept also claims that "global power and development potential is becoming decentralized, and is shifting towards the Asia-Pacific Region, eroding the global economic and political dominance of the traditional western powers" (Ministry of Foreign Affairs 2016, II: 5). This emphasis is not surprising considering that the Kremlin had already been in an attempt to develop its military capabilities long before the unfolding of the events in Ukraine with the goal of maintaining its position as a global player.

Russia's perception of the "Euro-Atlantic region" was also quite different in 2016 as also indicated by the foreign policy concept's warning about NATO and EU's intention to pursue "geopolitical expansion" and prevent Russia from becoming one of the centres of power in the multipolar international system (Ministry of Foreign Affairs 2016, IV: 61). It should be noted that although NATO has always been viewed as a hostile institution by Moscow, this was the first time that the EU was also openly accused of pursuing geopolitical expansion in a Russian official document. In this regard, Russia clearly blamed the West for the "serious crisis in the relations between Russia and the Western States" because according to the Russian leaders, both NATO and the EU refused "to begin implementation of political statements regarding the creation of a common European security and cooperation framework" (Ministry of Foreign Affairs 2016, IV: 61).

The latest version of Russian foreign policy concept can be viewed as a sign that Moscow has finally stopped seeing itself as the "victim" of the unipolar—or post-bipolar—world in which it has been treated unequally by the Western countries. This new perception inevitably urged the Kremlin to confront the West which was defined as a counterpart in the 2013 version of the foreign policy concept in (a) "building up a truly unified region without dividing lines through developing genuine partnership relations between Russia, the European Union and the United States"; (b) "creating a common space of peace, security and stability based on the principles of indivisible security, equal cooperation and mutual trust"; and (c) "creating a common economic and humanitarian space from the Atlantic to the Pacific" (Ministry of Foreign Affairs 2013, IV: 54–56).

Choosing the option of confronting the West in its strategy of becoming a rising power in a multipolar world order, Russia deliberately took the risk of being an isolated, but *global* power at any price. A major reason of the growing rift between Moscow and the West was their clashing strategic interests in Syria which was also later confirmed by the Russian military campaign in 2015 to prop up the regime of Bashar al-Assad. Another important reason was Russia's new struggle with the West in the sphere of propaganda and information warfare.

Yet, the epicentre of the new confrontation between Russia and the West shifted to Ukraine, which chose to adopt the Western vision of democracy rather than the Russian vision of "sovereign democracy" (Glebov 2009a). Such a development inevitably contradicted Russia's global aspirations. With the *Euromaidan* revolution, Ukraine confirmed its independent and sovereign will to succeed in its strategy towards integration with the EU, while rejecting the Russian counter-proposal for greater integration in the former Soviet space. Although the official position and sincerity of the Ukrainian political and economic elites in facilitating internal reforms and continuing the process of European integration are open to discussion (Glebov 2015), this excuse definitely did not give Russia the right to intervene in the domestic affairs of a sovereign state. This is even more important when one considers the Russian political discourse which vehemently rejects any kind of intervention in its own domestic affairs.

Yet, it seems that the Kremlin ultimately decided to punish Ukraine for attempting to move into the Western orbit. Russia also started to openly challenge the Western influence in Ukraine by employing new hybrid war tactics. This was one of the main reasons for Moscow's active role in the unfolding of the events in Donbas which aimed to pull Ukraine away from Europe and closer to Russia as well as the Russia-led integration mechanisms in the post-Soviet space. Not surprisingly, all these developments once again made NATO the main target of the Kremlin in the aftermath of the incidents in Ukraine.

Russia's New Confrontation with NATO

Russia updated its military doctrine in 2015 after its active involvement in Ukraine and decision to annex Crimea. The main external military threat to Russia's security was defined in the document as:

> [the] build-up of the power potential of the North Atlantic Treaty Organization (NATO) and vesting NATO with global functions carried out in violation of the rules of international law, bringing the military infrastructure of NATO member countries near the borders of the Russian Federation, including by further expansion of the alliance. (Rusemb.org.uk 2015, II: 12a)

The hints of Russia's approach regarding NATO in the new era can also be found in Foreign Minister Sergey Lavrov's speech on August 24, 2015 delivered during the Educational Youth Forum when he stated that "NATO-centrism" was one of the main causes of the developments in Ukraine:

> ...the only way is dialogue, respect for a negotiating partner's interests, and the desire to find consensus, which inevitably implies compromises without diktat or ultimatums ... I think if the same principles were accepted by our Western partners, there would have been no confrontation over the advance of NATO's military infrastructure towards Russian borders despite earlier promises to the contrary, nor would there have been the Ukrainian crisis, if things were done through the search for generally acceptable compromise rather than ultimatums, or a "black-and-white" understanding of developments, or the either-with-us- or-against-us dichotomy ... Thus, they gave up on the concept of a single and indivisible space of equal security in the Euro-Atlantic area, which had been proclaimed by their leaders. This NATO-centrism, this attempt to preserve the divides represent a systemic problem, while the rest, including the tragedy in Ukraine, is derived from this division into friend or foe. (Ministry of Foreign Affairs 2015)

To criticize Russia's approach about the concept of a single and indivisible space of equal security in the Euro-Atlantic area and to discuss who is responsible for the failure of this concept in practice are beyond the scope of this chapter. The details of this discussion can be found in other studies including an article by Glebov (2009b) which suggests the use of the concept of "New Euroatlantism." At the same time, however, it should be noted that the 2008 version of the Russian foreign policy concept touched upon this issue by indicating that Moscow maintained:

> its negative attitude towards the expansion of NATO, notably to the plans of admitting Ukraine and Georgia to the membership in the alliance, as well as to bringing the NATO military infrastructure closer to the Russian borders on the whole, which violates the principle of equal security, leads to new dividing lines in Europe and runs counter to the tasks of increasing the effectiveness of joint work in search for responses to real challenges of our time. (Kremlin.ru 2008, IV)

It is interesting to note that Russian officials refer to "NATO enlargement" as "the expansion of NATO"—which is also due to the nuances in the Russian language—and there is a direct relationship between the Moscow's syndrome about NATO's expansion in the post-1991 period and its decision to annex Crimea in March 2014. In fact, the annexation of Crimea was partly justified by President Putin when he hinted that NATO's intention to expand was one of the key causes for Moscow's motivation to have Crime "back home":

> If we don't do anything, Ukraine will be drawn into NATO sometime in the future. We'll be told: "This doesn't concern you," and NATO ships will dock in Sevastopol, the city of Russia's naval glory... if NATO troops walk in, they will immediately deploy these forces there. Such a move would be geopolitically sensitive for us because, in this case, Russia would be practically ousted from the Black Sea area. (The Washington Post 2014)

Yet, it should be emphasized that unlike 2008, the issue of admitting Ukraine to NATO was not on the agenda and Ukraine even officially possessed a non-aligned status since July 20, 2010. In other words, Putin's aforementioned statement contradicted the existing geopolitical reality. However, this reasoning quickly became incorporated into the Kremlin's anti-NATO rhetoric in an attempt to convince the Russian audience that the West was conspiring to initiate a "Russian Spring" at home. As a result, Crimea became some kind of "an impregnable fortress" (TASS 2015a) and a bridgehead against NATO in the Russian official discourse. The Kremlin is also interested to turn the peninsula into a colossal military base as an integral fortress of the "Russian world." Its spiritual significance as the cradle of the Orthodox faith also increases Crimea's significance for the Russian leaders' quest against NATO expansionism, Americanism and Westernization. Symbolically, the frontier between "us" and "them" for the Eastern Slavic peoples was also located in the ancient city of Chersonese—today's Sevastopol—from where Christianity spread to the region.

Putting such discourses aside, the Russian leaders' accusations about NATO and concepts like NATO-centrism can be regarded as a clear signal that Moscow wants to be taken seriously by the West and that it is ready to wage hybrid wars and launch pre-emptive strikes against any country—including those NATO members neighbouring Russia—daring to meet its security needs in a way that contradicts Russia's expectations (Glebov 2016).

GLOBAL IMPLICATIONS OF RUSSIA'S RESPONSE

With the annexation of Crimea, Russia started to flex its muscles in a "hard" security manner with a long-term confrontational perspective both at the regional and global levels. Yet, this is not only about the increasing number of provocations by Russian warplanes against NATO member states in a region extending from the Black Sea and Baltic Sea to North Sea and Atlantic Ocean or the Kremlin's strategic plans of strengthening its military presence in Crimea as a response to the West. It is neither only about the Kremlin's attempts to introduce some kind of an "import substitution" model against the Western economic sanctions—reminding Josef Stalin's policy of autarky during the times of Soviet industrialization. The real issue that needs to be highlighted here is that Russia seems to be prepared to confront the West in the global arena.

In his speech at the Valdai International Discussion Club on October 22, 2015, President Putin defined the "competition between nations and their alliances … absolutely natural" provided that "this competition develops within the framework of fixed political, legal and moral norms and rules" (Kremlin.ru 2015). He also said:

> Otherwise, competition and conflicts of interest may lead to acute crises and dramatic outbursts… What, for instance, could such uncontrolled competition mean for international security? A growing number of regional conflicts, especially in 'border' areas, where the interests of major nations or blocs meet. (Kremlin.ru 2015)

With these words, Putin actually justified the right of great powers to wage wars "especially in 'border' areas, where the interests of major nations or blocs meet" (Kremlin.ru 2015). It should be indicated that Ukraine and the Black Sea region are located in this "border" area where "such uncontrolled competition" takes place. Therefore, the Russian president implied that Russia had the right to intervene in Ukraine because the latter was a victim of the aggressive policies of NATO. This is another way of saying, "We attacked Ukraine because America prompted us to do so." However, even if one accepts Putin's argument about "uncontrolled competition"—which is probably the case for many experts of international relations—this cannot provide the basis for the annexation of the territory of another independent state since it also violates the very "fixed political, legal and moral norms and rules" that are underlined by Putin in the same speech (Kremlin.ru 2015).

Putin's approach means that Ukraine and some other states cannot escape becoming hostages of the global competition between Russia and the West. He poses an important question about who is responsible for the breaking down of the "fixed political, legal and moral normal rules." This is also a question directed to the US and its allies in order to understand whether they believe that great powers have a right to wage wars, even though this would mean a questioning of the Briand-Kellogg Pact of 1928, which renounced war as an instrument of national policy almost 90 years ago.

It is difficult for the US not to respond to such questions, and President Trump will sooner or later need to give the right answers taking into account that it was actually Russia which turned the West into an existential threat while securitizing its own discourse about the developments in Ukraine. It should be recalled for instance that the Kremlin blamed the West about the crisis in Ukraine from the very beginning. The Russian National Security Strategy of December 2015 stated that "the support of the United States and the European Union for the anti-constitutional coup d'état in Ukraine led to a deep split in Ukrainian society and the emergence of an armed conflict" (Ieee.es 2015, II: 17).

In the documentary which marked the first anniversary of the referendum that enabled Russia to take control of Crimea, Putin also described the Ukrainian revolution to oust Viktor Yanukovych in February 2014 as "an armed coup 'masterminded by our American friends' with the readiness to use nuclear weapons 'if necessary' " (Withnall 2015). "We were ready to do that," Putin said, when he was asked whether the Kremlin was prepared to place its nuclear forces on alert. The Russian leader added that he warned the US and Europe not to get involved, accusing them of engineering the ouster of the Russian-backed Ukrainian President Viktor Yanukovych and said, "That's why I think no one wanted to start a world conflict" (Meyer 2015).

Some scholars argue that "Russia's retaking of Crimea could give it a crucial head start in the event of a global conflict" (Kureev 2015). This is also closely related with the issue of nuclear safety and non-proliferation which became more urgent following the unfolding of the events in Ukraine. Considering Russia's efforts to nuclearize Crimea, the threat of the escalation of a nuclear rivalry between Russia and NATO is quite real especially in the Black Sea region. This means that Crimea may become not just a conventional, but also a nuclear "impregnable fortress" for Russia. As also indicated by Mikhail Ulyanov, head of the Russian foreign ministry's non-proliferation department, "Russia can deploy nuclear weapons in Crimea as the peninsula is part of its territory" (TASS 2015b).

At the same time, it should be mentioned that as one of the signatories of the 1994 Budapest Memorandum on Security Assurances, Moscow promised that it would "respect the independence and sovereignty and the existing borders of Ukraine, … refrain from the threat or use of force against the territorial integrity or political independence of Ukraine, and that none of their weapons will ever be used against Ukraine except in self-defence or otherwise in accordance with the Charter of the United Nations" (Msz.gov. pl 2014). Therefore, Russia's actions in Ukraine and Crimea violate not only the general principles of the international relations and the existing system of international law but also the global nuclear deterrence regime. It should also be noted for instance that parliamentarians from various EU countries identified the issue of Russia's nuclear weapons in Crimea as the most immediate security challenge for NATO (Schpeicher 2015).

Russia's deployment of nuclear weapons in the close vicinity of the NATO countries highlights the role of nuclear deterrence in Moscow's national security strategy (Peterson 2015). Some pundits argue that it is not a coincidence that Putin placed a renewed emphasis on Russia's nuclear capabilities:

> This is in part a reflection of Russia's continuing conventional military weakness …. What most alarms the West is the renewed emphasis in Russian rhetoric on nuclear rather than conventional forces. Threats to deploy short-range nuclear weapons in Crimea have been accompanied by veiled warnings of nuclear targeting against NATO members who might host ballistic missile defenses. (BBC News 2015)

At the beginning of 2018, Moscow also deployed its advanced ballistic Iskander missiles permanently in the exclave of Kaliningrad in the Baltic Sea region. With a range of up to 500 kilometres, the Iskander missiles pose a serious nuclear threat to many NATO countries. It is also very likely that Russia might consider deploying them in Crimea as the Iskander missiles are "an essential element of Russia's broader A2/AD [Anti-Access/Area-Denial] strategy" (Sukhankin 2017). Considering Russia's harsh criticisms to NATO's deployment of a missile defence system in its western borders, the NATO member states should be vigilant about the implications of a possible confrontation with Russia particularly in the Black Sea region.

THE BLACK SEA SECURITY KNOT

Alexander Vershbow, a distinguished US diplomat and former NATO Deputy Secretary General, stated that "the Black Sea is a springboard for Russia's efforts to extend its reach and influence far beyond its borders," noting that the region is in many ways the nexus of Russia's strategy aiming at re-establishing hegemony over its southern neighbourhood—a strategy based on disruption and destabilization rather than mutually beneficial cooperation. Given the political, economic and human rights implications of Russia's destabilizing policies, he indicated that all NATO allies were stakeholders in the security of the Black Sea (Parl.ca 2017).

In the face of Russia's considerable military build-up in the region, Vershbow suggested that NATO needed to consider a more persistent military presence in the Black Sea, especially when it came to maritime capabilities. In his view, Russia deployed advanced air defence systems (including the S-400) and coastal anti-ship defences, and turned Crimea into a bastion for Russian A2/AD capabilities that provided Moscow with the potential to impede the movement of regional forces and disrupt NATO's efforts to reinforce the defence of the member states (Parl.ca 2017). As noted by Andrew Budd, head of NATO's defence policy and capabilities directorate, Russia is moving modern weapons and military platforms to the region, creating a very effective A2/AD "bubble" and challenging the freedom of movement in the Black Sea area (Parl.ca 2017).

Are NATO and its allies in the EU ready to accept such challenges? The answer was partly articulated during NATO's Warsaw Summit in July 2016. In order to maintain the balance of power with Russia and be ready to protect the airspace of the Black Sea members properly, NATO changed its strategy in the Black Sea region and take a "retaliatory step of placing more modern air defence systems and fighter aircraft in Romania, Bulgaria and other Black Sea countries" (NATO.int 2016). NATO's perception of the changed military environment in the Black Sea region can be found in the Warsaw Summit Communiqué as well as the "Resolution on Stability and Security in the Black Sea Region" which was adopted during the NATO Parliamentary Assembly's annual session in Bucharest on October 6–9, 2017. In addition, during the NATO Parliamentary Assembly meeting which issued a strong declaration of support for states facing the Russian intervention, it was broadly accepted that Moscow's meddling in the affairs of the countries around the Black Sea was an issue of particular concern. As indicated by Paolo Alli, the president of NATO's Parliamentary Assembly, "supporting Ukraine, the Republic of Moldova and Georgia, is defending the whole of Europe and NATO as well" (NATO.pa.int 2017b).

It was also stated in the Warsaw Summit Communiqué that "Russia continues to strengthen its military posture, increases its military activities, deploys new high-end capabilities, and challenge regional security," while

NATO members informed that "[they] will also develop tailored forward presence in the southeast part of the Alliance territory" and assess "options for a strengthened NATO air and maritime presence" (NATO.int 2016). One of these options was assessed without a delay. During the Warsaw Summit, NATO allies declared Initial Operational Capability of NATO Ballistic Missile Defence (BMD), which was designed as a capability to defend the member states' populations, territory and military forces across southern Europe against a potential ballistic missile attack, including the most dangerous Russian Iskander missiles. These include the Aegis Ashore site in Deveselu, Romania, the early-warning BMD radar at Kürecik, Turkey, and an Aegis Ashore site at the Redzikowo military base in Poland.

Will this system be fully enough to deter Russia and counterbalance its ambitious military plans in the Black Sea region? The answer is probably negative, but such a BMD strategy in the Black Sea area is nevertheless an alarming signal for Russia. According to Alexander Khramchikhin, director of the Institute of Political and Military Analysis, for instance, "the key threat the U.S. missile defence system in Eastern Europe poses to Russia is the ability to instantly convert a missile defence base into an offensive one" (Russia Beyond 2016).

There are some recent developments that demonstrate the construction of a new security architecture in the Black Sea region. On August 15, 2018, the British Royal Air Forces (RAF) intercepted six Russian bombers flying close to NATO airspace over the Black Sea and forced them to return, while Eurofighter Typhoon jets were sent from the base in Romania to intercept Russian Su-24 Fencer bombers in the region on August 13 (Airforce Technology 2018). Such measures were taken in accordance with NATO's Enhanced Air Policing mission with the close cooperation of Romania (Airforce Technology 2018). It should be noted that four RAF Typhoons are deployed at the Mihail Kogalniceanu air base in southeast Romania where several hundred US troops are also stationed. This move was part of NATO's plans to strengthen the alliance's defence on its eastern flank following Moscow's annexation of Crimea in 2014. In addition, the US Air Force has four F-15C Eagles that are based in the neighbouring Bulgaria.

At the same time, the future of the Black Sea security also depends on the ongoing naval competition in the Black Sea. As Ambassador Vershbow noted, despite the positive steps taken in the last few years, there are still some significant gaps in NATO's deterrence posture in Europe—including gaps in maritime presence and insufficient air and theatre missile defence. This is why he suggested that NATO should consider a more persistent military presence in the Black Sea region, especially when it comes to maritime capabilities, fully in compliance with the Montreux Straits Convention of 1936 (Parl.ca 2017). NATO later confirmed its strategic intention "to use all available political and diplomatic means to seek de-escalation of tensions in the Black Sea region, and to support regional efforts to turn into an area of dialogue and cooperation" (NATO.pa.int 2017a).

CONCLUSION

With its intervention in Ukraine in February–March 2014, Russia became the first former superpower, the first nuclear state and the first permanent member of the UN Security Council to capture the territory of a neighbouring country. This shows that the EU's soft-power approach and strong belief in the omnipotence of normative methods have been insufficient to deter aggression in the European geopolitical space. In fact, Moscow quite successfully exploited the geopolitical purblindness of the West, while openly demonstrating its intention to use military force and undermine international law in order to defend its security interests and realize its geopolitical ambitions.

The annexation of Crimea revealed not only the different strategies of Russia and the EU, but also the differences in their methods to defend their strategic interests. While the EU as a normative power has limited soft-power instruments such as economic sanctions, Russia ultimately relies on its military capabilities and even disregards the diplomatic barriers of international organizations like the UN and Organization for Security and Cooperation in Europe (OSCE). Thus, Moscow did not worry much about the reaction of other countries when it resorted to direct military force in Ukraine and showed no reverence to the EU or the West when they criticized Russia for meddling in the affairs of Ukraine. In fact, the Russian involvement in Crimea was only confirmed by Putin after it became clear that it was impossible to hide it from the international community.

The war in Ukraine and Russia's military aggression takes us back to the times of the Cold War and reconfirms the arguments of neo-realists regarding the international order. This means that the whole system of regional and global security architecture in Europe is disturbed in a profound way and Russia poses a significant military threat to the Western community. This is rather ironic considering that Russia wants to be perceived as one of the main centres of the multipolar world order, but it actually destroys the foundations of that order through its actions in Ukraine. Any kind of world order that is based on multipolarity should be founded on the sustainability of the development and stability of the international system under mutual security guarantees capable of preventing a direct military confrontation between the main centres of power. Otherwise, this cannot be regarded as an order, but rather a state of permanent chaos where the risk of a world war is constantly higher.

Russia remains a great power, although already an isolated one. However, this might also mean a dangerous scenario for the future as isolation in foreign policy and political and economic stress at home might urge Moscow to become even more aggressive in order to find a way out of this situation. It should also be remembered that Russia is no longer committed to the creation of a common European and Euro-Atlantic security framework, which makes it even harder to achieve a breakthrough in its relations with the Western community. One possible way to initiate a new understanding between Russia and the West might be the sacrifice of Ukraine by the global powers for the sake of avoiding a direct confrontation between the two actors. However, as also indicated by the former US Secretary of State Rex Tillerson, Washington claims it will "never accept Russia's occupation and attempted annexation of Crimea" (The New York Times 2017). Therefore, it seems that the US and its allies are determined not to tolerate Russia's fait accompli over Ukraine. This means that the clash of interests between Russia and the West will not come to an end in the foreseeable future.

References

Airforce Technology. 2018. UK Typhoons Intercept Russian Su-24 Bomber over Black Sea. July 30. https://www.airforce-technology.com/news/uk-typhoons-intercept-russian-su-24

BBC News. 2015. Putin: Russia to Boost Nuclear Arsenal with 40 Missiles. June 16. http://www.bbc.com/news/world-33151125.

Glebov, Sergii. 2007. The Russian Black Sea Fleet and Ukraine's Security Strategy: Agenda 2017. In *Military Bases: Historical Perspectives, Contemporary Challenges*, ed. Luis Rodrigues and Sergiy Glebov, 181–187. Amsterdam: IOS Press.

———. 2009a. Constructing or Deconstructing Democracy? The Geopolitical Context of Ukraine's Democratic Choice. In *Identities and Politics During the Putin Presidency: The Foundations of Russia's Stability*, ed. Philipp Casula and Jeronim Perovic, 276–289. Stuttgart: Ibidem-Verlag.

———. 2009b. Concerning 'Strange' Relations: Extensive Perceptions of Security Spaces Within the Ukraine-Russia-NATO Triangle. *Russian Politics and Law* 47 (5): 52–65. https://doi.org/10.2753/RUP1061-1940470504.

———. 2015. Association Agreement Between Ukraine and the EU with Russia as Institutional Phenomenon of "Bad" and Good Governance. In *Governance and Participation: The Black Sea*, ed. Melanie Sully, 63–72. Vienna: Institute for Go-Governance.

———. 2016. Russia's Policy Towards the Black Sea Region and EU-Russia Relations. In *Avoiding a New 'Cold War': The Future of EU-Russia Relations in the Context of the Ukraine Crisis*, ed. Cristian Nitoiu, 57–63. London: LSE Ideas. http://www.lse.ac.uk/ideas/Assets/Documents/reports/LSE-IDEAS-Avoiding-a-New-Cold-War.pdf

Gov.uk. 2014. The UK Is Deeply Alarmed by the Escalation of Russian Military Intervention in Eastern Ukraine. August 28. https://www.gov.uk/government/speeches/the-uk-is-deeply-alarmed-by-the-escalation-of-russian-military-intervention-in-eastern-ukraine

Ieee.es. 2015. Russian National Security Strategy, December 2015—Full-Text Translation. http://www.ieee.es/Galerias/fichero/OtrasPublicaciones/Internacional/2016/Russian-National-Security-Strategy-31Dec2015.pdf

Kremlin.ru. 2008. Foreign Policy Concept of the Russian Federation. July 15. http://en.kremlin.ru/supplement/4116

———. 2015. Speech at the Valdai International Discussion Club. October 22. http://en.kremlin.ru/events/president/news/50548

Kureev, Artem. 2015. Russia's Military Overtures in Crimea Provoke a NATO Response. *Russia Direct*, July 28. http://www.russia-direct.org/opinion/russias-military-overtures-crimea-provoke-nato-response

Meyer, Henry. 2015. Russia Was Ready for Crimea Nuclear Standoff, Putin Says. *Bloomberg*, March 15. http://www.bloomberg.com/news/articles/2015-03-15/russia-was-ready-for-crimea-nuclear-standoff-putin-says

Ministry of Foreign Affairs. 2013. Concept of the Foreign Policy of the Russian Federation. February 18. http://www.mid.ru/en/foreign_policy/official_documents/-/asset_publisher/CptICkB6BZ29/content/id/122186

———. 2015. Foreign Minister Sergey Lavrov's Remarks and Replies to Questions at the Russian Terra Scientia Educational Youth Forum on Klyazma River, Dvoriki, Vladimir Region. August 24. http://en.mid.ru/en/web/guest/foreign_policy/news/-/asset_publisher/cKNonkJE02Bw/content/id/1680936

———. 2016. Concept of the Foreign Policy of the Russian Federation. December 1. http://www.mid.ru/en/foreign_policy/official_documents/-/asset_publisher/CptICkB6BZ29/content/id/2542248

Msz.gov.pl. 2014. Memorandum on Security Assurances in Connection with Ukraine's Accession to the Treaty on the NPT. February 6. https://www.msz.gov.pl/en/p/wiedenobwe_at_s_en/c/MOBILE/news/memorandum_on_security_assurances_in_connection_with_ukraine_s_accession_to_the_treaty_on_the_npt

NATO.int. 2016. Warsaw Summit Communiqué. July 9. https://www.nato.int/cps/en/natohq/official_texts_133169.htm

NATO.pa.int. 2017a. Lawmakers Debate Black Sea Tensions, Urge NATO to Stand Firm on Russia. October 7. https://www.nato-pa.int/news/lawmakers-debate-black-sea-tensions-urge-nato-stand-firm-russia

———. 2017b. NATO PA Backs Resolute Response to Security Challenges on Eastern and Southern Borders. October 9. https://www.nato-pa.int/news/nato-pa-backs-resolute-response-security-challenges-eastern-and-southern-borders

Parl.ca. 2017. Report of the Canadian NATO Parliamentary Association Respecting Its Participation in the 95th Rose-Roth Seminar. July 3–5. https://www.parl.ca/DocumentViewer/en/IIA/visit-report/9209232

Peterson, Nolan. 2015. Russia Sends Nuclear-Capable Bombers to Crimea. *The Daily Signal*, March 20. http://dailysignal.com/2015/03/20/russia-sends-nuclear-capable-bombers-to-crimea

Rusemb.org.uk. 2015. The Military Doctrine of the Russian Federation. June 29. https://www.rusemb.org.uk/press/2029

Russia Beyond. 2016. Russia to Open New Naval Base in Black Sea to Counter NATO. June 29. https://www.rbth.com/defence/2016/06/29/russia-to-open-new-naval-base-in-black-sea-to-counter-nato_607229

Schpeicher, Tatiana. 2015. Yevropeyskiye parlamentarii obespokoyeny ugrozami RF razmestit' v Krymu yadernoye oruzhiye. *RBC.ua*, June 9. http://www.rbc.ua/rus/analytics/evropeyskie-parlamentarii-obespokoeny-ugrozami-1433848437.html

Seib, Gerald F. 2017. Ash Carter Says Putin Is Making It Harder for U.S. to Work with Russia. *The Wall Street Journal*, January 6. http://www.wsj.com/articles/ash-carter-says-putin-is-making-it-harder-for-u-s-to-work-with-russia-1483698600

Sukhankin, Sergey. 2017. Russia Pours More Military Hardware into 'Fortress Crimea'. *Eurasia Daily Monitor* 14 (147). https://jamestown.org/program/russia-pours-military-hardware-fortress-crimea

TASS. 2015a. Deployment of Russian Nuclear Weapons in Crimea Possible—Foreign Ministry. March 11. http://tass.ru/en/russia/782071

———. 2015b. Polpred v Krymu ob'yavil poluostrov 'nepristupnoy krepost'yu'. February 19. http://tass.ru/politika/1779223

The New York Times. 2017. Tillerson Says the U.S. Will Never Accept Crimea Annexation. December 7. https://www.nytimes.com/2017/12/07/world/europe/rex-tillerson-russia-trump.html

The Washington Post. 2014. Transcript: Vladimir Putin's April 17 Q&A. April 17. http://www.washingtonpost.com/world/transcript-vladimir-putins-april-17-qanda/2014/04/17/ff77b4a2-c635-11e3-8b9a-8e0977a24aeb_story.html

Withnall, Adam. 2015. Vladimir Putin Says Russia Was Preparing to Use Nuclear Weapons 'If Necessary' and Blames US for Ukraine Crisis. *Independent*, March 16. http://www.independent.co.uk/news/world/europe/vladimir-putin-says-russia-was-preparing-to-use-nuclear-weapons-if-necessary-and-blames-us-for-10109615.html

Russia's Power Politics Towards Ukraine: Social Status Concerns and the Role of Emotions

Regina Heller

INTRODUCTION

One of the prominent narratives about the drivers of Russia's current coercive policy vis-à-vis Ukraine describes Russian conduct as an attempt of a regional power to defend its geopolitical supremacy over the region against Western influence, both institutionally (EU and NATO eastward expansion) and normatively (democratic political rule and values) (e.g. Mearsheimer 2014). Russian top officials have themselves rhetorically contributed to this geopolitical interpretation as they recurrently underlined that Russia holds special and "exclusive" rights in the region and that

This chapter draws on Regina Heller, "Defending Social Status: Why Russia's Ukraine Policy Is About More than Regional Leadership", *Rising Powers Quarterly* 3, no. 1 (2018): 137–59. http://risingpowersproject.com/quarterly/defending-social-status-why-russias-ukraine-policy-is-about-more-than-regional-leadership/

R. Heller (✉)
University of Hamburg, Hamburg, Germany
e-mail: heller@ifsh.de

E. Parlar Dal, E. Erşen (eds.), *Russia in the Changing International System*, https://doi.org/10.1007/978-3-030-21832-4_10

any attempts to penetrate what is informally still termed the "near abroad" will be pre-empted with adequate countermeasures (Kremlin.ru 2008). All this is rhetorically embedded into a global context, namely the idea that Russia has to fight against Western and in particular US "imperialism" or "colonialism" that creates instability in the world in favour of a new, "better" and more stable global order, in which the US is balanced by a multitude of regional poles including Russia.

This interpretation however ignores a number of paradoxes. First, in its coercive attempts to preserve regional primacy, Russia's leadership status is materially and ideationally more challenged than ever. Second, Russia has acted in Ukraine according to international principles whose validity it rejects precisely in this region—namely liberal interventionism and liberal humanism. These paradoxes require us to revise our thinking—both about Russia's motives and the logic of geopolitics. I suggest an alternative approach, which puts socio-emotional factors at the centre of attention. I argue that Russian "geopolitics" is not primarily driven by security-induced survival strategies and the goal to secure regional leadership, but to a significant extent by the Russian regime's moral expectations about Russia's legitimate and rightful place and role in world politics—its social status—as well as respective attempts to restore that status. I argue from a perspective of social psychology. From this perspective, Russia's policy has its origins in the country's elites' moral concern over international social status, that is, a positively distinctive identity in the international social order. In the neighbourhood, it is a traditional understanding of power and influence that constitutes this positive, collective identity. Social psychology and more recent findings from the International Relations (IR) research on emotions help us understand that Russian status concerns are embedded in negative experiences of status deprivation and misrecognition by the West throughout the post–Cold War era (Forsberg et al. 2014; Heller 2014; Larson and Shevchenko 2014). In order to better understand how regime identity shapes Russian foreign policy conduct towards Ukraine, I put forward the following hypotheses:

1. Risk assessments and judgements about the costs and gains of Russia's policy towards Ukraine are made on subjective, namely socio-emotional, grounds that tend to impede absolute payoffs. We should therefore see a number of costs and unintended effects incurring to Russia that tend to undermine the goal of securing or enhancing regional leadership.

2. The socio-emotional experience that is the structural basis for the regime's identity narrative is used as a strategic resource to produce status in the discursive space. We should therefore find strong evidence of emotions in the form of status-related moral argumentation in the official rhetoric justifying Russia's behaviour towards Ukraine.

In order to probe my claim, I will search for evidence of identity-induced attempts of social status restoration in Russia's Ukraine policy. In the chapter's second part, I outline the theoretical basis of my approach, drawn mainly from social psychology, IR emotions research and the power transition literature. In the third section, I trace the socio-emotional roots of the social status concerns of the Russian regime. In the fourth section, I show the way in which the Russian regime pursues its status-seeking strategy in the context of the ongoing conflict with Ukraine by (a) weighing the gains of Russia's aggressive status-seeking strategy vis-à-vis Ukraine against the costs, thereby assessing how far Moscow's power-politics enhances the country's regional power and influence; and (b) showing the strategic use of emotional markers, in particular moral justifications, in the official discourse that link back to and take up frames that are connected with past subjective experiences of status denial. In the fourth section, I summarize the findings and assess the added value of my perspective.

Identity and Emotions as Sources for Russian Power Politics Towards Ukraine

The status of major powers in international relations is measured along material capabilities (e.g. military and economic resources), but also the social recognition of major power status by other countries (Volgy et al. 2011, 7; Levy 1983). A power is "status-consistent" when it is legitimately recognized as having both capabilities and willingness, as being independent to become involved in international politics, and is expected to do so. A status-inconsistent power, on the contrary, faces a mismatch between capabilities, willingness and independence on the one hand and community-based status recognition on the other (Volgy et al. 2011, 10–12). While "status-overachievers" get status recognition from others, but lack the attributes to act accordingly, "status-underachievers" are willing and have the power to act as major powers, although they do not receive the recognition from other members of the international community. Status-overachievers are usually interested in keeping the status quo and they are assumed to defend their status in their neighbourhood at low costs and risks, while status-underachievers pursue more aggressive strategies in order to "resolve uncertainty around their status" and "create larger roles for themselves in international affairs" (Volgy et al. 2011, 11).

Here is where psychological elements come in. Status-underachievers are usually more willing to take greater risks and pay greater costs to achieve status-consistency. As they are, psychologically speaking, operating in a "domain of loss" that tends to neglect properly assessing the consequences and outcomes of events with clarity, decisions are prone to errors and miscalculations (McDermott 1998, 15). Moreover, decision-makers can interpret the domain they are operating in on the basis of either objective or subjective judgements. In the latter case, it is more important how an actor "feels" about the environment or a specific situation than the objective situation he/she faces. Psychologically inspired IR strands have for long acknowledged that the "feeling" of status recognition is emotionally relevant in international relations (Crawford 2000; Mercer 2006; Paul et al. 2014). One strand that explicitly links status and emotions is the Social Identity Theory (SIT). According to SIT, it is an actor's (i.e. decision-maker's) social identification and emotional attachment with a specific group (or collective) identity that gives relevance to subjective assessments of status. Larger collectives and their representatives (political decision-makers, people in high state functions) try to develop and preserve a positively distinctive identity and want to be accepted as a valuable member of their status-group or community (Tajfel 1978).[1]

Being recognized in one's (collective) self-identity is thus socially and emotionally important also for "states"—or what should be rather defined as composite actors in official state positions. Perceptions of misrecognition, unfair or deliberately harmful treatment trigger negative emotional reactions and attitudes that come close to what is described as "anger" in psychological studies on individual behaviour (Tajfel 1978)—as "negative phenomenological (or internal) feeling state associated with specific cognitive and perceptual distortions and deficiencies … subjective labelling, physiological changes, and action tendencies to engage in socially constructed and reinforced organized behavioural scripts" (Kassinove 1995, 7). It is important to note that anger is not only and primarily about aggression (Averill 1983), but a multitude of cognitive and behavioural short-term and long-term reactions that aim at reverting the discrepancy between the "as-is" situation and the desired and aspired status structure in a social relationship. Gerhards (1988, 12–13) clusters these reactions as behavioural and cognitive "coping strategies". Behavioural coping consists of active attempts to intervene in the social environment with the goal to change the status-power structure and, this way, modulate the virulent emotion. Cognitive coping refers to changes in the mental state through a re-interpretation of "self" and "other" representations, which is mainly based on moral categories.

It has been widely recognized that Russia's foreign policy is to a significant extent influenced by ideational concerns, in particular by the current political elite's consideration that the country deserves to occupy the status of a great power in international relations. This is a status which is consistent with Russia's historical identity, generated and consolidated under the Czarist empire and later on during the Cold War (Tsygankov 2006) and a status that—according to the current official narrative in Moscow—the West has denied Russia ever since the breakup of the Soviet Union (Forsberg et al. 2014). This vision of Russia as a major power mainly refers to the country's position as a powerful and influential actor in world politics.

The pre-occupation with Russia's status in the elite and public discourse is not new. For the Russian leaders, it was clear from the beginning that post-Soviet Russia should remain in a prominent position in world politics. After the dissolution of the Soviet Union and the end of the bipolar system, the question of Russia's national identity and role in world politics became a matter of intensive domestic debate among the public and the political elites (Tsygankov 2006). As early as 1993, a common denominator emerged in the debate, namely that Russia has always been and must continue to be a great power. As the old bipolar system vanished, Russia had to define itself in a new systemic structure of international relations. Then Foreign Minister Yevgeny Primakov was the first to establish the idea of an influential and powerful Russia in a multipolar world in the second half of the 1990s in Russia's foreign policy strategy. The idea of Russia as a great power relied on traditional conceptions, as prescribed in the Russian security culture, and has ever since been a constitutive component of Russia's foreign policy concepts. In fact, from the perspective of the Russian leadership and political elite, the country was seen as a "natural" member of the elite club of powerful states after the Cold War (Light 2014, 215).

Undoubtedly, post-Soviet Russia possesses the attributes to fulfil the criteria for being a major power in world politics. It holds the second largest arsenal of nuclear weapons after the US. Moreover, as the legal successor to the USSR, it is a permanent member of the United Nations Security Council (UNSC) and thus continues to hold an influential position in world politics. However, its economic potential and resources have significantly lagged behind the conceded power attributes throughout the 1990s, and greater Russian political influence in world politics has not materialized for a long time. Therefore, in Western political and academic circles, Russia was not perceived as having fulfilled the criteria for being a great power and rather seen as a status-overachiever for most of the post-Soviet period (Freire 2011).

In the late 1990s, with a still strong Euro-Atlantic orientation and the lack of economic resources to actively strengthen its international status, Russian representatives repeatedly complained about the Western "disrespect" and ignorance vis-à-vis Russian interests and reservations—for instance, in the case of NATO enlargement (Larson and Shevchenko 2014) or the NATO intervention in Kosovo in 1999 (Heller 2014). Status concerns gained momentum with the country's economic recuperation after the turn of the millennium and a more assertive rhetoric towards the West developed, which found its first expression in President Putin's speech at the Munich Security Conference in 2007 (Kremlin.ru 2007). In addition, a more assertive and uncompromising foreign policy that resembled the status-underachiever attitude, fed by feelings of anger and resentment over Western misrecognition, brought Russia increasingly in conflict with the West over social recognition and status. A statement made by Dmitry Rogozin, then Russian representative at NATO, immediately after the Russian-Georgian war of 2008 shows quite amply how such negative experiences of disrespect form emotional pre-dispositions and influence Russia's foreign policy behaviour: the West "… has now started to look at Russia differently—namely with respect—and I consider this to be Russia's key diplomatic achievement" (Russian Mission to NATO 2008).

In that sense, it can be stipulated that the Russian regime has adopted a status-underachiever perspective throughout the years. It bases its judgement of the international status structure and its own position in this structure on subjective, rather than objective grounds. The feeling of continued disrespect feeds feelings of anger and triggers attempts to reduce the emotional status discrepancy.

RUSSIA'S STATUS-SEEKING STRATEGY IN UKRAINE AND THE INFLUENCE OF EMOTIONS

Behavioural Level: Enhancing Russia's Leadership Status in the Neighbourhood

Material Costs

As a result of its interference in Crimea and Eastern Ukraine in 2014, after the escalation of the "Euromaidan" protests and dismissal of the pro-Russian Viktor Yanukovych government in Kiev, Russia has changed the geopolitical landscape in such a radical way that it now controls two Ukrainian territories—Crimea directly and the Donbas region indirectly. But keeping further control of these territories comes with significant long-term as well as unintended costs, supporting the assumption that Moscow strongly underestimated Ukrainian resistance and resilience to Russia's hybrid warfare. Although Russia invested comparably little financial resources for its immediate operations in both Eastern Ukraine and Crimea, it has faced considerable additional expenditures. As calculated by political analysts from the data taken from the Russian federal budget for 2017, "… the costs of the military involvement in Ukraine are estimated to amount to over $40 billion on military personnel and equipment, on refugees and on subsidies for Crimea" (The Moscow Times 2016). Moscow quite unwillingly took over the financial responsibility of the separatist entities in Donbas only after a year of violent conflict. In 2016, Russia started to bankroll pensions and social benefits as well as salaries to local employees in the public sphere and to the armed separatists. The International Crisis Group (2016, 2) calculated that "[i]f consistently maintained, this will cost [Russia] over $1 billion a year, a substantial sum for the Russian treasury in straitened economic times".

Information about the human costs of the military intervention vary and are contradictory, but estimates from 2016 based on information from the Russian Soldiers' Mothers Association points to over 2000 casualties (Shakov 2016). With regard to Crimea, Moscow has strengthened the integration of the peninsula into the Russian Federation, mainly by providing subsidies for economic development and modernization. Here, it equally faces long-term costs of modernization and social benefit transfers. These subsidies and investments already in 2015 were estimated as $4.5–7 billion annually (Berman 2015). Potential economic gains either cannot fully outweigh these investments—for instance, through the cancellation of the Kharkov Agreement securing the presence of the Russian Black Sea Fleet in Sevastopol until 2042 in exchange for "a $100 discount per thousand cubic meters for Ukraine's imports of Russian gas" (Bush 2014)—or are highly uncertain without the help of Western technology—for instance, through future assets from natural gas exploitation in the Crimean shoreline.[2]

The decision of the US and EU to impose sanctions on Russia as a reaction to its coercive policy towards Ukraine took the leadership in Moscow by surprise, although all in all, their impact on Russia's overall economy is assumed to be rather moderate (Russell 2016). The most serious and long-term effect is presumably the disintegration of the Russian firms from Western capital markets and a general worsening of the investment climate. Yet, both President Putin and Prime Minister Medvedev keep insisting that the economic repercussions of the Western sanctions helped to stabilize rather than exert more pressure on Russia's economy (Euronews 2016). They argue that the country is increasingly facing hostility from its geopolitical environment, which legitimizes the turn away from macro-economic development towards a militarized economy (Connolly 2016). The strategic subordination of the economy to short-term concerns of national security makes the overall costs of Russia's power politics particularly difficult to absorb and keeps Russia's geopolitical control over Ukraine unstable.

Consequences for Russia's Legitimacy as a Regional Leader

Power politics has strengthened Putin's rule and legitimacy in Russia, but not necessarily Russia's legitimacy as a leader in the region. Russia was indeed able to prevent Ukraine from moving closer to NATO, but it could not stop Kiev's rapprochement with the EU. On the contrary, Ukraine was even more determined to sign an agreement with the EU for the Deep and Comprehensive Free Trade Area (DCFTA). Political as well as public resistance against any kind of Russian interference in the political processes in the country has strongly increased.

Yet, Russia faces a legitimacy problem well beyond Ukraine. Its severe economic problems in combination with the more imperial attitude of its political elites with regard to the post-Soviet neighbours have resulted in a situation where not only the more critical and Western-oriented countries such as Ukraine and Georgia but also those that had so far been willing to cooperate—particularly those that joined the Eurasian Economic

Union (EAEU) which is Moscow's favourite regional integration project (Libman 2017)—have further distanced themselves away from Russia. The latter group of countries has embarked on a more cautious positioning and started to more independently renegotiate their relations with Russia.

Kazakhstan, for example, is one of Russia's most important partners in military, economic and political terms in the region. It is a member of the EAEU as well as the Collective Security Treaty Organization (CSTO). It has been highly interested in regional economic integration from the very beginning and is principally committed to joint projects with Russia. Since the Ukrainian crisis, however, Kazakhstan has become highly sensitive about the Russian attempts to constrain national sovereignty in Ukraine as well as Moscow's claims about its right and duty to protect ethnic Russians all across the post-Soviet space. Russian politicians have made similar statements that targeted Kazakhstan. In a statement, for instance, Putin claimed that Kazakhstan "never had a state" and that "Kazakhs never had any statehood" (RFERL 2014). The Kazakh authorities reacted by amending the country's penal code in order to punish those who threatened the country's territorial integrity and called for secession. Moreover, Kazakh President Nursultan Nazarbaev introduced more nationalistic elements in the domestic discourse regarding the EAEU. In August 2014, for example, he publicly recalled the country's right to withdraw from the EAEU in case its sovereignty was threatened (Tengrinews 2014). Another source of politicization within the EAEU was Russia's unilateral decision to impose counter-sanctions against the West. In Kazakhstan's view, Moscow displayed an increased selectiveness and violated its commitment to be bound by common rules in the field of economic policy coordination as this decision had to be taken after consulting the other EAEU members (Dragneva and Wolczuk 2017, 12).

While Russia's relations with Belarus had occasionally been ambivalent and problematic already before the Ukraine crisis, dissonances have considerably increased thereafter as well. Minsk, which is economically highly dependent on Russia, used Moscow's conflict with Kiev in combination with the overall weak Russian economic performance more strategically to enhance its own political and economic standing vis-à-vis Moscow and to ask for better conditions in the bilateral relationship. While Belarus joined Russia in March 2014 and voted against the UN declaration calling the Crimean referendum invalid, President Alexander Lukashenko later adopted a nationalistic "fraternization" rhetoric claiming solidarity with

Ukraine (Sedova 2017). This more critical rhetoric towards Russia evolved in the context of an ongoing economic dispute that was mainly about Russia's energy delivery and prices for Belarus (Lavnikevich 2017).

With regard to Armenia, another Russian ally in the post-Soviet space and equally dependent on Russia, the governmental relations did not significantly deteriorate. Both Yerevan and Moscow still benefit more from cooperation than conflict. However, the Ukrainian crisis amplified the ideological split that existed between the pro-Russian and pro-Western segments of the Armenian society (Minasyan 2015), which resulted in a new upheaval for more democracy in the country and the conclusion of a redesigned agreement with the EU in 2017.

Cognitive Level: A Discursive (Re)production of Russia's Global Power Status

Claiming International Status Through Moral Authority

The international community condemned Russia's annexation of Crimea as a violation of Ukraine's territorial integrity and referred to the assurances that were given by Russia to its neighbour after the dissolution of the Soviet Union in 1991 to respect and guarantee the borders then agreed upon. Likewise, Russia's military and political support to the pro-Russian separatists in Donbas was sharply criticized as the violation of Ukraine's sovereignty. Interestingly, Moscow's justification for its policy—first, that there was no annexation whatsoever, but that the Crimean people decided themselves with a referendum to secede from the Ukrainian state and seek integration with Russia; and second, that Moscow only protected its "compatriots" or ethnic minorities from a "criminal", "fascist" and therefore "illegitimate" regime in Kiev (Kremlin.ru 2014a)—makes a strong normative-ethical point, constructing the justification for the intervention along a security logic that takes on a non-state centric perspective of liberal humanism.

This is interesting because in the international context, Moscow was already quite critical about "humanitarian intervention" and the application of the principle of Responsibility to Protect (R2P) and stood at the forefront in criticizing the way it was applied by the Western powers in the past: "Events such as Kosovo, Afghanistan, Iraq, Libya, and Syria have, for Russia, become precedents by which Western powers have 'instrumentalized' the principle of humanitarian intervention, and later R2P, to further their own agendas internationally" (Snetkov and Lanteigne 2014, 122). In Kosovo, Russia accused the West of side-lining the UN, while in Iraq, it criticized the false pretences used by the West. In Libya, on the other hand, it witnessed that its "silent consent" (through abstention in the UNSC) to the international military intervention mandate was misused by the West for its own purposes.

This moral blaming along the argument that the West acts selfishly and abuses international norms was taken up again in Ukraine. It was applied in particular with regard to insinuated Western "orchestration" of the Euromaidan protests in Kiev. The West in the Russian perception not only supported the "unconstitutional" regime change in Ukraine but actively engineered the civil society forces that finally enacted the revolution (Kremlin.ru 2014a). The Russian framing suggests that the West displayed an interventionist practice which once again misrecognized the internationally formulated limits of ethically grounded external intervention; that it operated beyond international law; and that it followed the logic of the former US President George W. Bush: "You are either with us, or against us" (Ministry of Defence 2015). This is also supported by the statement by Vladimir Churkin, Russia's representative to the UN, who underlined that the Western policy towards Ukraine resembled a "game without rules" (Ministry of Foreign Affairs 2014).

Hence, rather than justifying their Ukraine policy as objectively "correct", Russian representatives sought to present their behaviour as morally "right", compared to a morally "wrong" Western approach. This distinction between the "good" Russian and the "bad" Western interventionist practice is also hinted in Putin's sarcastic comment about the Western protests to the annexation of Crimea as well as their reference to international law, where he stated that they have "finally called to their minds that there is something like international law. Thank you very much. Better late than never" (Kremlin.ru 2014a).

Re-claiming Great Power Status Through Moral Argumentation
A second important morality-based argument is constructed around the Western unfairness, unequal treatment and humiliation of Russia. Not only is the West blamed for ignoring (and violating) the rules of the international system, as explained earlier, but also it is blamed for ignoring and refusing Russia's equal "right" to be consulted and taken into consideration regarding the Western policy towards Ukraine. This right is on the one hand justified with historicism and historic re-interpretation, that is,

the construction of Russia-Ukraine relations as being "inseparable" (Kremlin.ru 2014a). On the other hand, there is also an emotionally inspired moral line of argumentation, which takes up the ruminating feeling of Russia being ignored by the West, blindsided, and put on a second-rank position in the international social order. This becomes obvious in official statements that reflect on the way in which Western integration models were introduced in the post-Soviet space. Officially, the cause for contention in Ukraine appeared to be the EU's association policy and that Russia had not been consulted on equal footing on these plans. However, in a relatively high number of statements, various speakers from Russia also refer to their right of being consulted as well as their former negative experiences with NATO as a proof of the Western "ignorance" and "betrayal" (Kremlin.ru 2014a).

In fact, much of the emotion-inspired rhetoric that emerged in the Russian discourse in the context of NATO enlargement and embarked on Russia's humiliation re-appeared prominently in the anti-Western discourse over the Ukraine conflict. One of them is the "Western dictate" image. Putin regularly criticized the West for its "dictate" vis-à-vis Russia and blamed the US to treat Russia as a "vassal". The dictate-vassal-image is not new. The first time it appeared was after NATO's military intervention in Kosovo in 1999 and it was invoked again in many occasions by Putin in the context of the missile defence issue (e.g. Pervy Kanal 2012). In the Ukrainian case, it was again extended from the initial context of NATO enlargement to the US and EU policy towards Ukraine. Russian officials argue that the EU forced Ukraine to cooperate and stop collaborating with Russia within the EAEU. Again, the economic terms of cooperation between Ukraine and the EU in the eyes of the Russian officials would lead to a situation in which the relations between Russia and Ukraine are "dictated by Brussels" (Medvedev 2014).

As much as the Russian leaders discursively discredit the Western intervention practices on moral grounds, thereby "undoing" the Russian mistakes, they also attempt to discursively fight against the perceived Western humiliation by turning the tables and rhetorically humiliating the West. In the following statement, for instance, Putin in a bitter tone suggested that the troubles the Western countries experienced after "meddling" in Ukraine's domestic affairs and ignoring Russia served them right: "The West would have been well advised to consider the consequences of its influencing the situation in Ukraine before" (Kremlin.ru 2014b).

The negative emotional attitude of *Schadenfreude*, that is, open displays of satisfaction about Ukrainian and Western political setbacks, is also frequently expressed in the following way: Ukraine does not deserve Russia's help as it did not listen to Moscow's warnings, and it must therefore now pay the price for its decisions which will cause "very hard times" for the country. Medvedev (2014), for instance, prophesized that "the hardest part still lies in front of our neighbours". Through such open expressions of satisfaction about the setbacks confronted by the West and Ukraine, Russian officials discursively reject to cooperate with the West on the solution of the Ukraine conflict.

CONCLUSION

Prominent explanations view Russia's policy in the Ukraine crisis and its subsequent geopolitical confrontation with the West as a proof of a power-driven strive for regional leadership. This chapter demonstrated that this explanation carries in itself a number of paradoxes which need further explanation. I argued that Russian geopolitics is primarily a function of enhancing its social status as a global power, and not securing regional leadership as a function of security in the first place. We need to understand Russia's aggressive stance as part of an attempt to restore a positively distinctive identity that is acceptable for the ruling elites in Russia. I based my assumptions on theoretical strands in IR that highlight the socio-emotional foundations of foreign policy and the relevance of social status recognition. I argued that the Russian political elite over the years developed an underachiever perspective that is firmly rooted in negative experiences and perceptions of misrecognition of its traditional international status by the West. Russia's past experiences and its unresolved status conflict with the West strongly inform Moscow's current Ukraine policy.

Behaviourally, the Russian leadership clearly acts out of the subjective assessment of a position of loss and pursues a highly risky and costly neighbourhood policy, which has limited geopolitical gains and neglects or miscalculates this policy's immediate and long-term costs and effects. While preventing Ukraine from rapprochement with NATO seems rewarding at first glance, it might turn out as highly counter-productive in the longer term. Moscow will need to provide subsidies to Eastern Ukraine and Crimea for years to come and find ways to pacify these regions and prevent the emergence of spaces of insecurity and instability. Ukrainian resistance and resilience as well as the Western responses to Russia's policies seem to have been underestimated by the status-fixated policy conduct of the Russian elite. Neglecting Russia's domestic modernization in favour of promoting a militarized economy will likely have even more serious long-term implications for Russia's economic and political leadership claim. Moreover, traditional Russian allies have already started to act more along their own strategic interests than on the basis of accepting Russia as the legitimate power centre in the region. If this trend continues, Russia will most likely fail to substantially enhance its material power and status resources in the post-Soviet space in the future.

The analysis of the cognitive level covered the official Russian discourse and rhetoric put forward in defence of Russia's aggressive stance towards Ukraine. The analysis revealed a second layer of meaning underneath the seemingly dominating geopolitical narrative, based on moral categories and invoking earlier negative experiences of status denial from the West. Putting into question the Western practices of intervention, Russia has created highly negative images of the West while depicting itself and its own intervention practices in a positive light. Second, earlier Russian discourses about Western disrespect and being side-lined in matters of European security architecture are re-activated, moralized and trans-formed into Russia's moral right to reject cooperation with the West for the solution of the Ukrainian conflict. In sum, all of this constitutes a strategic attempt to discursively transform the power-status relationship between Russia and the West with Russia de-legitimizing Western superiority and re-claiming a prime rank in a multipolar world order.

Russian policy conduct towards Ukraine and the neighbourhood is often described in an all too simplistic manner in categories of "status quo" or "revisionism". My analytical focus on the socio-emotional foundations of Russian power projection vis-à-vis Ukraine shows that it is not primarily about external security or domestic stability, but about the attempt to bring Russia's international status back into consistence with the regime's moral expectations about the appropriate regional and global order as well as Russia's legitimate place in it. I do not seek to undervalue the role played by external security considerations or domestic interests of powerful groups. Rather, I show how strongly earlier socio-emotional experiences can shape present moral expectations of a ruling elite, influence their risk assessments and form strategic resources for domestic and international debates at a time when the structure of the international system is being re-negotiated.

NOTES

1. While SIT assumes that status-seeking is primarily intrinsically motivated and directed at the approval of a certain social (collective) identity, it does not exclude that the intrinsic driver also co-constitutes external material status-goals.
2. There is "reportedly 45–75 trillion cubic metres of natural gas under the Black Sea" (Maritime Herald 2016).

REFERENCES

Averill, James. 1983. Studies on Anger and Aggression. *American Psychologist* 38 (11): 1145–1160. https://doi.org/10.1037/0003-066X.38.11.1145.

Berman, Ilan. 2015. Paradise Lost in Crimea: How Russia Is Paying for the Annexation. *Foreign Affairs*, September 8. https://www.foreignaffairs.com/articles/ukraine/2015-09-08/paradise-lost-crimea

Bush, Jason. 2014. Factbox: Costs and Benefits from Russia's Annexation of Crimea. *Reuters*, April 8. http://uk.reuters.com/article/uk-ukraine-crisis-crimea-costs-factbox-idUKBREA370NY20140408

Connolly, Richard. 2016. Towards Self Sufficiency? Economics as a Dimension of Russian Security and the National Security Strategy of the Russian Federation to 2020. *NATO Defense College*, July. http://www.ndc.nato.int/news/news.php?icode=964

Crawford, Neta C. 2000. The Passion of World Politics: Propositions on Emotion and Emotional Relationships. *International Security* 24 (4): 116–156. https://doi.org/10.1162/016228800560327.

Dragneva, Rilka, and Kataryna Wolczuk. 2017. The Eurasian Economic Union: Deals, Rules and the Exercise of Power. *Chatham House*, May. https://www.chathamhouse.org/sites/default/files/publications/research/2017-05-02-eurasian-economic-union-dragneva-wolczuk.pdf

Euronews. 2016. Medvedev: Syria, Ukraine and the Economic Crisis—An Exclusive Interview for Euronews. February 14. https://www.euronews.com/2016/02/14/medvedev-syria-ukraine-and-the-economic-crisis-an-exclusive-interview

Forsberg, Tuomas, Regina Heller, and Reinhard Wolf. 2014. Status and Emotions in Russian Foreign Policy. *Communist and Post-Communist Studies* 47 (3): 261–268. https://doi.org/10.1016/j.postcomstud.2014.09.007.

Freire, Maria Raquel. 2011. USSR/Russian Federation's Major Power Status Inconsistencies. In *Major Powers and the Quest for Status in International Politics*, ed. Thomas J. Volgy et al., 55–75. New York: Palgrave Macmillan.

Gerhards, Jürgen. 1988. *Soziologie der Emotionen: Fragestellungen, Systematik und Perspektiven*. Weinheim & München: Juventa.

Heller, Regina. 2014. Russia's Quest for Respect in the International Conflict Management in Kosovo. *Communist and Post-Communist Studies* 47 (3): 333–343. https://doi.org/10.1016/j.postcomstud.2014.09.001.

International Crisis Group. 2016. Russia and the Separatists in Eastern Ukraine. February 5. https://www.crisisgroup.org/file/194/download?token=No_5C5Ti

Kassinove, Howard. 1995. *Anger Disorders. Definition, Diagnosis and Treatment.* London: Routledge.

Kremlin.ru. 2007. Vystupleniye i diskussiya na Myunkhenskoy konferentsii po voprosam politiki bezopasnosti, Myunkhen. February 10. http://kremlin.ru/events/president/transcripts/24034

———. 2008. Interview with Euronews, Sotchi. September 2. http://en.kremlin.ru/events/president/news/1294

———. 2014a. Obrashcheniye prezidenta Rossii o situatsii v Krymu. March 18. http://kremlin.ru/events/president/news/20603

———. 2014b. Zasedaniye mezhdunarodnogo diskussionnogo kluba 'Valdai.' October 24. http://kremlin.ru/events/president/news/46860/photos

Larson, Deborah W., and Alexei Shevchenko. 2014. Russia Says No: Power, Status, and Emotions in Foreign Policy. *Communist and Post-Communist Studies* 47 (3–4): 269–279. https://doi.org/10.1016/j.postcomstud.2014.09.003.

Lavnikevich, Denis. 2017. Kak Belorusiya zarabatyvaet na rossiysko-ukrainskom konflikte? *Gazeta.ru*, January 4. https://www.gazeta.ru/business/2016/12/26/10450733.shtml#page6

Levy, Jack S. 1983. *War in the Modern Great Power System 1495–1975.* Lexington: University Press of Kentucky.

Libman, Alexander. 2017. Russian Power Politics and the Eurasian Economic Union: The Real and the Imagined. *Rising Powers Quarterly* 2 (1): 81–103. http://risingpowersproject.com/quarterly/russian-power-politics-eurasian-economic-union-real-imagined/

Light, Margot. 2014. Foreign Policy. In *Developments in Russian Politics*, ed. Stephen White, Richard Sakwa, and Henry E. Hale, 211–230. London: Palgrave Macmillan.

Maritime Herald. 2016. Ukraine Discovered Large Natural Gas Reserves. December 14. http://www.maritimeherald.com/2016/ukraine-discovered-large-natural-gas-reserves-in-black-sea-shelf/

McDermott, Rose. 1998. *Risk-Taking in International Politics: Prospect Theory in American Foreign Policy.* Ann Arbor: University of Michigan Press.

Mearsheimer, John J. 2014. Why the Ukraine Crisis Is the West's Fault: The Liberal Delusions That Provoked Putin. *Foreign Affairs* 93 (5): 77–89. https://www.foreignaffairs.com/articles/russia-fsu/2014-08-18/why-ukraine-crisis-west-s-fault

Medvedev, Dmitrii. 2014. Rossiya i Ukraina: zhyzn' po novym pravilam'. *Russia in Global Affairs*, December 15. http://www.globalaffairs.ru/global-processes/Rossiya-i-Ukraina-zhizn-po-novym-pravilam-17183

Mercer, Jonathan. 2006. Human Nature and the First Image: Emotion in International Politics. *Journal of International Relations and Development* 9 (3): 288–303. https://doi.org/10.1057/palgrave.jird.1800091.

Minasyan, Sergey. 2015. Armenia and Russia: Pragmatics and Stereotypes. *Russian International Affairs Council*, November 30. http://russiancouncil.ru/en/analytics-and-comments/analytics/armeniya-i-rossiya-pragmatika-i-stereotipy/

Ministry of Defence. 2015. Vystupleniye Ministra oborony Rossiyskoy Federatsii generala armii S.K. Shoigu na IV Moskovskoy konferentsii po mezhdunarodnoy bezopasnosti. April 16. http://mil.ru/pubart.htm?id=12016244%40cmsArticle

Ministry of Foreign Affairs. 2014. Vystupleniye postoyannogo predstaviteliya Rossiyskoy Federatsii pri OON V.I. Churkina na otkrytom zasedanii Soveta Bezopasnosti OON po situatsii na Ukraine. March 3. http://www.mid.ru/vistupleniya_rukovodstva_mid/-/asset_publisher/MCZ7HQuMdqBY/content/id/792739

Paul, T.V., Deborah W. Larson, and William C. Wohlforth. 2014. *Status in World Politics*. New York: Cambridge University Press.

Pervy Kanal. 2012. Interviyu na programme/dokumental'nyi film 'Kholodnaya politika' na Pervom kanale. February 2. https://www.1tv.ru/doc/pro-politiku/holodnaya-politika

RFERL. 2014. Putin Downplays Kazakh Independence, Sparks Angry Reaction. September 3. https://www.rferl.org/a/kazakhstan-putin-history-reaction-nation/26565141.html

Russell, Martin. 2016. Sanctions over Ukraine: Impact on Russia. European Parliamentary Research Service, Briefing EN PE 579.084. March. http://www.europarl.europa.eu/RegData/etudes/BRIE/2016/579084/EPRS_BRI(2016)579084_EN.pdf

Russian Mission to NATO. 2008. Ia predstavlyayu sil'nuyu Rossiyu. August 20. http://natomission.ru/society/article/society/artpublication/25

Sedova, Anna. 2017. Soyuz Rossii i Belorussii tresnul v Kieve. *Svobodnaya Pressa*, July 23. http://svpressa.ru/politic/article/177386

Shakov, Damien. 2016. Over 2,000 Russian Fighters Killed in Ukraine: President's Spokesman. *Newsweek*, July 3. http://europe.newsweek.com/over-2000-russian-fighters-dead-ukraine-presidentsspokesman-434295?rm=eu

Snetkov, Aglaya, and Marc Lanteigne. 2014. 'The Loud Dissenter and Its Cautious Partner'—Russia, China, Global Governance and Humanitarian Intervention. *International Relations of the Asia-Pacific Contemporary Politics* 15 (1): 113–146. https://doi.org/10.1093/irap/lcu018.

Tajfel, Henri. 1978. The Psychological Structure of Intergroup Relations. In *Differentiation Between Social Groups: Studies in the Social Psychology of Intergroup Relations*, ed. Henri Tajfel, 27–98. London: Academic.

Tengrinews. 2014. Nazarbaev napomnil o prave Kazakhstana na vychod iz EAES'. August 25. https://tengrinews.kz/kazakhstan_news/nazarbaev-napomnil-o-prave-kazahstana-na-vyihod-iz-eaes-260719

The Moscow Times. 2016. Kremlin Pledges $593M Boost for Crimean Economy in 2017. May 12. https://themoscowtimes.com/news/kremlin-proposes-593m-boost-for-crimean-economy-in-2017-56418

Tsygankov, Andrei. 2006. *Russia's Foreign Policy. Change and Continuity in National Identity*. Lanham: Rowman & Littlefield.

Volgy, Thomas J., et al. 2011. *Major Powers and the Quest for Status in International Politics: Global and Regional Perspectives*. New York: Palgrave Macmillan.

CHAPTER 11

Russia's New Policy Towards Aspiring Political Movements and Unrecognized States

Victor Jeifets and Nikolay Dobronravin

INTRODUCTION

Russian foreign policy has had many traditions including a tendency to deal with great powers or other influential sovereign states. Smaller and less influential states in the international system were often ignored or

This chapter draws on Victor Jeifets & Nikolay Dobronravin, "Russia's Changing Partners: Sovereign Actors and Unrecognized States", *Rising Powers Quarterly* 2, no. 1 (2017): 211–29. http://risingpowersproject.com/quarterly/russias-changing-partners-sovereign-actors-unrecognized-states/. The research was partially conducted at the Herzen State Pedagogical University of Russia, St. Petersburg, and supported by the Russian Science Foundation (grant number 14-18-00390, the section dealing with the Soviet Union and unrecognized states). It was also partially conducted at the St. Petersburg State University and supported by the Russian Foundation for Humanities (grant number 16-01-00138, the section dealing with the dualism of the Soviet foreign policy).

V. Jeifets (✉) • N. Dobronravin
St. Petersburg State University, St. Petersburg, Russia
e-mail: n.dobronravin@spbu.ru

© The Author(s) 2020
E. Parlar Dal, E. Erşen (eds.), *Russia in the Changing International System*, https://doi.org/10.1007/978-3-030-21832-4_11

treated with contempt by Moscow. During the Soviet period, non-official contacts with national liberation movements were made by "public" organizations such as the "Union of Soviet Societies for Friendship and Cultural Relations with Foreign Countries", rather than the Soviet state. However, since the collapse of the Soviet Union which brought the end of the bipolar world order and especially since the restart of the Cold War between Russia and the Western countries in the past few years, one can observe a certain change in the Kremlin's foreign policy regarding the issue of relations with non-recognized states around the world and/or would-be states across Russia's border.

The goal of this chapter is to evaluate Russia's evolving policy towards the aspiring political movements and unrecognized states in the post-Soviet period. To this end, following a brief discussion about the dualism (i.e. supporting world revolution versus protecting the national interests of Moscow) which was prevalent in the early Soviet policies regarding this issue, the chapter will proceed with a general assessment of the changes in Russia's approach in the aftermath of the collapse of the Soviet Union—making reference to diverse cases including non-Soviet (Western Sahara, Kosovo) and former Soviet (Nagorno-Karabakh, Transnistria, Abkhazia and South Ossetia) regions. Understanding Russia's position regarding these cases is important to evaluate its present perception and discourse about the situation of Crimea and Donbas region following the crisis in Ukraine.

Dualism in Early Soviet Policy

Even in the first decades of the Soviet era, during the period of global communist activities, relations with national liberation movements were led by the Communist International (Comintern), while the Soviet state officially preferred to deal only with sovereign state actors. Moscow's foreign policy during this period was based on a dualism which was aimed at the need to support the world revolution and secure the Soviet national interests at the same time. Yet, the early Soviet dualism resulted in a number of diplomatic conflicts. The objectives of Moscow in establishing relations with the bourgeois countries in the West were quite contradictory, as the Kremlin wanted peaceful coexistence only with their governments, and not the capitalist states (Zagladin 1990, 40–45). One basic principle in Soviet foreign policy was that that the interests of the governments and populations in the West could never be the same as long as capitalism existed in the world. The Soviet diplomacy was inspired by this principle, even when the idea of immediate world proletariat revolution was about to vanish. One should also note that Moscow saw the anti-imperialist movement as one of the precautions to deter an eventual Western intervention against the Soviet Union. In other words, official contacts with foreign states were viewed by Moscow simply as an instrument to maintain the balance in international relations, rather than the principal objective of the revolutionary Soviet foreign policy. The People's Commissar for Foreign Relations Georgi V. Chicherin told it clearly at the 14th Congress of the All-Union Communist Party (Bolsheviks) in 1925:

> We need urgently close contacts with the Communist parties of other countries... I wish much closer contact between the Narkomindel [People's Commissariat for Foreign Relations] and the Executive Committee of the Comintern... The previous situation of some discoordination between the Soviet diplomacy and local Communist parties, is, fortunately, over. We have managed to establish close and permanent (though unofficial, absolutely secret) contacts with the local Communist parties of different countries. (Blinov et al. 1991, 122)

The same approach was also recognized by Georgi Skalov ("Sinani"), the assistant to the Soviet envoy in Bukhara, who later became the chairman of the Latin American Secretariat of the Comintern:

> The main task of our Legation was not like the work of the common diplomats—it was the political preparation for the sovietisation of Bukhara and the organization of the Bukhara Communist Party. (Skalov n.d., 37)

A classic example of dualism in Soviet foreign policy was the activity of Stanislav Pestkovsky, the Soviet envoy to Mexico in the mid-1920s. We completely agree with Richardson's conclusion that, while Soviet diplomacy was trying to settle possible conflicts with the Mexican government, Comintern agents were provoking new conflicts (Richardson 1988, 102). As a matter of fact, the situation was more complicated as Pestkovsky was not only a diplomat but also a Comintern emissary (under the alias "Andrei") (Jeifets and Jeifets 2002). This dualism was not extraordinary, since the Soviet diplomats were either ex-revolutionaries or they usually returned to the Comintern after completing their diplomatic missions. This symbiosis reached the organizational level as well. The top administrators of the Soviet People's Commissariat (Ministry) for Foreign Affairs were also members of the Executive Committee of the Comintern.

The case of Mexico, however, was still different from the European countries. Soviet Union thought the Mexican revolution closely resembled the Bolshevik revolution, and thus there seemed to be no contradiction between diplomatic work and revolutionary activities. Pestkovsky, for instance, was designated as the envoy in Mexico City, as the person who was "able to fulfil the Comintern's American tasks" (Chicherin 1924, 76). He was trying to broaden the Mexican-Soviet relations, while simultaneously making pressure to the local Communist Party in order to change its leadership. As a result of this pressure, there was a rise of ultra-leftist feelings inside the party as well as a rupture between the authorities and left-wing militants.

Yet, the dualism in Soviet foreign policy was not absolute. Moscow placed some limits to the revolutionary activities of the Soviet diplomats and Comintern envoys, at least, in areas which were not promising many perspectives according to the Executive Committee of the Communist International (ECCI). For instance, the Ministry of Foreign Affairs and ECCI were ready to promote the communist activities in Mexico (without taking into account the possible worsening of official relations with the government), while they were unwilling to support the idea of an armed expedition to Venezuela (as proposed by Gustavo Machado, a Venezuelan revolutionary who was supported by Pestkovsky) with the purpose of overthrowing the dictatorship of Juan Vicente Gomez. In fact, Moscow did view Gomez not only as a dictator but also as an unconditional ally of US imperialism in Latin America.

However, the Soviet leadership did not see any prospects of triumph for the revolution in Venezuela and therefore did not want to waste time and money for such plans. The same approach also prevailed regarding the plans of an armed expedition to Cuba (developed by the Cuban revolutionary Julio Antonio Mella who was ready to reach a kind of agreement with bourgeois Unión Nacionalista with the purpose of overthrowing Gerardo Machado's dictatorship) or regarding a communist revolt in Colombia and Ecuador (with the support of the Rockefeller oil corporation). Moscow preferred to avoid direct participation in such projects of doubtful promise (Jeifets and Jeifets 2015). In the latter case, the ECCI was also concerned that the Communist revolt supported by the US-based oil corporation would lead to the creation of a quasi-independent Zulia state and thus to a serious reconfiguration of the political map of Colombia, Ecuador and Venezuela. In other words, Soviets were unwilling to grant support to non-state actors, if there was no definite chance for them to win and transform themselves into states—especially into communist states.

On the other hand, local contacts with would-be states and non-state actors across the Russian/Soviet border were often seen as an embarrassment for the official Soviet foreign policy. One such example was Mongolia's struggle for independence from China in the first decades of the twentieth century. At the local level, Russian merchants and military supported the independence of Mongolia, which was proclaimed in 1911. Russia and China then officially recognized the autonomy of Outer Mongolia under the Chinese suzerainty. After the Bolshevik revolution of 1917, this autonomy was abolished by China. Later, the White Russian and Mongolian forces expelled the Chinese and restored Mongolia's independence. In 1921, the Red Army and its Mongolian allies defeated the White Army. In 1924, in accordance with the Sino-Soviet Treaty, Mongolia was recognized as an integral part of China. The same year, the Mongolian People's Republic was proclaimed and the Soviet Union recognized the new state, although the treaty with China was not annulled.

Soviet diplomats were in favour of the autonomy of Outer Mongolia, while the Executive Committee of the Comintern saw Mongolia as an independent republic which would become a part of the Chinese federation after the eventual victory of the Communists in China (Perepiska 2008, 111 & 119). During World War II, Mongolia declared war on Germany. In 1944, the Soviet Union and US agreed on "the maintenance of the Republic of Outer Mongolia as an independent identity" (U.S. Department of State 1945, 378). After World War II, China recognized the independence of the Mongolian People's Republic. This recognition was then adopted by the People's Republic of China, but annulled by Taiwan. The conundrum continued until 1961, when Moscow and the West reached a deal which permitted Mongolia to join the United Nations (in exchange for the admission of Mauritania, which was previously vetoed by the Soviet delegation). The Mongolian People's Republic remained a client state of the Soviet Union until the 1980s (Murphy 1961; Luzyanin 2003).

Unrecognized States, Decolonization and Dissolution of the Soviet Union

Although the early Soviet dualism disappeared in time, there were some other challenges to Moscow's foreign policy. In the process of decolonization, quite a few states were proclaimed, but they were not recognized by the international community. Most of these states did not last long, while some of them were able to survive for several years and even decades. This group of quasi-sovereign international actors has remained relatively stable in numbers, and all of them tried to behave like "normal" states. There have been many attempts to describe these political entities. Various definitions included "unrecognized states", "de facto states", "self-proclaimed states", "state-like entities", "virtual states", "quasi-states", "states-within-states", "statelets" and even "non-state states". The phenomenon has attracted many scholars, including historians, political anthropologists and geographers (Berg and Toomla 2009; Caspersen 2011; Dobronravin 2013). Understandably, the analysis of such entities is often far from being academic. In the writings supportive of the countries that fell victim to "illegitimate state-building", the very existence of unrecognized states is negated through the consistent use of terms delegitimizing them—for example, "secessionist regions/entities", "separatist territories/regimes", "breakaway territories", "self-proclaimed republics" or "illegal entities" (but never "states").

Many—but not all—unrecognized states are fairly weak and depend on foreign assistance from a third state ("tutor state", "patron state", "external patron/sponsor", "kin-state"). In the twentieth century, the political discourse even included references to "puppet states", a rather clumsy term, as it covers both unrecognized and sovereign recipients of external assistance. Nowadays, such relations may better be defined as "outsourcing" (Popescu 2006). The outsourced functions of a patronized state usually include defence and foreign affairs. Nevertheless, no such entity has ever declared that it would not try to enter the arena of international relations. Full-scale recognition, including membership in international organizations, dominates the political agenda of all unrecognized states. All of them have formulated their own foreign policies, even if they are too weak to implement these policies without an external patron. Seaboard unrecognized states have even developed their own maritime policies, following the rules of 1982 United Nations Convention on the Law of the Sea (UNCLOS), even though they could not join the Convention. A number of legitimate or self-proclaimed subnational entities also emulate sovereign states—for example, in their approach to the seas, maritime boundaries and exclusive economic zones.

Before 1991, Soviet Union avoided open official contacts with unrecognized states. There were very few exceptions (e.g. Algeria in 1960–1962, Guinea Bissau in 1973–1974 or the communist-controlled Republic of South Vietnam in 1969–1975). Yet, in most other cases, no recognition was granted. An illustrative case was Western Sahara. The former Spanish Sahara was claimed by Morocco and Mauritania, while the adjacent Algeria supported the Sahrawis who opted for independence. In 1976, when the intervention of Moroccan forces had already begun, the Popular Front for the Liberation of Saguia el-Hamra and Río de Oro (POLISARIO) proclaimed the Sahrawi Arab Democratic Republic (SADR) without the consent of the former metropolitan state. The majority of the population moved to the refugee camps in Algeria together with the leadership of the new republic. By 1991, the parties to the conflict exhausted all possibilities for a military solution to the problem of Western Sahara, and a ceasefire was brokered by the UN. The POLISARIO front, the government of the self-proclaimed SADR now control about 20 per cent of the territory of the former Spanish Sahara, called "free zones" or "liberated territories". SADR established diplomatic relations with some countries of Sub-Saharan Africa and Latin America. The de facto republic also joined the African Union. The UN sees the Western Sahara as a territory to be decolonized. All the agreements reached under the auspices of the UN have been signed by the representatives of POLISARIO, and not by SADR. Russian policy towards Western Sahara has been influenced by the practical interests of the fishermen who used to deal with the Moroccan authorities. Neither the Sahrawi independence nor the annexation of the Western Sahara by Morocco has been recognized by the Soviet Union.

On the eve of the dissolution of the Soviet Union, some regions opted to break away from their republics: Nagorno-Karabakh from Azerbaijan; Abkhazia and South Ossetia from Georgia; Transnistria from Moldova; and Chechnya from the Russian Federation. When the new sovereign states were born (or recreated) out of the Soviet Union and recognized by the international community, these de facto entities were also eager to emulate them. For instance, the independence of the Republic of Azerbaijan was declared on August 30, 1991, and the Nagorno-Karabakh (Artsakh) Republic declared its independence from Azerbaijan only a few days later. This previously autonomous region was supported by Armenia as a kin-state. And from the perspective of Azerbaijan, this was the result of direct Armenian intervention and occupation. The Nagorno-Karabakh war continued until 1994, when the leaders of Azerbaijan and Armenia agreed on a ceasefire. Yet, until now, no sovereign state including Armenia has recognized the independence of the Nagorno-Karabakh Republic (Kaldor 2006; Dobronravin 2010, 163–66).

All the aforementioned breakaway territories, with the exception of Chechnya, were then transformed into relatively stable unrecognized states. Until 2008, there was a consensus in the world that no such entities should be granted official recognition. In the case of Chechnya, Moscow was able to cope with the crisis only after two wars and reconciliation with some of the Chechen secessionists. At the same time, it used all possible measures to prevent the international recognition of this breakaway region in the Caucasus. Russia's policy was then totally consistent, as neither Chechnya nor any other self-proclaimed states (e.g. Abkhazia and South Ossetia) were officially recognized by Moscow. The post-Soviet consensus on the non-recognition of breakaway entities remained in force for more than a decade under the Yeltsin and Putin administrations.

RUSSIA'S NEW FOREIGN POLICY: A REASSESSMENT

Russian foreign policy started to change by the end of Putin's second presidency and this shift also continued during the presidency of Dmitry Medvedev. Many observers in the West saw February 2007, which was marked by Putin's speech in Munich Security Conference and his visit to the Middle East, as a watershed in Russian foreign policy. Ariel Cohen from the Heritage Foundation was one of those people who described this shift as a rebirth of the Soviet and Russian imperial past:

> To a great degree, contemporary Russian rhetoric has come full circle and resembles the Soviet agenda before President Mikhail Gorbachev's perestroika (restructuring) and glasnost (openness) ... Russia is following the Soviet model of opposing first the British and then the American presence in the Middle East by playing to anti-Western sentiment in the "street" and among the elites. This is something that both Wilhelmine Germany and, later, Nazi Germany tried to do as well .... The image of a new Cold War may be too simplistic to describe the emerging relationship with Russia. In fact, Russian foreign policy has a distinctive late 19th century czarist, post-Bismarckian tinge: muscular, arrogant, overestimating its own power, and underestimating the American adversary that it is busily trying to recreate. This policy is likely to become a self-fulfilling prophecy with dangerous consequences and a high price in treasure and ultimately in blood. (Cohen 2007)

Cohen's description is worth attention primarily because such an approach has become quite common in the Western media. However, mixing together two periods of Russian history as well as various allusions to the past of Germany is contradictory and far from convincing. What remains, in Cohen's own words, is that "while it lacks the global reach of

Soviet ideology and the Soviet Union's military muscle, Russian policy nonetheless limits Washington's freedom to manoeuvre" (Cohen 2007).

By 2007, the relations between Russia and the West were overshadowed by the events in former Yugoslavia and the Western intervention in Kosovo, which resulted with the region's decision to secede from Serbia. The importance of these events should not be exaggerated, but they did play a certain role in the transformation of Russian foreign policy. Cohen noticed that "Russia threatened to apply the precedent of Kosovo independence to recognize the independence of Transnistria, Abkhazia and South Ossetia" and "supported secessionist statelets seeking to undermine the sovereignty of Moldova and Georgia" (Cohen 2007). The paradox was that Transnistria, Abkhazia and South Ossetia grew up as anti-secessionist entities within the former Soviet Union.

Cohen also referred to an interview of Putin with *Al Jazeera*. When asked about his decision to invite the Hamas officials to Moscow, he underlined the election victory of Hamas and claimed that "it is better to work with people who have influence among their country's people and try to transform their position through negotiations than to pretend that they do not exist" (Kremlin.ru 2007). Putin also confirmed that Russia had "very friendly relations" with the Lebanese government as well as Hezbollah and other political groups in Lebanon. This position was apparently different from Moscow's official state-to-state approach, but understandable in the context of Lebanon and particularly Palestine. In both cases, it would be infeasible for Moscow to keep contacts with only one local actor.

The change in Russian foreign policy became more pronounced in 2008, when the Republic of Kosovo proclaimed its independence from Serbia. The International Court of Justice (2010) concluded that "the declaration of independence of February 17, 2008 did not violate general international law" because "general international law contains no applicable prohibition of declarations of independence". Most Western states and several international organizations recognized Kosovo and established diplomatic relations with this new state. However, Russia saw this approach as rule-changing and a precedent for the recognition of Abkhazia and South Ossetia. After the August 2008 war with Georgia, President Medvedev signed the decrees recognizing the independence of Abkhazia and South Ossetia.

Russia continually displayed calm and patience. We repeatedly called for returning to the negotiating table and did not deviate from this position of ours even after the unilateral proclamation of Kosovo's independence. However our persistent proposals to the Georgian side to conclude agreements with Abkhazia and South Ossetia on the non-use of force remained unanswered. Regrettably, they were ignored also by NATO and even at the United Nations …. It is our understanding that after what has happened in Tskhinvali and what has been planned for Abkhazia they have the right to decide their destiny by themselves. The Presidents of South Ossetia and Abkhazia, based on the results of the referendums conducted and on the decisions taken by the Parliaments of the two republics, appealed to Russia to recognize the state sovereignty of South Ossetia and Abkhazia. The Federation Council and the State Duma voted in support of those appeals. A decision needs to be taken based on the situation on the ground. Considering the freely expressed will of the Ossetian and Abkhaz peoples and being guided by the provisions of the UN Charter, the 1970 Declaration on the Principles of International Law Governing Friendly Relations Between States, the CSCE Helsinki Final Act of 1975 and other fundamental international instruments, I signed Decrees on the recognition by the Russian Federation of South Ossetia's and Abkhazia's independence. (Kremlin.ru 2008)

The recognition of Abkhazia and South Ossetia did not mean that Russia was ready to recognize other de facto entities in the former Soviet space. For instance, recognition was not extended to Transnistria. In fact, Russia has supported the territorial integrity of Moldova, even though Russian forces have been stationed in Transnistria. More recently, Russian policy drifted towards more intensive contacts with would-be states and aspiring political movements. After Abkhazia and South Ossetia, no de facto entities were recognized, with the well-known exception of Crimea, but contacts with aspiring political movements became admissible at the official level.

The same dualistic approach is now common in Russia's policy towards the de facto states which were created outside Europe and post-Soviet Eurasia. For instance, Russia now has regular official contacts with the POLISARIO front as a party to the conflict in Western Sahara. At the same time, however, Moscow has refrained from recognizing Western Sahara as an independent state and a sovereign party to the conflict. In this regard, Foreign Ministry Spokesperson Maria Zakharova has reiterated Russia's official position:

We received a number of inquiries regarding the prospects for resolving the territorial dispute over Western Sahara. Indeed, the fate of this former Spanish colony has remained unresolved for over 40 years now. The efforts to develop an acceptable conflict resolution approach for the parties to the conflict—Morocco and the POLISARIO Front—undertaken under the auspices of the United Nations have been repeatedly disrupted for various reasons. Meanwhile, the fragile local status quo causes serious concern, because it is fraught with major challenges to regional security... We operate on the premise that lasting peace in Western Sahara can be achieved exclusively by political means. While maintaining contacts with all interested parties, we will continue to help create positive dynamics in order to achieve a Western Sahara settlement. (Ministry of Foreign Affairs 2018b)

As a rare exception, one can mention the conversation between Sergey Lavrov, Minister of Foreign Affairs, and young diplomats in 2017. Answering a question of a forum participant who presented himself as being "from the Sahrawi refugee camp, a diplomat", Sergei Lavrov said:

... Consultations are being held with all the stakeholders in the run-up to the adoption of such resolutions including the diplomats representing the Western Sahara at the UN. (Ministry of Foreign Affairs 2017)

However, taking into consideration the context of this conversation, Lavrov's answer cannot be treated as a recognition of the position advocated by the POLISARIO front.

In April 2012, as a spillover from the "Arab Spring" across the Sahara, the National Movement for Liberation of the Azawad (MNLA) proclaimed the independence of Azawad in the north of Mali. Within a few months, this de facto state was crushed by the jihadists who were then defeated by the French and their European and West African allies. In 2013, MNLA opened a political dialogue with the Malian government. Russia supported this dialogue as it was based on the inviolability of Mali's territory (Ministry of Foreign Affairs 2012). The situation suddenly changed in March 2014, when a delegation of MNLA visited Moscow and met with Mikhail Bogdanov, Deputy Minister of Foreign Affairs and Special Presidential Representative for the Middle East. The level of the talks apparently came as a shock to the Mali leadership. From the West African perspective, this visit was explained as an attempt by MNLA to find a patron state, taking into account Moscow's reputation of "never letting its friends down" (MEMRI 2014). Although Russia did not support Azawad's independence, MNLA's visit to Moscow heralded a new approach in Russia's foreign policy. Later, there were several public meetings held between Russian officials and various delegations from Syria and Libya, who represented the armed opposition to the governments which were recognized by Russia and the UN. Even taking into account the complexity of the situation in the Middle East, open official contacts with such actors may be seen as a novelty in Russian foreign policy.

In 2016, a new Russian Foreign Policy Concept was adopted, marking a new step in the development of the Russian approach to various international issues. According to this document, "assisting the establishment of the Republic of Abkhazia and the Republic of South Ossetia as modern democratic States, strengthening their international positions, and ensuring reliable security and socioeconomic recovery remains a priority for Russia" (Ministry of Foreign Affairs 2016, clause 57). This meant that Russia would continue to seek wider international recognition and guaranteed security for these two entities (seen as "modern democratic states"), as well as their socio-economic recovery. As for the Transnistrian issue, the Concept stressed the need to respect "the sovereignty, territorial integrity and neutral status of the Republic of Moldova" as well as a future "special status" for Transnistria (Ministry of Foreign Affairs 2016, clause 58). Other post-Soviet de facto states were only mentioned within the context of conflict regulation, with references to "the Nagorno-Karabakh conflict" and "the internal conflict in Ukraine" (Ministry of Foreign Affairs 2016, clauses 56 & 58).

In relation to the Middle East and North Africa, the Concept stated that Russia "consistently promotes political and diplomatic settlement of conflicts in regional States while respecting their sovereignty and territorial integrity and the right to self-determination without outside interference", and as for Syria, "Russia supports the unity, independence and territorial integrity of the Syrian Arab Republic as a secular, democratic and pluralistic State with all ethnic and religious groups living in peace and security and enjoying equal rights and opportunities" (Ministry of Foreign Affairs 2016, clauses 92 & 93). The guiding principles of Russian foreign policy were defined as "independence and sovereignty, pragmatism, transparency, predictability, a multidirectional approach and the commitment to pursue national priorities on a non-confrontational basis" (Ministry of Foreign Affairs 2016, clause 3g).

Russia and the Ukrainian Conundrum Since 2014

The role of Russia in the Ukrainian "revolution of dignity" and the proclamation of several people's republics (e.g. Kharkov, Donetsk, Lugansk and Odessa) in 2014 attracted much more international attention than Russia's contacts with the non-governmental forces in Africa and Middle East. From the Western and post-revolutionary Ukrainian perspective, Russian policy towards Ukraine was defined as a hybrid war, sometimes in an exaggerated way. Zarembo (2016, 4), for instance, argued that "the artificial nature of the separatism in Eastern Ukraine and instigation of conflict by Russia makes this type of conflict unprecedented in global practice".

The surviving people's republics in Donetsk and Lugansk were seen as a mere smokescreen for a direct Russian intervention. When the leadership of the Lugansk People's Republic invited US Senator John McCain to visit and monitor the local elections, McCain (2015) said, "While I do not typically monitor the elections of imaginary countries, I am grateful for this unique invitation. If the so-called 'Lugansk People's Republic' is interested in democratic elections, I suggest its adherents put down their weapons and participate in the next round of elections in a free and united Ukraine". Interestingly, the Western field reports from eastern Ukraine were often more balanced and took into account the local sources of the rebellion against the "revolution of dignity" (Judah 2015). Moscow recognized the short-lived independence of Crimea before the region made a referendum to join the Russian Federation. On the contrary, regular contacts between Russian officials and the leadership of the Donetsk and Lugansk republics have not led to the recognition of these two republics.

The case of Crimea has parallels with the early Soviet experience, not to mention the short-lived republics of Central Lithuania or Hawaii, even though it is something unprecedented in the post-1991 history of Russia and Ukraine. The attitude towards Donetsk and Lugansk followed the post-2008 line of Russian foreign policy, in negation of the idea that the "guided independence" of Kosovo was unique and could not present a precedent for secession elsewhere in the world (for the discussion on this subject, see Summers 2011).

Until now, supporting the rebel entities, Russia has never treated them as independent states comparable to Abkhazia or South Ossetia.

The official discourse oscillated between the terms used in Donetsk/Lugansk and Kiev, never going as far as questioning Ukraine's sovereignty in the region. At a news conference on Russian diplomacy in 2017, Lavrov was confronted with a question: "How important is it for Russia to preserve those pseudo-state entities in eastern Ukraine? The Minsk Agreements say nothing about the DPR or LPR, which you mention so often". The Minister answered: "It refers to some districts of the Donetsk and Lugansk regions. Since this is not a court hearing and I am addressing journalists, I'll permit myself to speak about events in a descriptive manner" (Ministry of Foreign Affairs 2018a).

Russia's approach towards the breakaway republics in the southeast of Ukraine showed itself most clearly in Moscow's reaction to the killing of Alexander Zakharchenko, president of the non-recognized Donetsk People's Republic on August 31, 2018. Putin officially expressed his "deep condolences following the tragic death of Head of the Donetsk People's Republic Alexander Zakharchenko" in the following statement:

> Alexander Zakharchenko was a true leader for his people, a brave and determined man and a Donbas patriot. He protected his homeland during a difficult time, bore a great personal responsibility and led his people. The contemptible murder of Alexander Zakharchenko is further evidence that those who have chosen a path of terror, violence and fear do not want to search for a peaceful political solution to the conflict or have a real dialogue with the people in the southeast, but thrive on destabilization to bring the people of Donbas to their knees. This will not happen. I believe that the organizers and executors will be punished for what they did. I would like to once again express my condolences to Alexander Zakharchenko's family and friends and to all the people of Donbas. Russia will always stand together with you. (Kremlin.ru 2018)

This statement did not include any direct references to Ukraine. However, from the geographical point of view, the vague reference to "southeast" implicitly indicated that the territory in question was still seen as part of Ukraine. On the other hand, the expressions "people of Donbas" and "Donbas patriot" could well be applied to the citizens of a sovereign state.

On the same day, Russia's Foreign Ministry issued another statement with a slightly different wording:

Tragic news from Donetsk—Head of the Donetsk People's Republic Alexander Zakharchenko was killed in a terrorist attack. We express our condolences to Alexander Zakharchenko's friends and family and wish prompt recovery to the wounded and injured in the blast, and we wish Donbas residents courage and stamina. We are confident that an investigation will be held soon and that all the circumstances of that crime will be established and the perpetrators and their sponsors will be identified. However, it is clear that the goal of the terrorist attack was to derail the process of peaceful political settlement in Donbas and the implementation of the Minsk Agreements. It looks especially cynical against the backdrop of the recently announced "back-to-school" ceasefire. The assassination of one of the signatories of the Minsk Package of Measures runs along Kiev's logic of a military solution to the internal Ukrainian crisis. Such actions carry the serious risk of destabilizing the situation in southeast Ukraine. We call on Kiev to stop relying on terrorism to resolve Ukraine's domestic issues. We hope that responsible Ukrainian politicians will find the strength to stop the party of war and prevent the escalation of the confrontation in Donbas. (Ministry of Foreign Affairs 2018c)

Seen through the prism of international relations, the latter statement explicitly confirmed that the territory in question remained part of Ukraine, both geographically and politically. The statement by the Foreign Ministry referred to the "Donbas residents", rather than "people of Donbas". Yet, it should be noted that both statements apparently used the term "Donbas" (abbreviated from the Donets Basin) in the same sense as Donetsk People's Republic.

CONCLUSION: NEW PRAGMATISM IN RUSSIA'S FOREIGN POLICY

Modern Russia's "hybrid" approach to de facto entities and aspiring political movements is by no means a new phenomenon. It was practised by major Western European powers long before it entered Russian foreign policy. The same approach was used by the West after the dissolution of the Soviet Union. For example, the US recognized Russian Federation as the successor to the dissolved Soviet Union in December 1991. Since then, relations between the two countries have experienced significant changes, but the official recognition of Russia by the US has never been questioned. At the same time, the US "Captive Nations" law, which was adopted during the Cold War, remained in place, stating:

... the imperialistic policies of Communist Russia have led, through direct and indirect aggression, to the subjugation of the national independence of Poland, Hungary, Lithuania, Ukraine, Czechoslovakia, Latvia, Estonia, White Ruthenia, Rumania, East Germany, Bulgaria, mainland China, Armenia, Azerbaijan, Georgia, North Korea, Albania, Idel-Ural, Tibet, Cossackia, Turkestan, North Viet-Nam, and others. (GPO.gov 1959)

The list of "captive nations" still includes supposedly subjugated states within the borders of Russia, namely Idil-Ural and Cossackia. From the Russian side, no government in Moscow has supported the independence of any self-proclaimed entity on the territory of the US.

In 2015 and 2016, the Anti-Globalization Movement of Russia organized two conferences of aspiring political movements and de facto states titled "Dialogue of Nations: Right of Peoples to Self-Determination and the Construction of a Multipolar World". Among the participants, there were representatives of independence movements from Texas, California, Hawaii and Puerto Rico, as well as an African-American party from the US. Contrary to the widespread accusations in the media, these conferences did not receive official support from the Russian Federation. An attempt by the Anti-Globalization Movement of Russia to get a multi-million presidential grant for a similar conference in 2017 was unsuccessful. Thus, it can be argued that the Russian government has no intention of supporting any such "congress of separatists" in the nearest future.

In conclusion, it seems that Russia has adopted a more pragmatic policy regarding aspiring political movements and de facto entities in the last few years. Moscow no longer treats official or semi-official contacts with such actors as prejudicial to its relations with sovereign states. The boundary between various levels of contacts in Russian foreign policy has become blurred, as it has long been the case in the practice of the Western powers. All in all, this new pragmatism seems to have granted the Russian leaders a greater manoeuvring space and dynamism in foreign policy.

References

Berg, Eiki, and Raul Toomla. 2009. Forms of Normalisation in the Quest for De Facto Statehood. *The International Spectator* 44 (4): 27–45. https://doi.org/10.1080/03932720903351104.

Blinov, N.V., V.D. Nadtocheev, and E.D. Orehova. 1991. Rech' narodnogo komissara inostrannyh del SSSR G.V.Chicherina na XIV syezde VKP (b). *Kentavr*, October–November: 122.

Caspersen, Nina, ed. 2011. *Unrecognized States in the International System.* London: Routledge.

Chicherin, G.V. 1924. Letter to G. E. Zinoviev, Moscow, July 4. *The Archive of the Foreign Policy of Russian Federation.* The Mexican Department, Inventory 4, Folder 1.

Cohen, Ariel. 2007. How to Confront Russia's Anti-American Foreign Policy. *The Heritage Foundation,* June 27. https://www.heritage.org/europe/report/how-confront-russias-anti-american-foreign-policy

Dobronravin, Nikolay. 2010. Oil, Gas, Transit and Boundaries: Problems of the Transport Curse. In *Resource Curse and Post-Soviet Eurasia: Oil, Gas, and Modernization,* ed. Vladimir Gel'man and Otar Marganiya, 149–170. Lanham: Lexington Books.

———. 2013. *Modernizatsiia na obochine: vyzhivanie i razvitie nepriznannyh gosudarstv v XX—nachale XXI veka.* St. Petersburg: EUSP Press.

GPO.gov. 1959. Public Law 86–90. July 17. https://www.gpo.gov/fdsys/pkg/STATUTE-73/pdf/STATUTE-73-Pg212.pdf

International Court of Justice. 2010. Accordance with International Law of the Unilateral Declaration of Independence in Respect of Kosovo. July 22. https://www.icj-cij.org/files/case-related/141/141-20100722-ADV-01-00-EN.pdf

Jeifets, Victor, and Lazar Jeifets. 2002. *Stanislav Pestkovski. Tovarisch Andrei: Dvoinoi portret v meksikanskom interiere.* St. Petersburg: Clio.

———. 2015. The International Insertion of the Communist Left-Wing Anti-Gómez Tendency of the Venezuelan Exiles, the First Years. *Izquierdas* 25: 1–28.

Judah, Tim. 2015. *In Wartime: Stories from Ukraine.* London: Allen Lane.

Kaldor, Mary. 2006. *New and Old Wars.* Cambridge: Polity.

Kremlin.ru. 2007. Interview with Arab Satellite Channel Al-Jazeera. February 10. http://en.kremlin.ru/events/president/transcripts/24035

———. 2008. Statement by President of Russia Dmitry Medvedev. August 26. http://en.kremlin.ru/events/president/transcripts/1222

———. 2018. Condolences over the Tragic Death of Alexander Zakharchenko. August 31. http://en.kremlin.ru/events/president/news/58425

Luzyanin, S.G. 2003. *Rossiya—Mongoliya—Kitaj v pervoj polovine XX veka. Politicheskie vzaimootnosheniya v 1911–1946 gg.* Moscow: Ogni.

McCain, John. 2015. Statement by Senator John McCain on Invitation from Russia-Backed Rebels to Monitor Elections. September 14. https://www.mccain.senate.gov/public/index.cfm/2015/9/statement-by-senator-john-mccain-on-invitation-from-russia-backed-rebels-to-monitor-elections

MEMRI. 2014. The National Movement for the Liberation of Azawad Looks to Russia as an International Partner. April 13. https://www.memri.org/reports/national-movement-liberation-azawad-looks-russia-international-partner

Ministry of Foreign Affairs. 2012. On Beginning of Inner-Malian Political Dialog. December 7. http://www.mid.ru/en/foreign_policy/news/-/asset_publisher/cKNonkJE02Bw/content/id/131358

———. 2016. Foreign Policy Concept of the Russian Federation. November 30. http://www.mid.ru/en/web/guest/foreign_policy/official_documents/-/asset_publisher/CptICkB6BZ29/content/id/2542248

———. 2017. Remarks by Foreign Minister Sergey Lavrov at the First Global Forum of Young Diplomats in the Framework of the World Festival of Youth and Students, Sochi. October 16. http://www.mid.ru/en/foreign_policy/news/-/asset_publisher/cKNonkJE02Bw/content/id/2904546

———. 2018a. Foreign Minister Sergey Lavrov's Statement and Answers to Media Questions at a News Conference on Russian Diplomacy in 2017, Moscow. January 15. http://www.mid.ru/en/foreign_policy/news/-/asset_publisher/cKNonkJE02Bw/content/id/3018203

———. 2018b. Briefing by Foreign Ministry Spokesperson Maria Zakharova, Svetlogorsk. August 15. http://www.mid.ru/en/press_service/spokesman/briefings/-/asset_publisher/D2wHaWMCU6Od/content/id/3319709

———. 2018c. Statement by the Foreign Ministry. August 31. http://www.mid.ru/en/foreign_policy/news/-/asset_publisher/cKNonkJE02Bw/content/id/3334568

Murphy, George G.S. 1961. On Satelliteship. *Journal of Economic History* 21 (4): 641–651. https://doi.org/10.1017/S0022050700109118.

Perepiska I.V. Stalina i G. V. Chicherina s polpredom SSSR v Kitae L. M. Karahanom. 2008. Moscow: Natalis

Popescu, Nicu. 2006. "Outsourcing" De Facto Statehood: Russia and the Secessionist Entities in Georgia and Moldova. *Centre for European Policy Studies Policy Brief*, no. 109. https://www.ceps.eu/publications/outsourcing-de-facto-statehood-russia-and-secessionist-entities-georgia-and-moldova

Richardson, W.H. 1988. *Mexico Through Russian Eyes: 1806–1940.* Pittsburgh: Pittsburgh University Press.

Skalov, G. n.d. Avtobiographiia. *The Russian State Archive of the Social and Political History*, Fund 495, Inventory 65a, Folder 4569.

Summers, James, ed. 2011. *Kosovo: A Precedent? The Declaration of Independence, the Advisory Opinion and Implications for Statehood, Self-Determination and Minority Rights.* Leiden/Boston: Martinus Nijhoff Publishers.

U.S. Department of State. 1945. Foreign Relations of the United States. Conferences at Malta and Yalta, 1945. http://digital.library.wisc.edu/1711.dl/FRUS.FRUS1945

Zagladin, N.V. 1990. *Istoriia uspehov i neudach sovetskoi diplomatii.* Moscow: Mysl.

Zarembo, Kateryna, ed. 2016. Conflict Settlement Practices Around the World: Lessons for Ukraine. *Institute of World Policy*, February 11. http://iwp.org.ua/en/publication/dosvid-vregulyuvannya-konfliktiv-u-sviti-uroky-dlya-ukrayiny

CHAPTER 12

Russia's "Modern" Foreign Policy Tools in Crimea and Syria

Philipp Casula

INTRODUCTION

The swift Russian annexation of Crimea has puzzled Western politicians and scholars alike. The EU and US have reacted by imposing sanctions on selected individuals of the Putin regime and continued to expand them to different sectors of Russia's economy, but so far to no avail. Rather, the integration of Crimea into Russia has continued at a fast pace. Analysts have reacted by drawing parallels to the Cold War, identifying a neo-imperialist course in Russia's foreign policy or referring to expansionism as a means to secure the popularity of the Russian regime (Petersson 2014). Similarly, the scale and intensity of Russia's military intervention in the

This chapter draws on Philipp Casula, "Russia's Foreign Policy from the Crimean Crisis to the Middle East: Great Power Gamble or Biopolitics?" *Rising Powers Quarterly* 2, no. 1 (2017): 27–51. http://risingpowersproject.com/quarterly/russias-foreign-policy-crimean-crisis-middle-east-great-power-gamble-biopolitics/

P. Casula (✉)
University of Basel, Basel, Switzerland
e-mail: ph.casula@unibas.ch

© The Author(s) 2020
E. Parlar Dal, E. Erşen (eds.), *Russia in the Changing International System*, https://doi.org/10.1007/978-3-030-21832-4_12

205

Syrian conflict came to the surprise of all those who regarded Moscow as struggling with Western-imposed sanctions and incapable to wield power beyond its direct neighbourhood.

In the present chapter, Crimea and Syria will serve as case studies to highlight how different forms of power have been wielded by Russia.[1] The chapter unfolds three basic approaches of political theory—particularly following Foucault's interpretation (2007)—in order to underscore the changing preferences in the choice of foreign policy tools adopted by the Putin regime in these most recent international crises. The basic tenets taken into consideration are "sovereignty", "reason of state" and "biopolitics". Employing these concepts implies a selective reading of Foucault and consciously disregards other approaches to power he has developed (Foucault 1982). This deliberate choice has the clear advantage of providing a coherent framework of analysis. Furthermore, *Security, Territory, Population* (2007) is one of the few texts in which Foucault openly develops ideas pertaining to international relations, while generally he is much more concerned with the domestic arena of power in the liberal societies (Selby 2007, 332). The chapter locates itself in the field of the growing literature of International Governmentality Studies (IGS), which includes "a whole series of investigations that are putting Foucault's hypotheses to work across full spectrum of concerns and topics that animate IR" (Walters 2012, 83).

Theoretically, the chapter shows that IGS can encourage *both* a constructivist and a realist reading of international relations. The possibility of a realist interpretation runs against the expectations of what is usually feasible with a Foucauldian approach, as Foucault is generally posited in the realm of post-structuralism. It also runs against the actual use of Foucauldian terminology in the works of authors such as of R. B. J. Walker, Richard Ashley, Jim George or Cynthia Weber.

Empirically, the chapter analyses how Russia used the tools associated with the forms of power of sovereignty, reason of state and biopolitics since the collapse of the USSR and especially after the annexation of Crimea. The chapter's main claim is that Russia's military interventions in Crimea and Syria do not represent a break with the previously professed principles of Russian foreign policy. Rather, Russia has adopted the entire repertoire of devices, means or mechanisms available to modern states: all the tools of sovereignty, reason of state and biopolitics remain present in both domestic and foreign policy. The comparison between Russia's use of power suggests that in the Near Abroad, Russia adopts a de-territorializing *biopolitical stance*, undermining the sovereignty of other former Soviet republics and highlighting a *Russkii mir* (i.e. the Russian world, or what Russian pundits conceive as the space inhabited by Russians beyond the borders of the Russian Federation), while beyond the borders of the former USSR, it plays the *territorial game of sovereignty*, stressing nation-states in their current borders and their non-violability, emerging as a "defender of territoriality" (Nunan 2016, 12), while selectively undermining their sovereignty itself. Methodologically, the chapter will adopt a discourse-analytical stance and scrutinize key documents published by the Russian government, including Russian federal laws and speeches by key politicians.

BIOPOLITICS IN CRIMEA AND THE NEAR ABROAD

If biopolitics means defining a *bios*, a life or a population, then Russian foreign policy assumed a biopolitical dimension, emphasizing increasingly the importance of a vaguely defined "Russian life" in the Near Abroad. "Biopolitics deals with the population, with the population as political problem, as a problem that is at once scientific and political, as a biological problem and as power's problem" (Foucault 2003, 245). Put differently, biopolitics is the power exercised on the population. It does not aim at or relate to a specific territory and its relation to the sovereign or the state is the focal point of all political activity. It is hence a de-territorialized form of power that transgresses the borders. The tool Foucault associates with biopolitics is *security* (Foucault 2007, 4). Security encompasses all the means to steer, regulate and govern a population taking into account its inherent qualities (Gros 2012). "Security is related to normality and liberty, not to war and survival, nor with coercion and surveillance. It differs from sovereignty and discipline as it is a cost calculation inside a series of probable events" (Bigo 2008, 96).

Humanitarian interventions fit into the scheme of security because they claim to be specifically aimed at preserving threatened lives and go well beyond simple military activity. Rather, they involve occupation, state-building, economic development and infrastructure improvements. While sovereignty requires a territory to be delimited, biopolitics requires a *population* to be identified. The population that is increasingly coming into play and becoming a factor determining or legitimizing Russian foreign policy in the Near Abroad is the community of ethnic Russians in the post-Soviet space. Who is exactly to be considered as belonging to the group of *sootechestvenniki* (compatriots) is, however, everything but clear.

Already under Yeltsin, efforts have been undertaken to define the "compatriots" and develop a strategy towards this population. The efforts under Yeltsin, Medvedev and Putin to provide clarity about what it means to be a Russian *sootechestvennik*, however, resulted in rather vague laws. The Federal Law No. 99-FZ "On State Policy toward Compatriots Living Abroad", which was adopted in May 1999 and amended in July 2010, offers a very broad definition (Garant.ru 2010). It even underlines the principle of self-identification as the basis for being recognized as a *sootechestvennik* (Casula 2014, 8–9). Thus, theoretically anyone can make a claim to Russianness and hence to the specific rights connected to this identity. The concept of "compatriots" as defined in the law seems to be malleable or have different degrees (Shevel 2011, 89).

The law reflects the discussions that have been raging for years and reflects the demands raised in the wider political discourse. Kholmogorov and Isaev, for example, underline that Russianness is above all about the culture. Isaev stresses that "not soil and blood, but language and culture" determine being Russian, and that Russianness "is a declarative right. Following this logic, for Russia, s/he is Russian, who declares herself or himself to be so. In Russian culture there is not a single argument that would allow questioning such a demand. Whoever says 'I am Russian', cannot not be answered negatively on cultural grounds" (Isaev 2006, 8). Kholmogorov (2006, 266) hints that one might also become Russian by serving the Russian state—an argument which gained importance in the context of considerations to open the Russian army to the Commonwealth of Independent States (CIS) citizens, who would then be eligible for Russian citizenship. Such an assumption might also pave the way for declaring all pro-Russian militiamen in Donbas as Russian citizens.

While a concern for Russians in the former Soviet republics was present already in the 1990s, it only gained momentum in Russian foreign policy in the mid-2000s.[2] In 2005, Putin highlighted that the end of the USSR, "for the Russian people, became a real drama" (Putin 2008, 272). On March 18, 2014, after the Euromaidan revolution and the events in Crimea, he repeated: "Millions of people went to bed in one country and awoke in different ones, overnight becoming ethnic minorities in former Union republics" (Kremlin.ru 2014b). Moreover, security concerns became visible regarding the issue of migration to Russia, ensuring the flows of people between Russia and neighbouring countries in order to tackle the perceived demographic problems, which Putin declared as the most pressing problem in Russia—something that he called the problem of "love, women, and children" (Putin 2008, 330). The ageing population, the high (male) mortality rate and the low birth rate threaten Russia as a state. This is viewed as a defence policy issue and the problem can be alleviated by an inflow of Russians from other CIS members (Rotkirch et al. 2007, 351–52).

Thus, the care about the compatriots also has a foreign policy dimension. The defence of the Russian citizens or Russian-speaking populations abroad became a key issue and the rationale for justifying the exertion of pressure on neighbouring countries, and recently Putin has again vowed to protect the rights of the compatriots (Goble 2018). The compatriots also figure prominently in the 2013 version of the "Concept of the Foreign Policy of the Russian Federation", which underlines that "particular attention will be paid to providing support to compatriots living in the CIS Member States [*sootechestvennikov, prozhivaiushchich v gosudarstv-uchastnikakh SNG*], as well as to negotiating agreements on the protection of their … rights and freedom … ensuring comprehensive protection of rights and legitimate interests of Russian citizens and compatriots residing abroad [*rossiiskich grazhdan i sootechestvennikov*], and promoting, in various international formats, Russia's approach to human rights issues" (Ministry of Foreign Affairs 2013). The intervention in South Ossetia in 2008 was explicitly made on the grounds of saving the lives of the *sootechest-venniki* (Kremlin.ru 2008a, b).

With regard to Crimea and Ukraine, Putin adopted a similar rhetoric. However, since the Crimean people had no Russian passport and the legal category of "citizens" was absent, he drew on a broader understanding of compatriots, and stated that in Ukraine "live and will live millions of ethnic Russians, russophone citizens, and Russia will always defend their interests with political, diplomatic, and legal means" (Kremlin.ru 2014a). Whereas under Medvedev in 2008, Russia still manoeuvred to define the South Ossetians as Russians in legal terms, under Putin this policy has tilted towards a broader interpretation of compatriots, which can be defined in ethnic, linguistic or cultural, and *not only* legal terms. Under Putin's tenure since 2012, a shift occurred towards stressing a civilizational definition of Russianness, making it broader on the one hand because it refers to multiethnicity (*mnogonatsionalnost'*) and yet assigning to ethnic Russians a special role as "state-forming" people (*gosudarstvoo-brazuyushchiy narod*) within Russia on the other. These positions come along using the terminology borrowed from Russian nationalism, which the Russian official discourse had widely avoided beforehand (Malinova 2015, 132–34).

With this shift to biopolitics, Russia also allotted to the former Soviet republics a special place in its foreign policy not only due to their geographical proximity and close socio-economic ties with Russia but also because their populations include Russian or Russian-speaking minorities, and thus actual or potential compatriots. In this light, it seems that the Kremlin displayed greater interest in the population of the CIS than the territory they inhabit. In this way, Russia reserved the right to intervene to protect this population with whomever it claims to have "close historical, cultural and economic ties". As Putin underscores, "protecting these people is in our national interests... We cannot remain indifferent if we see that they are being persecuted, destroyed and humiliated" (Kremlin.ru 2014a). Or as succinctly put by Foreign Minister Lavrov: "Russian citizens being attacked, is an attack against the Russian Federation" (RT 2014). Such an interpretation of compatriots means that the current Russian foreign policy explicitly recognizes a mismatch between the sovereign territory of the Russian Federation and the population for which Russia claims responsibility.

Reason of State: Stability, Diplomacy and Balance of Power

Reason of state means putting the state's interests above all other political goals—and here the "realist" potential of Foucault's power triptych comes to the fore. Reason of state describes the knowledge necessary to form, preserve, strengthen and expand the state. Bogislaw Chemnitz wrote in 1640 that reason of state is "a certain political consideration that is necessary in all public matters, councils and plans, which must strive solely for the preservation, expansion, and felicity of the state, and for which we must employ the most ready and swift means" (Foucault 2007, 257). In this perspective, the state is the sole principle and aim of reason of state, supplanting the key place held beforehand by the prince under the principle of sovereignty: "The ruler's task is ... to enable the state to survive and thrive in an environment where it must exist and compete alongside other states" (Walters 2012, 26).

The key tool of reason of state is a military-diplomatic technology that consists of securing and developing the state's forces through a system of alliances and organization of military forces (Foucault 2007, 296), producing a balance or equilibrium (Walters 2012, 27). Also, the economy becomes a tool in the hand of reason of state. In a mercantilist understanding, the economy has to contribute to the state's power and wealth (Foucault 2007, 101). This logic has never completely changed: while reason of state originated in the seventeenth century, it still continues to be applied explicitly or implicitly—not only by Russia but by all nation-states albeit with different degrees of intensity. Furthermore, reason of state explicitly allows breaking the law if it serves the interests of the state (Foucault 2007, 262–64).

Gaddy and Hill (2013) argue that the state is a "mythic entity" in Russia. They define Putin as a statist—or a *gosudarstvennik* or *derzhavnik*—appointed to serve the Russian state and restore its greatness. And indeed the state's greatness plays an important role as a rhetorical device to justify policy. Putin's well-known statement made in 2005 that "the collapse of the Soviet Union was the biggest geopolitical catastrophe of the century" (Putin 2008, 272) perfectly reflects the reason of state thinking and shows that Putin at least wished others *to think* that he had the state's interests in mind. The statement also underscores that in his vision, present-day Russia is a temporal extension of the Soviet Union. Hence, the Soviet demise means a weakening of the Russian state, its institutions and its reach. Restoring Russia's power has been a clearly stated goal of Putin's tenure, from the very beginning, and it is also in line with the principles already defended by the former Russian foreign and prime minister Yevgenii Primakov in the 1990s (Primakov 2004). The handling of the national economy and especially the crackdown on the political ambitions of the Russian oligarchs provide another good example to demonstrate how Russian policies are in line with reason of state. In a mercantilist fashion, Russian oligarchs have been put at the service of the state. In Russian political discourse, hints abound regarding such an understanding of the economy (Fadeev 2006, 141; Kokoshin 2006, 96; Orlov 2006).

In view of this statist thinking, two foreign policy tenets of the current leadership come to the fore: a preference for stability over democracy and the striving for a balance of power. Firstly, the stability over democracy principle is important both for domestic and foreign policy. Hence, in the Kremlin's view, Syria's Bashar al-Assad is better than a "radical" and split opposition, while Ukraine's Viktor Yanukovych is better than the "fascists" in power. Official Russian discourse abhors any revolutionary scenario that might change the balance of power in the disfavour of Russia. As Kolonitsky (2014) commented, "after 23 years apart, Russians and Ukrainians have shaped very different narratives from the same Soviet memories. Soviet culture romanticized and sanctified revolution .... The very term revolution has come to carry negative connotations for Russians". Indeed, while Russia's opposition at first managed to mobilize 50,000 Muscovites to protest against the Kremlin's actions in Crimea, later even critical voices such as Dmitri Bykov (2014) cautioned against a "Ukrainian euphoria" and a Russian "patriotic trance" as well as revolutions in general. The Kremlin itself obviously rejects any revolutionary scenario. Statements such as "no revolution, no counterrevolution" (Putin 2008, 80) must be seen both against the backdrop of the domestic economic and political "chaos" of the 1990s and the so-called Colour Revolutions in Russia's neighbourhood in the 2003–2005 period, which left a deep mark in the Kremlin's thinking (Saari 2009). Hence, Russia seems to be a status quo power, whatever that status quo is unless, of course, change is to the advantage of the Russian state, as also exemplified by the Crimean case. Russia has always played a special role in the Crimean peninsula and this special role was threatened by feared pro-European takeover in Kiev. The same holds for the Donbas region: Russia could accept to have only indirect influence over this territory, but not its complete loss to Europe. Hence, in these two cases, Russia was willing to break international law to maintain the influence it had before.

Secondly, Russia's official vision abhors any turbulence in the international balance of power. For Moscow, this balance is threatened because the West has been creeping closer to Russia's borders—even swallowing former Soviet satellites—and obstructing the planned Eurasian Union. The latter in particular became a cornerstone for the Russian attempts to maintain a balance of power and strengthen the bonds between the former Soviet republics (Putin 2011). Since at least 2002, the former Soviet space became the top priority of Russian foreign policy as also declared by Putin (2008, 106–28). In his view, the interests of the CIS and Russia coincide mainly due to a shared history and culture, while common economic interests, issue of immigration and Russian diaspora are all elements that stress the importance of the former Soviet Union for Russian foreign policy (Ministry of Foreign Affairs 2013).

The Near Abroad in this regard has turned into a "Russian sphere of identity" or a *Russkii mir* that goes beyond the borders of the Russian Federation (Zelevev 2014). A key factor in this identity-based conception of belonging to Russia is the memory of the World War II and how it has been interpreted by the Russian official narrative (Malinova 2015, 88–127). In this sense, the Russian foreign policy is unambiguous about the central ideational role the CIS plays for Russia. Hence, "Russia intends to actively contribute to the development of interaction among CIS Member States in the humanitarian sphere on the ground of preserving and increasing common cultural and civilizational heritage", while Ukraine has been earmarked "as a priority partner within the CIS" (Ministry of Foreign Affairs 2013).

The Syrian intervention also includes a reason of state thinking because it is not about the defence or expansion of Russian territory itself. Actually, it even contradicts the thinking in terms of sovereignty as it represents a breach of Syrian sovereignty. Russia's position regarding this issue is less about being concerned about Syria, and more about its own relations with the West and especially the balance of power with the US in the Middle East. In other words, from a reason of state perspective, Russia's main concern is to maintain an equilibrium between the pro-Russian and pro-Western forces, and also generally prevent the West from once again dictating the course of events in the Middle East. Therefore, the intervention in Syria is a means to reassert Russia as a global player.

Sovereignty, "Sovereign Democracy" and the Syrian Crisis

Commenting on the Russian occupation of Crimea, US President Barack Obama—apparently with Thomas Hobbes in mind—claimed that Russia had "a more traditional view of power", according to which "ordinary men and women … surrender their rights to an all-powerful sovereign" (The White House 2014). Indeed, the concept of sovereignty dates back to the Renaissance and is thus associated with the post-medieval modernization of monarchic power (Singer and Weir 2006, 451). Sovereignty asks: "How can the territory be demarcated, fixed, protected, or enlarged?" (Foucault 2007, 65). Sovereignty is circular, as it is concerned with upholding itself. In sovereignty, there is no utopian *telos* or a specific vision for the state and society, and thus it seems a good match for post-Soviet and post-utopian societies. The end of sovereignty is self-preservation through authority and law (Singer and Weir 2006, 448)—or in short: "the good proposed by sovereignty is that people obey it" (Foucault 2003, 136).

The traditional tools of sovereignty to uphold the relationship between prince and territory are laws (internally) and war (externally). Sovereignty "consists in laying down a law and fixing a punishment for the person who breaks it" (Foucault 2007, 5). The hint at "punishment" aptly shows that legitimate violence is a built-in feature of sovereignty. These themes of sovereignty, concern for territory and use of laws to defend the relationship between the sovereign and territory all play a role in contemporary Russian politics. It is not a coincidence that for many years in Putin's tenure, "sovereign democracy" has been a key notion used by Russian pundits to describe the Russian political system, until Medvedev (2006) officially dismissed the term. However, while the term was put aside, its importance in the political practice maintained its significance (Averre 2007) and anteceded the hype about sovereignty in Western European right-wing populist discourse.

The insistence on sovereignty means two things. Firstly, sovereign democracy, as aptly summarized by Putin, implies that "Russia is an independent, active participant of international life, and it has, like other countries, national interests, which you have to take into account and to respect" (Kremlin.ru 2014b). However, Russia perceives itself not as any other country, but as a great power with clear spheres of influence. This is in line with the classic precepts of sovereignty in terms of a territory, which has to be defended and preserved—both in terms of the Russian territory itself and in terms of its spheres of influence. The key texts of sovereign democracy reflect this concern for Russian uniqueness. For instance, Surkov (2008, 10) argues that while the "democratic order" of Russia emerged out of the "European civilization", Russia contains a unique character. It is true that the sense of belonging to Europe includes an adoption of the "European economic model" because "the European way is the path of success, of growth" (Surkov 2008, 95). However, this belonging to Europe should have certain limits because it can also mean giving up one's sovereignty. Nikonov (2007) for instance estimates that the EU member states transfer "60–70 percent of the sovereign functions to Brussels". Glazev also recently echoed Nikonov, pointing out that any association with the EU means transferring sovereignty over the economy to Brussels (Echo Moskvy 2014). Karaganov (2004, 2005) also criticized any kind of adoption of the European norms as a loss of sovereignty. Hence, the sense of belonging to Europe that was visible in the early Russian texts on sovereign democracy was flawed from the very beginning due to concerns about preserving Russia's uniqueness and the belief of the Russian leaders that belonging to Europe does not include a sacrifice of sovereign power (Nikonov 2003).

Secondly, as early as 2000, Putin promised a "dictatorship of law" (Kremlin.ru 2000). The influence of the executive branch of power on the judiciary weighs heavily, precisely because the Russian leadership so zealously strives to build its power on law. Thus, political lawsuits became common practice in contemporary Russia. The executive branch exploits the courts to use the law against political opponents, treating them as if they were criminals, just because they threaten to destabilize the existing system. The punk-musicians of *Pussy Riot*, for instance, were convicted on *hooliganism* charges, a broadly defined infraction.[3] Additionally, what comes into play is the prevailing legal culture. According to these legal traditions, the police officers, prosecutors and judges see themselves as a team that shares the goal to convict a criminal and serve the interests of the state (Reznik 2012). Indeed, after the turbulent 1990s, Putin's regime has continuously emphasized and promised order, stability and lawfulness. In this regard, the Kremlin's policies lack any utopian element, both internally and externally (Prozorov 2010, 272). Basically, the existing system is supposed to remain in place as it is. Putin has been unambiguous about this: "It is time to say firmly that... there will be neither revolution, nor counterrevolution" (Putin 2008, 80).

Law also plays a key role in Russia's foreign policy. Referring to the Western conduct in international affairs, Putin stressed that "our approach is different: we proceed from the conviction that we always act legitimately. I have personally always been an advocate of acting in compliance with international law" (Kremlin.ru 2014a). And again, he condemned Russia's "Western partners", claiming that they "prefer not to be guided by international law in their practical policies, but by the rule of the gun .... They act as they please: here and there, they use force against sovereign states .... To make this aggression look legitimate, they force the necessary resolutions from international organizations, and if for some reason this does not work, they simply ignore the UN Security Council and the UN overall" (Kremlin.ru 2014b).

The same theme resurfaced in the context of the Syrian crisis. Foreign Minister Lavrov complained about the Western conduct in the Middle East and underscored that the West "need[s] to be trained that the affairs can only be conducted on the basis of equality of rights, balance of interests, and mutual respect" (Embrussia.ru 2013). For Lavrov, the West acted illegally in Libya and Iraq, dragging these countries into chaos. Such an interpretation of events has also allowed the Russian leaders to claim to have acted differently in Syria.[4] Yet, there is an interesting contradiction in Russia's attitude. On the one hand, Moscow insists on respecting international law. In the UN Security Council, for instance, it vetoes resolutions and still enjoys a status on par with other great powers. As a matter of fact, Russia and China repeatedly vetoed resolutions against Syria since the outbreak of the civil war in that country. If the UN is bypassed by Western powers—as it happened in 1999 or 2003—Russian officials deplore the breach of international law and the abuse of the concept of humanitarian intervention. It should be noted that when Russia was consented about the intervention in Libya, it promptly caused a rift in the Russian top-echelons of power (BBC 2011), with many Russian observers highlighting that the West overstepped the mandate granted by the UN Security Council Resolution No. 1973. Since then, the Russian position regarding the humanitarian interventions has further stiffened. Any Western intervention in Syria, for instance, has been regularly dismissed, while Russia's own military intervention in that country was regarded as legitimate on the grounds that it was launched on the official invitation of the Syrian government.

On the other hand, Russia itself has been very flexible in interpreting international law and especially the "Responsibility to Protect" (R2P) doctrine in its direct neighbourhood, invoking an international legal framework whenever possible to support its foreign policy actions.[5] Both in the case of Georgia's two breakaway republics Abkhazia and South Ossetia, and later in the case of Crimea, Russia claimed it sought to protect the local populations against the alleged reprisals of the Georgian and Ukrainian forces. Especially regarding Crimea's annexation, multiple legal steps were swiftly taken in order to maintain a lawful facade. An important point here was that the forces that seized key positions in Crimea on February 27 remained unidentified at first. Russia continuously denied to have occupied foreign soil and it took Putin almost a month to formally acknowledge his decision to send Russian troops to Crimea.[6] On March 16, a referendum was hastily conducted on Crimea and a day later, the peninsula declared independence, which was promptly recognized by Russia. Only two days later, on March 18, Putin signed the "Treaty on Accession of the Republic of Crimea to Russia" and received the consent of the Supreme Court on March 19. On March 20, the treaty was ratified by the State Duma by a 443-1 vote with no abstentions and by the Federal Council on March 21. This procedure, including the go-ahead of the court, also circumvented Federal Law 6-FKZ (2001) that would have required Ukraine's consent to Crimea's decision to be incorporated into Russia. This prima facie perfectly legal procedure reflects the two tenets of sovereignty: the concern about territory on the one hand, and the emphasis on lawfulness as a means to exercise power on the other.

Regarding the intervention in Syria, the biopolitical dimension has less importance in Russia's rationale of power. Reports on the conflict in the Russian media often underscored the threat posed to the Orthodox communities.[7] The Russian intervention is, hence, presented as if it was conducted with the aim of protecting a religious community, which has been important for the Russian people. Curanović (2012) has stressed the rising importance of the Russian Orthodox Church for shaping foreign policies. The predominant rationale, however, corresponds to the sovereign and territorial form. Borrowing from Nunan (2016, 17), a "post-territorial morality" seems to dominate the Russian foreign policy discourse in the Near Abroad, while regarding the Syrian case and possibly the "Far Abroad" in general, I would argue that the defence of the "territoriality of the nation-state" prevails as the rationale of power. Still, it could be claimed that Russia's intervention has actually undermined Syrian sovereignty, with Russia—and more importantly Iran—having a greater influence in Syria's decision-making (Lesh 2017).

Russian foreign policy statements concerning Syria repeatedly underlined the country's territorial integrity, sovereignty and the illegitimacy of foreign intervention. For example, Putin picked up the classic circular argument of sovereignty in his following statement: "We are not protecting the Syrian government, but international law. We … believe that preserving law and order in today's complex and turbulent world is one of the few ways to keep international relations from sliding into chaos. The law is still the law, and we must follow it whether we like it or not" (Kremlin.ru 2013).

The Dushanbe declaration of the Shanghai Cooperation Organization's 2014 summit is also full of allusions regarding the sovereign rationale of power. For instance, the SCO heads of state stressed the need "to strengthen the legal foundations of international relations" and, referring to UN principles, reciprocally respect "sovereignty, independence, territorial integrity of state, [and] … non-interference in internal affairs". The declaration specifically mentioned the support for "sovereignty, unity and territorial integrity" of Syria as well as the "independence, sovereignty and territorial integrity" of Afghanistan (Kremlin.ru 2014c). By the same token, Lavrov stressed twice that "it is necessary to fully respect Syria's sovereignty, territorial integrity and unity … [to] respect for the sovereignty, independence, unity and territorial integrity of the Syrian Arab Republic as a multiethnic, multi-religious, democratic and secular state" (Ministry of Foreign Affairs 2016).

Additionally, it should be highlighted how Russia has employed not only its sovereign apparatus (i.e. international law and war) but also the tools of reason of state. As mentioned earlier, if the military-diplomatic technology consists of securing and developing the state's forces through a system of alliances and the organization of military forces, then this perspective brings to our attention the alliances that Russia succeeded to establish in order to contain the Syrian crisis—such as a division of labour with Iran and Turkey in Syria. Russia is also one of the few states that is on good terms with almost all of the regional actors including the Assad regime, Turkey, the Syrian Kurds, Iran and Israel.

CONCLUSION

This chapter has shown that IGS can simultaneously imply a realist and a constructivist reading of international relations. The definition of a *Russkii mir* or "compatriots" refers to the field of identity politics and constructivism—thoroughly explored by Tsygankov (2013)—while the territorial exercise of sovereign power reflects the main tenets of realism. The main empirical argument advanced in this chapter has been that Russian foreign policy adopts all mechanisms of modern power; however, it fields different rationales in varying degrees depending on whether the foreign policy regards the "Near Abroad"—that is, the post-Soviet space—or the "Far Abroad"—the other countries. In the former case, Russia is inclined to advance a biopolitical rationale, as exemplified by the intervention in Georgia 2008 and the Crimean crisis of 2014. In the latter case, sovereignty is the predominant rationale, as demonstrated by Russia's Syria policy.

The concern for an ill-defined population outside of Russia means that there is a de-territorialized form of power at work that transgresses the borders of the post-Soviet states including Russia. Thus, their sovereignty is put into question. Because of this mismatch between the territory of the Russian Federation and the *Russkii mir* or the Russian "sphere of identity", Russian foreign policy contains an expansionist potential aimed at preserving the Russian influence over territories where the "compatriots" live. The biopolitical rationale seems to prevail over the rationale of sovereignty, but it does not exclude the fact that elements of both forms can go hand in hand. Indeed, the Crimean example shows how at the beginning of the crisis, Russia argued in biopolitical terms ("save compatriots"), but then moved on to employ tools associated with sovereignty and built a whole legal edifice to justify the incorporation of Crimea into the Russian Federation. To claim that a biopolitical *turn* is taking place in Russian foreign and domestic policies may be too bold, which would also run against Foucault's own position. Such a claim would also mean denying any modern subjectivity for pre-Putin Russia. Rather, what is at stake here is a continuum of forms of power in Russia. While the reason of state and sovereignty are "more traditional" forms of power, they are not outdated and continue to play a role in Russian foreign policy, for example in Syria.

Claims about saving lives play a smaller role concerning Russia's intervention in Syria. While there have been attempts to cast the Russian military deployment as an effort to save the Syrian Orthodox Christians—and kill "terrorists"—more thrust has been invested in playing the sovereignty and reason of state game, employing the military and diplomatic apparatus and focusing on Syria's sovereignty and territoriality.

Notes

1. Hence, "forms of power" and "tools" are not the same: three forms of power (sovereignty, reason of state and biopolitics) are associated respectively with three tools of power ("law and war", "military-diplomacy-economy" and "security") as will be discussed in more detail further.
2. A debate over the Russian diaspora was an element to justify Russian military involvement in Georgia, Tajikistan and Moldova in the 1990s. For details of the political debates, interests and Russian military actions see, for example, Jackson (2003).
3. For the specific meaning of *hooliganism* in the Russian context, see Konecny (2004).
4. Valerii Zorkin produced a key text regarding Russia's official stance on international law and sovereignty. First published in 2004, the book has been reprinted several times. Zorkin fervidly defends state sovereignty as well as the principles of the "Westphalian system" (Zorkin 2006).
5. UN Security Council Resolution No. 1674 of April 28, 2006 underscores the states' responsibility to protect their population and the possibility to limit their sovereignty in case they fail to ensure this protection.
6. Putin acknowledged the Russian troops' intervention in a Q&A session on Russian TV on April 17, 2014. He also stressed his personal role as well as the role of Russian special forces in *Krym—Put' na rodinu*, released on March 15, 2015, on channel Rossiya-1. See BBC (2015).
7. See, for example, Anastasiya Popova's reports on Syria for Russian television, especially https://vera.vesti.ru/video/show/video_id/286720

REFERENCES

Averre, Derek. 2007. 'Sovereign Democracy' and Russia's Relations with the European Union. *Demokratizatsiya* 15 (2): 173–190. https://doi.org/10.3200/DEMO.15.2.173-190.

BBC. 2011. Medvedev Rejects Putin 'Crusade' Remark over Libya. March 21. http://www.bbc.co.uk/news/world-europe-12810566

———. 2015. Kak Rossii udalos' vzyat' Krym bez boya? March 20. https://www.bbc.com/russian/russia/2015/03/150320_crimea_film_battle

Bigo, Didier. 2008. Security: A Field Left Fallow. In *Foucault on Politics, Security and War*, ed. Michael Dillon and Andrew W. Neal, 93–114. New York: Palgrave Macmillan.

Bykov, Dmitri. 2014. Ukrainskaia eyforiya, patrioticheskiy ekstaz Kryma i dukh vtoroy revolyutsii. *Sobesednik*, March 25. http://sobesednik.ru/dmitriy-bykov/20140325-dmitriy-bykov-ukrainskaya-eyforiya-patrioticheskiy-ekstaz-kr

Casula, Philipp. 2014. Russia's and Europe's Borderlands. Between Sovereign Intervention and Security Management. *Problems of Post-Communism* 61 (6): 6–17. https://doi.org/10.2753/PPC1075-8216610601.

Curanović, Alicija. 2012. *The Religious Factor in Russia's Foreign Policy*. London: Routledge.

Echo Moskvy. 2014. Gotova li Rossiya k samoizolyatsii. May 20. http://echo.msk.ru/programs/beseda/1323436-echo/#element-text

Embrussia.ru. 2013. Foreign Minister Sergey Lavrov's Interview in the 'Sunday Evening with Vladimir Solovyev' Program on 'Russia' TV Channel, Moscow. February 10. http://www.embrussia.ru/node/263

Fadeev, Valerii. 2006. Rossiya—eto energeticheskaya sverkhderzhava. In *Suverenitet—sbornik*, ed. Nikita Garadzha, 133–146. Moscow: Yevropa.

Foucault, Michel. 1982. The Subject and Power. *Critical Inquiry* 8 (4): 777–795. https://doi.org/10.1086/448181.

———. 2003. *Society Must Be Defended*. New York: Picador.

———. 2007. *Security, Territory, Population*. New York: Palgrave Macmillan.

Gaddy, Clifford, and Fiona Hill. 2013. *Mr. Putin: Operative in the Kremlin*. Washington: Brookings.

Garant.ru. 2010. Federal'ny zakon 179-FZ. July 23. http://base.garant.ru/198858/#block_13

Goble, Paul. 2018. Moscow to Boost Protection of Russians Abroad and Make It Easier for Many to Return. *Eurasia Daily Monitor* 15 (156). https://jamestown.org/program/moscow-to-boost-protection-of-russians-abroad-and-make-it-easier-for-many-to-return

Gros, Frédéric. 2012. *Le principe sécurité*. Paris: Gallimard.

Isaev, Andrei. 2006. *Yedinaya Rossiya: Partiya russkoy politicheskoy kultury*. Moscow: Evropa.

Jackson, Nicole J. 2003. *Russian Foreign Policy and the CIS: Theories, Debates and Actions*. London: Routledge.

Karaganov, Sergey. 2004. Rossiya i Yevropa: vmeste ili po sosedstvu? *Rossiyskaya Gazeta*, September 2. http://www.rg.ru/2004/09/02/evropa.html

———. 2005. Rossiya i Yevropa: buduscheye v dal'nem pritsele. *Rossiyskaya Gazeta*, September 30. http://www.rg.ru/printable/2005/09/30/es.html

Kholmogorov, Yegor. 2006. *Russkiy natsionalist*. Moscow: Yevropa.

Kokoshin, Andrei. 2006. Real'ny suverenitet i suverennaya demokratiya. In *Suverenitet—sbornik*, ed. Nikita Garadža et al., 89–130. Moscow: Evropa.

Kolonitsky, Boris. 2014. Why Russians Back Putin on Ukraine. *New York Times*, March 12. http://www.nytimes.com/2014/03/12/opinion/why-russians-back-putin-on-ukraine.html

Konecny, Peter. 2004. Library Hooligans and Others: Law, Order, and Student Culture in Leningrad, 1914–38. *Journal of Social History* 30 (1): 97–128. https://doi.org/10.1353/jsh/30.1.97.

Kremlin.ru. 2000. Poslaniye Federal'nomu Sobraniyu Rossiyskoy Federatsii 2000. July 8. http://kremlin.ru/events/president/transcripts/21480

———. 2008a. Zayavleniye v svyazi s situatsiyey v Yuzhnoy Osetii. August 8. http://kremlin.ru/events/president/transcripts/1042

———. 2008b. Dmitry Medvedev Has Declared August 13 a Day of Mourning for the Humanitarian Disaster in South Ossetia. August 12. http://en.kremlin.ru/events/president/news/1076

———. 2013. The Syrian Alternative. September 12. http://en.kremlin.ru/events/president/news/19205

———. 2014a. Vladimir Putin: Otvetil na voprosy zhurnalistov o situatsii na Ukraine. March 4. http://kremlin.ru/transcripts/20366

———. 2014b. Obrashchenie Prezidenta Rossiyskoy Federatsii. March 18. http://kremlin.ru/transcripts/20603

———. 2014c. Dushanbe Declaration of the SCO Heads of State. September 12. http://kremlin.ru/supplement/4750.

Lesh, David W. 2017. Iran Is Taking over Syria: Can Anyone Stop It? *New York Times*, August 29. https://mobile.nytimes.com/2017/08/29/opinion/iran-syria.html

Malinova, Olga. 2015. *Aktual'noe proshloe*. Moscow: Rosspen.

Medvedev, Dmitri. 2006. Dlya prostvetaniya vsekh nado uchityvat' interesy kazhdogo. *Ekspert*, July 24. http://expert.ru/expert/2006/28/medvedev

Ministry of Foreign Affairs. 2013. Concept of the Foreign Policy of the Russian Federation. February 18. http://www.mid.ru/en/foreign_policy/official_documents/-/asset_publisher/CptICkB6BZ29/content/id/122186

———. 2016. Foreign Minister Sergey Lavrov's Remarks and Answers to Media Questions at a Joint News Conference Following Trilateral Talks with Iranian Foreign Minister Mohammad Javad Zarif and Turkish Foreign Minister Mevlut Cavusoglu. December 20. http://www.mid.ru/en/vistupleniya_ministra/-/asset_publisher/MCZ7HQuMdqBY/content/id/2574870

Nikonov, Viacheslav. 2003. Rossiya-2013: nezapdny Zapad. *Rossiya v globalnoy politike*, September 3. http://www.polity.ru/articles/nezapad.htm

———. 2007. Yeshche raz o suverennoy demokratii. In *PRO Suverennuyu demokratiyu*, ed. Leonid V. Poljakov, 317–320. Moscow: Yevropa.

Nunan, Timothy. 2016. *Humanitarian Invasion: Global Development in Cold War Afghanistan*. Cambridge: Harvard University Press.

Orlov, Dmitri. 2006. Byt' li Rossii 'energiticheskoy sverkhderzhavoy'? *Izvestia*, March 17. http://www.izvestia.ru/news/310285

Petersson, Bo. 2014. Taking the Shortcut to Popularity: How Putin's Power Is Sustained Through Ukraine. *Russian Analytical Digest* 148: 6–9. http://www.css.ethz.ch/rad.

Primakov, Yevgenii. 2004. *Russian Crossroads: Toward the New Millennium*. New Haven/London: Yale University Press.

Prozorov, Sergei. 2010. Ethos Without Nomos: The Russian Georgian War and the Post-Soviet State of Exception. *Ethics & Global Politics* 3 (4): 255–275. https://doi.org/10.3402/egp.v3i4.5665.

Putin, Vladimir. 2008. *Izbrannyye rechi i vystupleniya*. Moscow: Knizhnyi mir.

———. 2011. Novyi integratsionnyi proyekt dlya Yevrazii. *Izvestiya*, December 3. http://izvestia.ru/news/502761

Reznik, Henri. 2012. Nashi sudy—eto chinovniki v mantiyakh. *Russian Reporter* 38 (267). http://www.rusrep.ru/article/2012/09/26/reznik

Rotkirch, Anna, Anna Temkina, and Elena Zdravomyslova. 2007. Who Helps the Degraded Housewife? Comments on Vladimir Putin's Demographic Speech. *European Journal of Women's Studies* 14 (4): 349–357. https://doi.org/10.11 77%2F1350506807081884.

RT. 2014. Lavrov: Kiev Issued 'Criminal Order' Allowing Use of Weapons Against Civilians. April 23. http://rt.com/shows/sophieco/154364-lavrov-ukraine-standoff-sophieco

Saari, Sinikukka. 2009. European Democracy Promotion in Russia Before and After the 'Colour' Revolutions. *Democratization* 16 (4): 732–755. https://doi.org/10.1080/13510340903083018.

Selby, Jan. 2007. Engaging Foucault: Discourse, Liberal Governance and the Limits of Foucauldian IR. *International Relations* 21 (3): 324–345. https://doi.org/10.1177/0047117807080199.

Shevel, Oxana. 2011. *Migration, Refugee Policy, and State Building in Postcommunist Europe*. Cambridge: Cambridge UP.

Singer, Brian C.J., and Lorna Weir. 2006. Politics and Sovereign Power: Considerations on Foucault. *European Journal of Social Theory* 9 (4): 443–465. https://doi.org/10.1177%2F1368431006073013.

Surkov, Viacheslav. 2008. *Teksty 97-07: Stat'i i vystupleniya*. Moscow: Yevropa.

The White House. 2014. Remarks by the President in Address to European Youth. March 26. http://www.whitehouse.gov/the-press-office/2014/03/26/remarks-president-address-european-youth

Tsygankov, Andrei. 2013. *Russia's Foreign Policy*. Lanham: Rowman & Littlefield Publishers.

Walters, William. 2012. *Governmentality: Critical Encounters*. London: Routledge.

Zelevev, Igor. 2014. Posle Kryma: Novaya vneshnepoliticheskaya doktrina Rossii. *Vedomosti*, April 7. http://www.vedomosti.ru/newspaper/articles/2014/04/07/novaya-vneshnyaya-politika-rossii

Zorkin, Valerii. 2006. Apologiya Vestfal'skoy sistemy. *Rossiyskaya Gazeta*, August 22. http://www.rg.ru/2006/08/22/zorjkin-statjya.html

Assessing Russia's Middle East Policy After the Arab Uprisings: Prospects and Limitations

Alexey Khlebnikov

INTRODUCTION

Since the beginning of the 2010s, Russian foreign policy towards the Middle East has started to become much more assertive. This has coincided with a new stage in the global and regional developments which significantly changed the existing regional power balances and security architecture: gradual decline of the "unipolar world" and rise of multiple power centres; "regionalization" of global politics which provided a greater role for regional powers, institutions and security alliances; and another wave of what Moscow perceived as "regime changes"—that is, the Arab uprisings which launched the process of a grand transformation in the Middle East.

These major trends have influenced Russia's policy in the Middle East and conditioned its strategy for the future. Moscow largely perceived the revolutionary movements in the region which started in 2010 as the result of the influence of external powers. This perception has become a key factor defining Russia's Middle East policy ever since. As the Arab uprisings

A. Khlebnikov (✉)
Russian International Affairs Council, Moscow, Russia

© The Author(s) 2020
E. Parlar Dal, E. Erşen (eds.), *Russia in the Changing International System*, https://doi.org/10.1007/978-3-030-21832-4_13

225

accelerated the regional transformation, the US, EU, Russia and major regional actors (especially Saudi Arabia, Turkey and Iran) have been scrambling to find policy solutions that take into account the new realities in the "post-Arab uprisings" period while also safeguarding their own national interests. This is why it is important to understand the current regional context in terms of the emerging security system and power balances because it has a huge impact on global and regional powers' policies in the Middle East.

This chapter seeks to evaluate the development of Russia's foreign policy towards the Middle East. The first section focuses on the regional context in the light of the fragmentation of the Arab world as well as the regional security system. The second section deals with the implications of the grand transformation taking place in the Middle East, while the third section elaborates on the reasons for Russia's more assertive policies towards the region. The last three sections discuss the pragmatic interests of Russia in the Middle East in the light of its security and economic concerns.

REGIONAL CONTEXT: FRAGMENTATION OF THE ARAB WORLD AND REGIONAL SECURITY SYSTEM

With the fragmentation of the traditional twentieth-century security system in the Middle East which was centred around three major Arab states—Egypt, Iraq and Syria—and traditional non-Arab actors—Iran, Turkey and Israel—the region has entered a period of instability and turbulence. Since the 2003 war in Iraq and later the 2011 uprisings in Egypt and Syria, that system has been dismantled. With the decline of the aforementioned traditional Arab powers, Saudi Arabia has emerged as a new power broker in the region and a Riyadh-led alliance of the oil-rich Gulf monarchies has significantly increased its role in the Middle Eastern affairs.

Saudi Arabia and Qatar have been involved in the Syrian conflict financing various radical groups which aimed at ousting the regime of Bashar al-Assad (Egorov et al. 2016). They have invested a lot in this goal which makes it very difficult for them to simply give up and let Iran enjoy its rising regional influence. A grand stand-off between Iran and Saudi Arabia which is portrayed in sectarian terms further exacerbates the instability in the region.

In addition, the Saudi-led war launched in Yemen against the Houthi rebels created a new "hot spot" in the region providing the radical Islamic groups with a safe haven and also undermining the image of the Gulf states as they have been incapable of winning the war they initiated. Besides, the huge financial aid coming from the Gulf Cooperation Council (GCC) countries to Egypt turned once an influential regional player into a paralyzed giant with important unresolved economic, social and political issues. Egypt is now largely dependent on external financial aid and thus unable to seriously influence the resolution of any regional issue.

On the one hand, all these processes seem quite natural and logical as the Saudi-led GCC formation is trying to fill the vacuum left by Iraq, Egypt and Syria due to its fear about the rise of Iranian and Turkish influence in the region. On the other hand, these processes exacerbate regional confrontation along sectarian lines which brings the Middle Eastern order to the verge of collapse.

Throughout the second part of the twentieth century, the security system established in the Middle East was based on three major pillars: (a) lack of unity among the Arab states and their inability to unite and create a strong regional force, (b) emergence of various partnerships between the Arab states and non-Arab regional actors, and (c) involvement of global powers (US and Soviet Union) to support different actors in the region. This security system provided the Middle East with a relatively simple and more or less working system of checks and balances. In addition, non-Arab actors except Israel played a quite marginal role in the Middle East affairs.

Today, when almost the entire territory between Turkey, Iran and the Persian Gulf is in chaos, Ankara, Tehran and Riyadh aim to exploit this situation to increase their influence in the region, which means that today we have three regional centres of power in the Middle East. They can also be regarded as "pillars of stability/instability" depending on how one perceives them. Russia has been working hard to maintain and develop positive relations with all three countries which can be quite challenging as they often have different—if not always conflicting—interests and approaches regarding the regional crises in Syria, Iraq, Yemen and Libya as well as regional issues such as the Iranian nuclear deal and the US involvement in the Middle East.

In this context, Egypt's role is also crucial as it is the most populous country in the region and a traditional key to regional stability. Destabilization of Libya which had a population of 6 million people and Syria which had a population of 21 million people caused the largest post-World War II refugee crisis and an unprecedented pressure on Europe. One can only imagine what would happen if a country of 90 million people becomes destabilized like Libya or Syria. This compels Saudi Arabia (and other regional and global actors) demonstrate genuine interest in the security and stability of Egypt, since otherwise the Saudi kingdom itself could be set on fire. It also helps to understand the rationale for the generous aid of the Gulf states that have already provided Cairo with over $40 billion since 2013 (Young 2016; Walsh 2017; Harb 2017).

As stated before, we also witness a significant change in a key regional dynamic—the strengthened role of Iran and Turkey as the two non-Arab powers in the regional affairs. This development challenges the influence of Saudi Arabia and the GCC and risks a deeper confrontation between the regional actors. Moreover, this change is taking place at a time when a set of events defines the transformation trend in the region: the Arab uprisings, gradual decline of the US role in the Middle East (considering that the new US administration is likely to continue the policy of limited involvement in the region); increased number and role of non-state actors; ongoing wars in Syria, Yemen and Libya; rise of Islamic radicalism; and low oil prices (Seib 2016).

The Grand Transformation

Due to all these developments, the current period in the Middle East can be characterized as a "grand transformation" which will most likely result in the formation of a new regional security architecture. The war in Syria plays the most important role in this context as all major regional and global actors have been involved in one way or another in the Syrian crisis. Results of the Syrian civil war and power struggle among the involved powers will define the parameters of the newly formed regional security system. Some scholars even indicate that the turbulent processes that we witness across the Middle East are clear testimonies of the emergence of a brand new world order (Naumkin 2018).

This is why major regional actors like Turkey, Iran and Saudi Arabia desire to protect their interests and positions in Syria. In addition, we should consider the US unwillingness to be further involved in Syria and the Middle East which is a major factor that prompts the regional powers to flirt with Russia. The regional rivalry between Turkey, Iran and Saudi Arabia urges all three states to improve their relations with Moscow in order to use the Russian support as an effective diplomatic card against each other. In the Syrian context, Turkey and Iran have more common interests with each other—for example, the Kurdish issue—than they have with Saudi Arabia, which has also allowed Tehran and Ankara to develop a working partnership with Moscow. This can also be regarded as a significant example showing how regional actors with a fair amount of disagreements with each other are able to form an effectively functioning format of interaction.

Russia's achievement in bringing Iran and Turkey on board in Syria has effectively side-lined the US and Saudi Arabia, while giving Moscow the opportunity to demonstrate that its approach regarding the Syrian issue has been more fruitful than Washington's. Moreover, by establishing close links with Turkey and Iran, Russia has acquired greater influence over the regional dynamics. For instance, Turkey is a NATO member which makes it a convenient interlocutor and a useful channel for transmitting messages between Russia and the West.

However, the newly formed Iran-Russia-Turkey "bloc" in Syria brings in certain difficulties which might work against the interests of its members. First, these three countries have numerous disagreements among themselves regarding the resolution of the issues in the Middle East. Second, they are all non-Arab states which weakens the legitimacy of their policies in the eyes of the Arab public. According to the survey of Zogby Research Services (2016), for instance, the favourability ratings of both Turkey and Iran have been in decline in the Arab world, although the situation started to slightly change in 2018. In addition, many people in the Arab countries see Russia's role in the region negatively, although its favourability ratings have been improving in Saudi Arabia and Egypt. This is also a major reason behind Russia's efforts to include Riyadh and Cairo in a more extensive manner in the formation of the new security system in the Middle East.

For Russia, Saudi Arabia is one of the most important Arab states in terms of its economic power and political influence outside its borders and thus it can be a valuable contributor to the new regional security architecture. The same applies for Egypt which is the most populous Arab country and which has an important peace treaty with Israel as well as the traditional support of Washington. In addition, Cairo's policies do not always coincide with those of Riyadh regarding key regional issues—for example, Syria, Yemen and Iran—which makes it a more flexible actor in the eyes of Russian leaders.

This is why Russia has been interested in developing close ties with Egypt. In 2018, the two countries celebrated the 75th anniversary of the establishment of their diplomatic relations. During his official visit to

Russia in October 2018, Egypt's President Abdel Fattah al-Sisi said that Moscow has always supported Cairo in times of trouble (Federation Council 2018). The two states have been successfully developing their economic and military-technical cooperation despite Egypt's traditionally close ties with the US. Cairo also serves as an additional channel of communication between Russia and the Saudi-led GCC as well as a strategic gate opening to the African continent. Partly as a result of Egypt's constructive intermediary role between Russia and Saudi Arabia, the relations between Moscow and Riyadh have also improved in the last few years—particularly following King Salman's ground-breaking visit to Russia in October 2017. Yet, it should be noted that Russia has been improving its relations also with Qatar which demonstrates Moscow's willingness to develop its ties with all regional actors in the Middle East.

Another important dimension of the grand transformation taking place in the Middle East is the changing attitudes of the regional actors towards Russia, although this is also closely related with the US behaviour in the Middle East. For instance, despite Trump's commitment to Saudi Arabia's security concerns in the region, Riyadh still feels uncomfortable due to the US approach in Syria which prioritizes defeating the Islamic State of Iraq and the Levant (ISIL) and Jabhat al-Nusra (renamed Hayat Tahrir al-Sham). As Saudi Arabia is much more concerned about the rise of Iranian influence in the Middle East, it has sought closer ties with Russia to make sure that the Iran's designs in the region remains in check (Seib 2016).

Reasons Behind Russia's More Assertive Policy in the Middle East

In 2011, the Russian government came to a conclusion—mainly due to the Arab uprisings—that it needed to change its Middle East policy in order to counter the trend of "regime change" which also previously impacted the countries of the former Soviet Union in the 2000s (e.g. Ukraine, Georgia and Kyrgyzstan). Moscow still remembers those "colour revolutions" and believes that the West supported those mass protests with the masterplan to apply the same scenario for Russia in the future (Roxburgh 2012). The Kremlin interpreted the pro-democracy protests of the early 2010s that swept Russia in the same vein. It is also important to highlight the crisis in Ukraine that started in late 2013 and culminated in 2014 as Moscow perceived it as another example of Western-sponsored "regime change" in the close vicinity of Russian borders. As a result, it decided to take serious steps to revert this trend by supporting the Syrian government forces and reinforcing its presence in the Middle East

Another important factor which convinced Moscow to adjust its Middle East policy was the developments that took place in Libya. The Western military operation in Libya in March 2011 made the Russian leaders feel deceived as Moscow had chosen not to use its veto power in the UN Security Council in order to facilitate the solution of the humanitarian crisis in that country. However, the Western countries used the UN mandate to eliminate the regime of Muammar Qaddafi, causing further chaos in Libya along with a new refugee crisis in Europe and strengthening the rise of Islamic radicalism across the region. In short, Moscow saw the events in Libya as a proof of the opportunistic and destructive nature of the Western policies in the Middle East.

Despite such negative drivers, there was a positive factor which provided Russia with the opportunity to enhance its position in the region. Moscow has attentively followed the US moves in the Middle East capitalizing on the gradual decline of the American involvement in the region which started during the Obama administration. The regional countries started to watch the US policies with greater concern since 2010–2011 when Washington abandoned its long-time allies in the Middle East—particularly President Hosni Mubarak of Egypt. The fall of the one-man regimes in Tunisia and Egypt sent a strong signal to the Arab countries that they could not fully rely on the US support anymore.

The military coup in Egypt in 2013 was another important turning point in this regard. After the ouster of Islamist President Mohammed Morsi by the Egyptian army, Washington decided to suspend its annual aid to Cairo which amounted to $1.3 billion. Saudi Arabia and the UAE, which supported the 2013 coup as well as the new Egyptian president al-Sisi, however, opposed the rise of Muslim Brotherhood across the region as they viewed it as a threat to their own political systems (Khlebnikov 2015). These developments opened a room of manoeuvre for Moscow in its relations with all three countries. For instance, Russia started to establish very close relations with the new leadership in Cairo and signed a $3.5 billion arms deal—first of its kind between the two countries since the 1960s and 1970s—which was followed by additional financial and military contracts (Sputnik News 2014; Kozhanov 2016).

Another blow to the relations between the US and its Arab allies came when the Obama administration signed a nuclear deal with Iran in July

2015. This development particularly alarmed Riyadh which started to question the US security commitments to Saudi Arabia in its regional rivalry with Iran. The other GCC members also realized that they needed to diversify their portfolio of partners which is a major reason for the interest of Egypt, Qatar and UAE in intensifying their political and economic ties with Moscow.

The same logic also applies to Turkey, which resented the US decision not to extradite Fetullah Gülen, who is believed to be the mastermind of the failed coup attempt that took place in Turkey in July 2016. More importantly, both the Obama and Trump administrations continued to provide military support for the Syrian Kurds—particularly the Democratic Union Party (PYD) and its armed wing People's Protection Units (YPG) which Ankara simply views as terrorist organizations due to their close links with the Kurdistan Workers' Party (PKK). The growing rift between Turkey and the US in these two issues drew Ankara closer to Moscow in the region and contributed to the deepening Turkish-Russian-Iranian cooperation in Syria.

UTILIZING A MORE PRAGMATIC APPROACH TOWARDS THE MIDDLE EAST

Although some experts claim that Russia's role in the Middle East will continue to grow at the expense of the declining US influence, this is quite arguable. It is true that Russia's intensified involvement in the Syrian conflict signifies a remarkable return to the Middle East as well as the restoration of the Russian political, economic and military influence in the region; however, Moscow's actions did not change the regional balance of power. In addition, it should be noted that Russia neither has a desire nor has the capacity to further expand its involvement in the region. The Russian policy in the Middle East remains largely reactionary in this sense.

Historically, the Middle East has been of marginal importance for Russia. Even during the Cold War, the region was viewed as just one of the "battlefields" where the Soviet Union tried to confront and limit US influence. This situation has not changed much in the post-Soviet period. For instance, none of Russia's foreign policy documents in the 1990s and 2000s have prioritized the Middle East. In the most recent version of the Russian Foreign Policy Concept which was released in late 2016, the Middle East is listed as the fifth most important region in Russian foreign policy—below the post-Soviet space, Euro-Atlantic region, Arctic and Asia-Pacific, and only above Latin America in terms of Russia's foreign policy priorities (Ministry of Foreign Affairs 2016).

However, it should be noted that for the first time, 2016 Foreign Policy Concept also listed the Middle East among Russia's top priorities as a primary source of terrorism and instability which directly threatens Russia's national security. In this sense, the region has indeed grown in importance for Moscow in the last few years. As of now, Moscow's policy towards this region is driven by two factors: security concerns (in particular fighting terrorism) and economic interests. It can even be argued that Russia tries to implement a variation of the "leading from behind" approach in its Middle East policy which was previously pioneered by the US during the Obama period. Moscow clearly understands that it does not have enough resources and power to increase its involvement and challenge the traditionally strong US influence in the region.

Moreover, a greater influence in the Middle East comes together with additional responsibilities which could create an extra—and probably unaffordable—burden for Moscow. The sharp drop in the global oil prices in the 2014–2015 period, absence of structural economic reforms and Western sectoral sanctions launched after the crisis in Ukraine in 2014 have all negatively impacted Russia's economy and caused significant domestic challenges for the Russian leadership. This is why Moscow has been trying to exploit the current situation in the Middle East with the goal of increasing its benefits and making sure that the costs of involvement do not exceed the profits.

Prioritizing Security

Fighting Terrorism

The spread of instability and rise of terrorism in the Middle East pose a direct threat to Russia's Muslim neighbourhood and therefore its own national security. Moscow portrays its Middle East policy as a better and more effective alternative to the "failed" Western approach towards the conflicts in Iraq, Libya and Afghanistan, which practically resulted in the erosion of sovereignty and collapse of state institutions in those countries. In comparison, Russia believes that its military campaign in Syria helped avoid a similar scenario, prevented the country from collapsing and mitigated the security risks at home.

According to the figures provided by the Russian Federal Security Service (FSB) and Russia's Interior Ministry, over 4000 Russian citizens and over 5000 people from the former Soviet republics have been fighting in the ranks of terrorist organizations in Syria (Vedomosti 2017). This has created significant concerns about Russia's national security especially because of the extremist ideologies that might particularly become stronger in Russia's North Caucasus and Volga regions as well as Central Asia. In order to mitigate the security risks that are related with this situation, the Russian security services have tightened their control over the Muslim communities and enhanced their cooperation with local religious leaders as well as their intelligence counterparts in the Middle East. This approach finally culminated in the deployment of Russian military personnel in Syria. In this regard, Moscow thought it would be a better idea to fight the terrorists in Syria rather than at home.

The same rationale—securitization of bilateral ties (i.e. an anti-terrorist alliance)—has been masterfully used by Moscow to ensure better relations with the regional actors. Russia's partnership with Iran and Turkey in Syria is mainly centred on the issue of fighting terrorism. Similarly, Moscow-Cairo agenda is also heavily loaded with security issues—military-technical cooperation, joint anti-terrorist drills, a draft agreement for Russian warplanes to use Egyptian military bases, and so on.

Russia's Muslim Minority

Russia's Muslim population is estimated to be between 15 and 20 million which also makes it the European country with the largest Muslim minority (Pew Research Center 2017). In addition, the Russian officials argue there are up to 10 million Muslim migrants who reside in Russia either legally or illegally. In this sense, it is clear that Moscow cannot ignore its relations with the Middle East as the developments with regard to the broader Muslim world (or *ummah*) can have serious implications on Russia's own Muslim communities.

Foreign influence on Russia's Muslim communities is not something new. Especially during the two Chechen wars of the 1990s, radical Islamist ideas spread quickly in the North Caucasus and the Russian state failed to reverse this trend. The path from separatism to Islamism in the first Chechen war has been perceived by many Russian leaders as a consequence of the influence of external powers—particularly Saudi Arabia (International Crisis Group 2012). Russian leadership is convinced that Saudi financing and ideological support played a prominent role in triggering the jihadist movements in Afghanistan in the 1980s and Chechnya in the 1990s.

It should also be emphasized that the oil-rich Gulf monarchies funnelled a lot of money into building new mosques, educating a new generation of muftis, sending missionaries and spreading non-traditional ideologies in Russia's Muslim regions, as the Russian state did not have a strong control over its Muslim communities in the 1990s and 2000s. In addition to Wahhabism, the ideologies of Muslim Brotherhood and Tablighi Jamaat also made their way into Russia in the post-Soviet period (APN 2017). Furthermore, Islamic scholars who have been educated in countries like Saudi Arabia, Pakistan and Egypt also became active in disseminating Islamist ideas among the Muslim people of Russia who predominantly practise Hanafi Islam—one of the four religious Sunni Islamic schools of jurisprudence.

Therefore, by developing its relations with the Middle East countries, Moscow acquires additional leverage to observe and control their religious activities in Russia and the former Soviet space. The Kremlin also uses Ramzan Kadyrov, the head of the Chechen republic, as a significant figure in its policies towards the Middle East, as Kadyrov positions himself as a representative of all Russian Muslims and builds close ties with the ruling families in Saudi Arabia, Bahrain, Jordan and UAE. In addition, it should be noted that the Russian military police units first deployed in Aleppo and later in other parts of Syria predominantly consisted of Chechens and Sunni Muslims, allowing Moscow to establish a better communication with the local population which is also predominantly Sunni.

Global Power Status

Fighting ISIL and playing a major role in the resolution of the conflict in Syria raised Russia's regional status, discredited the myth about Russia's isolation in global politics and improved Moscow's chances for negotiating other issues with the West such as the Ukraine crisis. More importantly, Russia's intense military and diplomatic interaction with the US, Israel, Jordan, Iraq, Iran, Turkey and the Gulf states positioned Moscow as the only actor capable of maintaining close contacts with all parties involved in the Syrian crisis.

Since the start of its direct military involvement in Syria, Russia has been developing a close military coordination with all the actors in Syria. As Syrian skies became more crowded with the fighter jets of Syria, Russia and the US-led international coalition, ensuring the safety of these aircraft and preventing a clash or accident between them required much closer coordination. This was also in line with the general policy of Moscow which has long been calling for the exchange of intelligence and coordinates in order to fight the terrorists more effectively and avoid striking the "wrong targets" that could spark a new regional crisis and jeopardize diplomatic efforts.

In addition, launching the Astana platform with Turkey and Iran on Syria and establishing the mechanism of de-escalation zones and ceasefires which have so far proven to be effective shows that Russia is a diplomatic actor capable of reducing the degree of violence and bringing the warring parties to the negotiating table. Moscow also recently demonstrated its ability to play a constructive role in conflict resolution due to its diplomatic efforts for mediation between the rival political factions in Libya.

Demonstration of Russian Military Capabilities

For the first time after the collapse of the Soviet Union, Russia is using military force far away from its borders. What is more important is that the Syrian operation enabled the Russian army—particularly the Russian air forces—to gain very valuable combat experience after the major military reform which was initiated in 2008, after the Russo-Georgian war. The military operation in Syria significantly enhanced the mobility and coordination between the different branches of the Russian military. It also demonstrated Russia's ability to quickly deploy significant numbers of military units abroad and showcased Moscow's capacity to effectively project power beyond its own borders which is a crucial aspect of being perceived as a global power.

Russia has set up its first and only permanent military base in the Middle East in Latakia (Khmeymim) in Syria which now guarantees the Russian military presence in the region. Russia's former naval facility in Tartus is also going to be upgraded and turned into a military naval base capable of hosting up to 15 military vessels and even nuclear-powered submarines. In December 2017, the Russian parliament approved the agreements signed with the Syrian government for the lease of the Tartus and Khmeymim bases to Russia for 49 years with an automatic 25-year prolongation (RIA 2017). This has put Russia on par with the US, UK, France and Turkey which also have military bases in the Middle East.

In spite of these developments, it should be noted that Russia's current economic problems significantly limit its capacity to undertake further military expansion in the region, although it may have such plans in mind for the longer term. Moreover, as also stated earlier, such an objective requires more responsibilities and financial burden which Moscow is not willing to take. There are reports about Russia's plans to build new military bases in Egypt, Libya and Sudan, but these might be over-exaggerated due to Russia's economic limitations. Moscow might only aim at securing additional docking opportunities in the region to be able to maintain its fleet operations there. Yet, these developments nevertheless confirm the changed attitude of regional actors towards Moscow and thus highlight the existing opportunities for Russia in the Middle East.

Economic Pragmatism

In addition to the security drivers, Russia's Middle East policy is also defined by economic pragmatism. Following the de-ideologization of its foreign policy after the disintegration of the Soviet Union, Moscow has started to view the Middle East as an attractive market and intensified economic cooperation in the 2000s laid the foundations of a deeper political partnership between Russia and the countries in the region.

Moscow quite successfully utilized the Soviet heritage and used its old partners—Algeria, Egypt, Iraq, Iran and Libya—as outposts for expanding its economic activities in the Middle East. Having learnt the lesson that ideologically driven economic cooperation may conflict the Russian national interests, Moscow's approach in the region is now based on pragmatic economic concerns. For instance, Russia lost billions in contracts in oil and railway sectors due to the civil war in Libya (Reuters 2011). Since then, it has become more cautious in its economic policies in the Middle East, attempting to diversify its portfolio of economic cooperation.

Moscow's economic interests in the region are mainly located in three key areas: military-technical cooperation, energy and Arab investments in Russia.

Military-Technical Cooperation

In the post-Arab uprisings period, Russia managed to improve its economic position in the Middle East and signed several multi-billion arms deals. The most important one was the $3.5 billion agreement signed with

Egypt envisaging the delivery of new fighter jets, helicopters, air defence and coastal defence systems (Kozhanov 2016). Since 2012, Russia has also revived its military-technical cooperation with Iraq and signed arms contracts worth more than $4 billion for the delivery of a wide range of Russian weapons including jets, helicopters and tanks (Nikolsky 2017).

Since Moscow deployed its military to Syria in September 2015, it has also demonstrated cutting-edge weapons and successfully tested them in real combat. The Syrian operation has allowed Russia to discover the shortfalls and glitches of these weapons at relatively low cost and improve them for the future. It also greatly enabled Moscow to showcase its new weapons for prospective customers such as the advanced Su-34 and Su-35 fighter jets, Kalibr cruise missiles, S-400 air defence system and Pantsir-S1 air defence artillery system. According to some estimates, Russian arms exports have received a boost from $6 to $7 billion as a result of the "marketing effect" of the military campaign in Syria (Luhn 2016). Algeria, Turkey, Saudi Arabia, UAE and Pakistan which have long been buyers of the US arms, all became interested in purchasing the Russian weapons.

Although the Middle East is one of the fastest growing markets for arms sales, its share in Russia's arms export is still only about 11 per cent (SIPRI 2018). However, there are prospects for increasing Russia's market share in the region. If Russia ultimately manages to secure and implement its arms deals with Turkey, Saudi Arabia and Egypt, this might incentivize these countries to solidify their military-technical cooperation with Moscow in the long run. However, considering that all three countries have traditionally been the major clients of the US in the military sphere, it would be unrealistic to expect them to completely re-orient towards Russia.

Energy Cooperation

Russia's economic interests in the energy sphere are concentrated in the oil and gas sector as well as the construction of nuclear power plants (NPPs). Russian energy companies Rosneft, Gazpromneft and Lukoil work across the region quite successfully. They are also looking for new opportunities to participate in off-shore projects in Egypt, Iran and Lebanon and restore their positions in Libya.

The 2014–2015 period was crucial for the energy cooperation between Russia and the Middle East. Due to the sharp drop in global oil prices, Russia found itself on the same side with the Organization of Petroleum

Exporting Countries (OPEC). In December 2016, despite having stark differences regarding Syria and Iran, Russia and the Saudi-led OPEC managed to strike a deal that reduced their oil production. This agreement somewhat stabilized the oil prices and demonstrated that Moscow and its non-traditional partners in the Middle East were capable of making and maintaining strategic deals in the sphere of energy.

Russia is also seeking to secure its interests in developing civil nuclear energy projects in the Middle East. In 2014, it signed a package of agreements for the construction of up to eight new nuclear reactors in Iran. Moscow also has a contract worth over $20 billion to create the entire nuclear industry in Egypt to construct the country's first nuclear power plant (NPP) in El Dabaa and provide training to the Egyptians to operate it. It is also exploring opportunities to build NPPs in Jordan, Saudi Arabia and UAE which currently develop their own strategy for civil nuclear industry.

Foreign Direct Investments

It is important to underscore that the 2014 crisis over Ukraine and the subsequent Western economic sanctions against Russia played an important role in Moscow's reconsideration of its economic policies. In this new context, Russia has started to view the Middle East as an alternative partner which could compensate the Western sanctions' effect in the financial and agricultural sectors to a certain extent. By 2016, for instance, Egypt, Iran and Israel have all increased their export of food products to Russia, while Moscow increased its export of grains to the Middle East.

The US and EU sanctions also limited Russia's access to the Western loans and technologies, prompting Moscow to look for alternative sources of foreign direct investment (FDI). The investment funds of the Middle Eastern countries conveniently accommodated Russia's demands and by 2017 the Russian Direct Investment Fund (RDIF) signed a number of contracts and memorandums of understanding with the investment authorities of Saudi Arabia, Bahrain, Kuwait, Qatar and UAE. In addition, the Qatar Investment Authority bought 19.5 per cent of the shares of Russia's oil giant Rosneft, invested in the Russian bank VTB as well as the Pulkovo airport in St. Petersburg and signed a $2 billion deal with RDIF. Saudi Public Investment Fund, on the other hand, signed a deal with RDIF which envisaged the investment of $10 billion into the Russian economy (Vedomosti 2015). By now, Riyadh has already invested up to $2 billion in Russian economy.

Conclusion

According to the report of Zogby Research Services (2017) at least two-thirds of the respondents in Egypt, Lebanon, Jordan, Saudi Arabia, UAE, Turkey and Iran indicate that having good relations with Russia is important for their countries. It is also worth noting that relations with Russia are regarded more highly in these countries in comparison with the previous year. Results of this poll are quite indicative and confirm Russia's strengthened influence in the region.

Russia definitely enhanced its position in the Middle East, and its military campaign in Syria became a pivotal moment which convinced many regional actors to treat Moscow's interests in the region seriously. However, there are certain limitations on Moscow's long-term strategy in the Middle East. So far, it predominantly used "hard power" to achieve its goals in the region. Yet, to convert these successes into political dividends in the longer term is a rather challenging task. When the military dimension of the Syrian conflict comes to an end and political items start dominating the agenda, it will most likely create many problems for Russia (Khlebnikov 2018). For instance, disagreements with Turkey, Iran and the US over Syria are expected to exacerbate, while the economic burden of Syria's reconstruction is not something Moscow can carry alone. On the other hand, finding a political formula for Syria which will take into account the interests of all involved parties seems rather illusionary.

So far, Russia has chosen to enhance its ties with the regional actors who have more capacity and power to influence the military situation on the ground. Being an integral part of the Middle East, Turkey and Iran are naturally interested in playing a greater role in the region. By bringing them together, Moscow tries to test a new regional format where major Middle Eastern powers can work together. Russia maintains ties with all the main actors in the region which enables it to become an important power broker in the Middle East. Being equidistant from all parties in the conflicts in Syria, Yemen and Libya as well as the Palestine-Israeli dispute and the intra-GCC rift, Russia shows its intention to become a mediator in the broader regional context.

In the coming years, Russia will likely develop its regional policy in two major directions: (a) playing the role of a mediator by creating a functioning mechanism which helps regional powers solve their problems with each other, (b) influencing the state of affairs in the region by not becoming heavily involved, while reaping the benefits provided by the regional environment. For now, the regional environment in the Middle East works in Moscow's favour. However, if the situation changes and the US decides to substantially increase its influence in the region or if another economic crisis obliges Moscow to concentrate on its domestic problems, Russia might find it hard to maintain its role in the Middle East. Therefore, it is important to keep in mind that Russia's steady re-emergence as a leading power in the Middle East is not viewed as an end in itself. Moscow is interested in expanding its influence in the Middle East as long as such an opportunity exists in the regional setting. It is neither ready, nor willing to take extra responsibilities which could create higher risks for its domestic and global interests. Yet, in order to maintain its new role in the region, Moscow will first need to find a formula that would allow it to stay relevant in the regional realities of post-war Syria.

References

APN. 2017. Skhemy finansirovaniya islamskogo radikalizma v Rossii. April 3. https://www.apn.ru/index.php?newsid=36175

Egorov, Oleg, Ruslan Mamedov, and David Narmania. 2016. Anti-government Extremist Organizations in Syria. *Russian International Affairs Council*. http://russiancouncil.ru/en/syria-extremism#top

Federation Council. 2018. President of the Arab Republic of Egypt Delivered a Speech at the Federation Council. October 16. http://council.gov.ru/en/events/news/97122/

Harb, Iman K. 2017. An Economic Explanation for Egypt's Alignment in the GCC Crisis. *Arab Center Washington DC*, August 9. http://arabcenterdc.org/policy_analyses/an-economic-explanation-for-egypts-alignment-in-the-gcc-crisis

International Crisis Group. 2012. The North Caucasus: The Challenges of Integration, Ethnicity and Conflict. October 19. https://www.crisisgroup.org/file/1385/download?token=vR9sgEUX

Khlebnikov, Alexey. 2015. The New Ideological Threat to the GCC: Implications for the Qatari-Saudi Rivalry. *Strategic Assessment* 17 (4): 17–28. http://www.inss.org.il/wp-content/uploads/systemfiles/adkan17_4ENG_7_Khlebnikov.pdf

———. 2018. Moscow Has Won the War in Syria, But Can It Win the Peace. *The Middle East Eye*, September 6. https://www.middleeasteye.net/opinion/moscow-has-won-war-syria-can-it-win-peace

Kozhanov, Nikolay. 2016. Arms Exports Add to Russia's Tools of Influence in Middle East. *Chatham House*, July 20. https://www.chathamhouse.org/expert/comment/arms-exports-add-russia-s-tools-influence-middle-east

Luhn, Alec. 2016. Russia's Campaign in Syria Leads to Arms Sale Windfall. *The Guardian*, March 29. https://www.theguardian.com/world/2016/mar/29/russias-campaign-in-syria-leads-to-arms-sale-windfall

Ministry of Foreign Affairs. 2016. Foreign Policy Concept of the Russian Federation. December 1. http://www.mid.ru/en/foreign_policy/official_documents/-/asset_publisher/CptICkB6BZ29/content/id/2542248

Naumkin, Vitaly. 2018. The Middle East: Birth Pains of a New World Order? *Valdai Club*, October 16. http://valdaiclub.com/a/highlights/the-middle-east-birth-pains-of-a-new-world-order

Nikolsky, Alexey. 2017. Irak aktiviziruyet zakupki oruzhiya v Rossii. *Vedomosti*, July 25. https://www.vedomosti.ru/politics/articles/2017/07/25/725919-irak

Pew Research Center. 2017. Europe's Growing Muslim Population. November 29. http://www.pewforum.org/2017/11/29/europes-growing-muslim-population

Reuters. 2011. Gaddafi Fall Cost Russia Tens of Blns in Arms Deals. November 2. https://www.reuters.com/article/russia-libya-arms-idUSL5E7M221H20111102

RIA. 2017. Committee of the Federation Council on Defense Approved the Agreement on the Navy Base in Tartus. December 25. https://ria.ru/syria/20171225/1511640481.html

Roxburgh, Angus. 2012. *The Strongman: Vladimir Putin and the Struggle for Russia*. London/New York: I.B. Tauris.

Seib, Gerald F. 2016. Listen Closely: Donald Trump Proposes Big Mideast Strategy Shift. *The Wall Street Journal*, December 12. http://www.wsj.com/articles/listen-closely-donald-trump-proposes-big-mideast-strategy-shift-1481561492

SIPRI. 2018. Trends in International Arms Transfers, 2017. March. https://www.sipri.org/sites/default/files/2018-03/fssipri_at2017_0.pdf

Sputnik News. 2014. Russia, Egypt Initial Arms Contracts Worth 3.5 Billion. September 17. https://sputniknews.com/military/20140917193024553-Russia-Egypt-Initial-Arms-Contracts-Worth-35-Billion

Vedomosti. 2015. Saudovskaya Araviya investiruyet $10 mlrd v Rossiyu. July 6. https://www.vedomosti.ru/economics/articles/2015/07/07/599480-saudovskaya-araviya-investiruet-10-mlrd-v-rossiyu

———. 2017. Putin nazval chislo rossiyan, voyuyushchikh na storone boyevikov v Sirii. February 23. https://www.vedomosti.ru/politics/news/2017/02/23/678892-putin-nazval-chislo-rossiyan

Walsh, Declan. 2017. Despite Public Outcry, Egypt to Transfer Islands to Saudi Arabia. *The New York Times*, June 14. https://www.nytimes.com/2017/06/14/world/middleeast/egypt-saudi-arabia-islands-sisi.html?_r=0

Young, Karen E. 2016. Declining Gulf States' Financial Support Adds to Egypt's Currency Woes. *The Arab Gulf States Institute in Washington*, March 15. https://agsiw.org/declining-gulf-states-financial-support-adds-to-egypts-currency-woes

Zogby Research Services. 2016. Middle East 2016: Current Conditions and the Road Ahead. (November). http://www.zogbyresearchservices.com/s/SBY2016-FINAL.pdf

———. 2017. Sir Bani Yas Public Opinion 2017. (November). http://www.zogbyresearchservices.com/s/SBY2017-Final.pdf

Printed by Printforce, the Netherlands